Jane Auste

# Jane Austen and the Buddha

*Teachers of Enlightenment*

KATHRYN DUNCAN

Jefferson, North Carolina

LIBRARY OF CONGRESS CATALOGUING-IN-PUBLICATION DATA

Names: Duncan, Kathryn, author.
Title: Jane Austen and the Buddha : teachers of enlightenment /
Kathryn Duncan.
Description: Jefferson, North Carolina : Toplight, 2021 |
Includes bibliographical references and index.
Identifiers: LCCN 2021044604 |
ISBN 9781476685830 (paperback : acid free paper) ∞
ISBN 9781476644455 (ebook)
Subjects: LCSH: Austen, Jane, 1775-1817—Criticism and
interpretation. | Buddhist philosophy in literature. | BISAC: LITERARY
CRITICISM / European / English, Irish, Scottish, Welsh |
RELIGION / Buddhism / General (see also PHILOSOPHY / Buddhist) |
LCGFT: Literary criticism.
Classification: LCC PR4038.B77 D86 2021 | DDC 823/.7—dc23
LC record available at https://lccn.loc.gov/2021044604

BRITISH LIBRARY CATALOGUING DATA ARE AVAILABLE

ISBN (print) 978-1-4766-8583-0
ISBN (ebook) 978-1-4766-4445-5

Front cover: (top) Portrait of Jane Austen from
James Edward Austen-Leigh's *A Memoir of Jane Austen*, 1870;
(bottom) bas-relief of the Buddha (Shutterstock);
background illustration by Anastasia Lembrik (Shutterstock)

Printed in the United States of America

Toplight is an imprint of McFarland & Company, Inc., Publishers

*Box 611, Jefferson, North Carolina 28640
www.toplightbooks.com*

*For Mom and Amy,*
*my dearest loves*

# Acknowledgments

I wish to thank all of the people who directly and indirectly helped with this book. Particularly, I must thank Michael Austin, my friend and one of the best writers and smartest people I know; he read every chapter and encouraged me through the long writing process.

I wish to thank my students. I had the good fortune to teach two classes on Austen from a Buddhist perspective. Working with my students gave me new ideas and encouraged me. I especially appreciate the work of former student Leona Wilde who designed my blog.

Thanks to Gary Mitchem from McFarland who believed in this project in its early days and whose interest inspired me to keep going when writing was tough.

I have numerous friends to thank, including Jill Rupert, Aly Marino, Carol Ann Moon, Jalika Waugh, Chrissy Connor, Owen Robertson, Alissa Flores, Erin Sizemore, Jennifer Toole, Anne Barngrover, Chantelle MacPhee, Mike Malloy, Martha Tanner, Jacqueline Foertsch, Jennifer Trost, Johanna Lane, Lisa Anderson, and Gianna Russo who is one of the earliest with whom I shared my idea who told me that the hairs on her arm stood up; she introduced me to Pema Chödrön.

Thank you to the South Central Society for Eighteenth-Century Studies who heard many conference papers where I tried out my ideas with special thanks to Kevin Cope, Baerbel Czennia, Brett McInelly, Susan Spencer, Phyllis Thompson, Samara Cahill, and Ashley Bender.

I thank my parents, which includes my more than stepmom, Lynda Duncan, my adopted father, Gene Zimmerman, and his wife Emily Ann, my father, Raymond Duncan, who taught me a love of words and introduced me to the first Buddhist author whom I read, and my mother, Amy Thompson, who gave me the kind of unconditional love that one might think only exists in fiction.

Most importantly, I thank my daughter, Amy, my light, my love, my dearest one who inspires me daily with her creativity and resilience.

# Table of Contents

# Preface

Ever since I learned to read, I've read constantly. I mean constantly, as in while brushing my teeth or doing my hair constantly. My parents had to tell me to put the book down at the dinner table. I used to climb the pine trees to reach the roof of what we called the clubhouse in our backyard and read there to avoid disturbance. I read my first adult novel in fifth grade as a result of positive peer pressure. All the girls were reading Daphne du Maurier's *Rebecca*. I'm pretty sure that none of us fully understood it, but we all read it. I moved on to romances, liking historical ones best, and seventh grade introduced me to Charles Dickens. I was hooked by *A Tale of Two Cities*, becoming unabashedly an Anglophile devouring British novels, preferably centuries old, ever since. (I later would name my pets Pip, Oliver, Charlie, Rose, and Fezziwig in Dickens' honor.) Inevitably, I became an English professor specializing in British literature. I tried to avoid that fate (who wants to go to school another six years?) by majoring in journalism, but I washed out as a business reporter after five months, quitting because no 22-year-old should awaken every day filled with dread. As miserable as I was, probably because I was miserable, I still read—a lot—even increasing my misery with reading *Sophie's Choice*, for example, and sobbing. I was like the young Ebenezer Scrooge at boarding school in *A Christmas Carol* where Robinson Crusoe and Ali Baba became his friends during a sad and lonely time. Books were my friends and comforters.

I don't remember when I first read Jane Austen. I know it was *Pride and Prejudice* (of course), and it was for fun. I was in love. It was romance, historical, and British, filled with humor that I somehow got as a twentieth-century American girl reading on her own. This was before the Austen resurgence where seemingly every year

1

produced another Austen film adaptation. I knew her through words on the page only, and I read all of her novels.

I'm also an avid re-reader. I've decided this is because I'm an anxious reader. Characters become so alive for me that I can't wait to find out what will happen next, so I zoom hurriedly through books, reading for plot, always dreading the end of a good book because it feels like parting with a friend yet rushing to finish, needing to know what happens next. Then I reread if the book is good because I want to see how the author did it. So I read for who and what, reread for how and why. I've read most of Dickens' work more than once and all of Austen's major novels more times than I can count. Really. I hesitate even to hazard a guess.

I think this anxious reading style of mine also explains my attraction to Austen. Her work is soothing. Pick up *Pride and Prejudice* for the first time knowing nothing of it, and you still feel reassured all will be well. The proper characters will pair off correctly. That amazing, reassuring Austen narrative voice makes clear that even if in reality there's no way Elizabeth Bennet gets Darcy, Austen has created a world where she will—and his £10,000.

Yet I reached a point in my life as an English professor where I could not read any fiction for pleasure. I'd settled strictly into re-reading, finishing the Harry Potter series and immediately going back to the first book more than once. Eventually, I couldn't even manage that. I'd start a book, never get very far, and quit. This was completely unlike me. In the past, even if I didn't like a book, I finished it because it bothered me not knowing what happened. There were very few books I'd not finished in my life. This was entirely new territory for me.

The reason for this is that I was facing more than one major personal crisis. My mother was suffering from slowly progressive dementia. As she got worse, I found myself at a loss on how to help her from four hours away, especially since she would not accept my help. My marriage was failing in similarly slowly progressive fashion. It's not so much that it was slowly getting worse because it had been painful for a long while but that slowly I was moving toward the unavoidable conclusion that I would have to leave, a prospect made much worse because it meant giving up half custody of my young daughter. There were inevitably issues at work, too. I was lucky insofar as I had my health (minus minor illnesses due to stress), but all other areas of my life were crumbling around me. I think I was so overloaded on personal anxiety that there was no room in my psyche for the problems of fictional friends, even those I knew well such as Emma, Elinor, and Elizabeth who all got their happy endings. It was too much.

Eventually, I could read one book: Austen's *Persuasion*. I would finish it and start over again. It was the only novel I read through completely (other than books required for work) for more than a year. Austen makes sense given what I noted above about anxiety. Her reassuring, carefully constructed worlds produce enough dramatic tension for pleasure, not too much for anxiety. Yet, of all of her books, *Persuasion* seems the least likely candidate as the one book I could read during this difficult point in my life. It is the least comedic and contains the most hazard.

As part of the process of working through my personal pain, I started reading about Buddhism, drawn to these ideas because the heart of the Buddha's teachings is suffering, its sources, and the ability to transform it. Fiction, in the past, allowed me to escape my own suffering by entering into the worlds (and heads) of others. Buddhism, with its emphasis on practice, gave me not an escape but a tool to cope with suffering.

Buddhism, *Persuasion*, and heartbreak all came together after my divorce when I took (bear with me) a BuzzFeed quiz asking "Which Jane Austen heroine are you?" The answer was Anne Elliot. What? I should be Elizabeth Bennet! I'm hilarious, known for my wit. I retook it: Anne. I took it four times, and every time it was Anne. It all came together. Of course I'm Anne, for Anne is, of all Austen's characters, the most long suffering and most loyal, holding onto her love for Wentworth just as I had in staying in a marriage no longer working. And then I knew: I read and reread *Persuasion* alongside Buddhism because it is a novel about suffering. In fact, all of Austen's novels, even the most comedic, are about suffering, and the successful heroines are those who cope with their suffering in Buddhist fashion.

With every assignment I give as a professor, I tell my students they must know their purpose and audience. That determines everything. It's a bit problematic for me. I'm an academic writing about Austen and Buddhism, which sounds pretty academic. Only academics don't include personal experience in their work, which I've already done, and by now I should have a bunch of bibliographic references. In addition, my discipline of English does not welcome this kind of argument where I wish to make claims about universals. Because misguided claims about universals have led to terrible-isms, particularly sexism and racism, most academics hear the words *universal human nature* and cringe. (I know. I've gotten the cold shoulder and snide comments at conferences when I've tried.)

For these reasons, I don't see this as purely an academic book for an academic audience. Beyond that, I'd like to reach a larger audience than fellow academics because I hope I have helpful insights to share that might be applied to readers' personal lives. I envision this book's audience to include the many Janeites out there. My hope is to offer a new perspective on Austen. An even more general reader may engage with this text. We all suffer. It's part of the human condition, and we don't have to be Buddhists to see this. Many of us have turned to fiction for solace. I'm confident what I have seen in Austen would open up other texts as well; for example, in re-reading Dickens' *Great Expectations* from a Buddhist perspective, I had new insight into Pip's suffering. Even those not enamored of Austen (I pause to wonder how this is possible) but lovers of literature might be a part of my audience. Lastly, someone interested in Buddhism from a new angle might be among my readers.

However, just as I'm not saying Austen was a Buddhist, I am not Buddhist either. I jokingly refer to myself as Buddhish. The great religions share at their core a central message of love. I'm uninterested in doctrine and fascinated with religious teachings on love from Hinduism, Islam, and Christianity as well as Buddhism. The path to peace for me has been Buddhism in all likelihood because the brand of Buddhism I've read comes from those more interested in the practice of mindfulness and transcending suffering than on doctrine. For me, that has been Thich Nhat Hanh, the Dalai Lama, Charlotte Joko Beck, and Pema Chödrön. I suppose my purpose is implied in my discussion of audience. I wish to offer insight into suffering via a discussion of Austen and Buddhism in the very humble hope that I may contribute to alleviating suffering for at least one person.

# Introduction

"No man's knowledge here can go beyond his experience."
—John Locke, *An Essay Concerning Human Understanding*

"A teacher cannot give you the truth. The truth is already in you. You only need to open yourself—body, mind, and heart."
—Thich Nhat Hanh, *The Heart of the Buddha's Teachings*

"We have all a better guide in ourselves, if we would attend to it, than any other person can be."
—Jane Austen, *Mansfield Park*

I am not arguing that Jane Austen knew anything about Buddhism, but there is overlap between Buddhist ideas about enlightenment and the British Enlightenment, the period during which Austen wrote. The British Enlightenment is generally thought of as spanning the "long eighteenth century," from 1660 to 1815, and represents an epistemological shift: a change in how people viewed and interacted with the world. Rather than depend entirely upon the Catholic church to explain the world, as people had during the medieval era, or turning back to ideas from antiquity, as the Renaissance did, the Enlightenment offered up a new notion of reality. Its stories, to use zen teacher David Loy's term in *The World Is Made of Stories*, serve as the roots of modern Western culture, particularly the United States. For example, our modern economic system owes much to eighteenth-century philosopher Adam Smith, and our contemporary scientific method rests upon the ideas of early empiricist Sir Francis Bacon. As Peter Knox-Shaw's work *Jane Austen and the Enlightenment* argues, Austen's novels very much embody the important ideas of the Enlightenment: science, reason, and social reform as well as "an emphasis on the limits of individual heroism" and distrust of doctrine (5). Austen's novels also contain characteristics of Buddhist enlightenment.

The most important Enlightenment thinker for our purposes is seventeenth-century philosopher John Locke, who wrote *Two Treatises of Government* and *An Essay Concerning Human Understanding*. In Locke's *Essay*, we find the essential overlap between the British Enlightenment and Buddhist enlightenment: the emphasis on experience. Locke argued that all knowledge starts with the senses. He believed that people are born as blank slates with no innate ideas and get to know the world entirely through their senses. Understanding comes from direct experience that produces simple ideas, and all knowledge builds from there via reflection on more complex ideas. To know something, Locke believed, we must experience it directly for ourselves.

The Buddha similarly privileged experience, explicitly acknowledging that his wisdom came from personal experience. We need to remember that the Buddha was not a god but an individual. He began life as Siddhartha Gautama, an Indian prince whose father protected him from all suffering. Eventually, though, Siddhartha witnessed human suffering firsthand. He consequently renounced wealth and went in search of enlightenment, leaving the palace to join ascetics on his quest. After many years of difficult practice, the Buddha failed to achieve enlightenment. He left his fellow ascetics, eventually meditating under the Bodhi Tree where he understood the origin and cure for suffering: the Four Noble Truths. The Buddha prefaced his first teaching by saying, "I tell you that if I have not experienced directly all that I have told you, I would not proclaim to you that I am a free person" (qtd. in Thich Nhat Hanh, *Heart* 7). Because each person has the Buddha within, that is, has the potential to achieve Buddhahood or enlightenment, Thich Nhat Hanh notes the importance still for the primacy of personal experience in the creation of ideas. "When our beliefs are based on our own direct experience of reality and not on notions offered by others, no one can remove these beliefs from us" (*Living* 220).

With the emphasis on personal experience comes a commensurate emphasis on the individual. Naturally with attention on the eye—as in knowing the world through our senses—there comes an interest in the I, the individual and his perception of the world. The individual is the maker of knowledge. Modern-day psychology has its roots in Enlightenment ideas where philosophers such as Locke and David Hume attempted to understand how the individual mind perceives the world and creates ideas. At the same time, the British Enlightenment was concerned with the individual's place within a larger societal structure. It was a stratified society that still believed in a place for everything (everyone) and everything (everyone) in its (her) place.

We can see this in one of the eighteenth century's most popular poets, Alexander Pope. His poem "Essay on Man" quietly owes a debt to Locke with his description of people using their senses to know the world. He then proceeds to insult his reader as a "vile worm" with accusations of "madness, pride, impiety" for questioning humankind's place in the universe. Pope argues for God's universal order with humans occupying their correct place, writing: "All are but parts of one stupendous whole, / Whose body Nature is, and God the soul" (lines 267–8); he exhorts, "Know thy own point" (line 283) and closes his poem with "Whatever is, is right" (line 294). Pope's poem underscores the Enlightenment's foundation being the individual tempered by the individual's place within society.

My own previous research on eighteenth-century British pirates demonstrates this same worry over the individual not remembering his proper place. Pirates were represented as the worst of all possible criminals, even dehumanized, for their complete disregard for society's rules and structures. Pirates were reviled for taking individualism to extreme. Even as the individual became so important as knowledge creator, therefore, there was anxiety about taking that too far and a strong sense of the interconnectedness of individuals for the good of the greater society. The culture was hierarchical, balancing the individual and interconnectedness. The eighteenth century, therefore, was a time of moderation in all things.[1]

The Buddhist enlightenment shares this notion of interconnectedness, while still stressing individual experience. And, similarly, there is an emphasis on moderation, called the Middle Way, in Buddhism. Because Buddhism advocates the dropping of concepts, experience is paramount. Zen teacher Charlotte Joko Beck emphatically declares that "there *is* no authority outside of my experience" (emphasis in original 16). Yet, while enlightenment must be found at the individual level, Buddhists see all life as interconnected. Thich Nhat Hanh proclaims that we can recognize what he calls *interbeing* simply by looking at a flower, which exists thanks to the coming together of clouds that produce rain, sun, and the light produced by the sun, the soil, etc. All of these elements come together to form the flower and "interare." In this way, Buddhists share Pope's vision of connection and interdependence and a consequent belief in the Middle Way, a balance between extreme asceticism and intemperance.

In practice, the Middle Way means not asking Buddhists to disengage or to ignore emotions but to adopt multiple perspectives and to approach life in a calm manner, not allowing emotion to take over. Like the British of the eighteenth century, Buddhists recognize the stakes of connectedness. One person's fear and anxiety or enlightenment impact all of those around her.

This energy we feel in the presence of others allows us to read those around us, crucial since we live together as a species. Though not using this language, both versions of (the) enlightenment recognize that we are social animals. We are, therefore, finely attuned to others, an evolutionary adaptation called Theory of Mind by evolutionary psychologists.

Evolutionary psychology builds upon Charles Darwin's theory of natural selection, claiming humans not only adapted physically to their environment but also psychologically. Those psychological traits that best ensured the carrying forth of one's genes became adaptations. Theory of Mind means mind reading, not in a clairvoyant fashion, but in registering the body language and action of others and thereby ascribing motivation and emotion. We observe behavior and create narrative around that behavior (often times incorrectly). Such an adaptation would be crucial in early societies where interpreting the reaching for a weapon during a hunting party might save the observer's life if the weapon were meant to harm the observer rather than prey. Theory of Mind matters throughout time because of potential life and death consequences but, more applicably, because we live in societies that evaluate and categorize. Theory of Mind is necessary to negotiate the social world and achieve status.

Because of Theory of Mind, then, we all tell stories. The stories we tell ourselves create or mitigate suffering as do the stories created about us and the stories that we read. As Loy argues, "The life we are thrown into is a storied one where the task of interpretation is unavoidable and always incomplete" (25). Problems arise because we struggle with this idea of incomplete stories, strongly preferring certainty, and we often misinterpret.

Enlightenment thinkers understood this, though of course not couching their concerns in the language of evolution or Buddhism. Locke's *Essay* created great interest in education since he (falsely) argued that everyone is born a blank slate with no prior knowledge. If this is the case, then it matters very much what an individual sees, tastes, hears, touches, smells—and reads.

Such concern coincides with the proliferation of a new genre, the novel.[2] The increased interest in the individual, her place in the world, and how the mind worked combined with an increase in print materials available overall to readers of the eighteenth century created the novel. Here was an opportunity to read about an average person's life in an accessible form. With the novel, readers could witness how characters created their own stories, how Pamela, the eponymous heroine of a popular mid-century novel, interpreted her experience in the same way that readers were daily interpreting their own lives via Theory of Mind.

Novels largely traced the average person's experience (though perhaps an average person with a more adventurous life than typical) and often chronicled the lives of women. Because women were seen as the weaker sex, there was a great deal of concern over their reading material. Samuel Richardson, for example, created his own footnotes to his novel *Clarissa*, feeling that his first published novel, *Pamela*, had been misunderstood. (And he was very annoyed by the parodies.) Charlotte Lennox's *The Female Quixote* follows Arabella as she gets herself into misadventures due to reading the world around her as if it operated the same way as the French romances she has read. With the rise of the stories in novels, the eighteenth century recognized how the stories we consume become a part of the stories we tell.

Buddhism also has great interest in consumption, defined broadly as those experiences to which we expose ourselves. In Buddhism, there are the Five Precepts, updated by Thich Nhat Hanh as the Five Mindfulness Trainings, a distillation of the Buddha's teachings to serve as guidelines for living mindfully. The Fifth Training begins with, "Aware of the suffering caused by unmindful consumption, I am committed to cultivating good health, both physical and mental, for myself, my family, and my society by practicing mindful eating, drinking, and consuming" (*The Mindfulness Survival Kit* 122).

Thich Nhat Hanh defines consumption, like the eighteenth century, via the senses and notes that we are inundated with sensory material, some of which can be toxic to our well-being both physically and emotionally. Like the eighteenth-century novelists Richardson or Lennox, then, Buddhism recognizes how what we input—what we read—impacts our understanding and the stories we go on to create for ourselves.

Austen's stories embody the principles shared by both enlightenments. The individual's experience is at the heart of Austen's novels, as is how differing perceptions and the stories that arise from those perceptions can create happiness or suffering. For Austen's characters, Theory of Mind is not necessary to negotiate a world of predators but is vital in the social settings of all of Austen's novels.[3] The title alone of *Sense and Sensibility* proves Austen's dedication to the Middle Way. Austen also provides overt commentary on consumption whether it be Anne Elliot giving Captain Benwick advice on what to read to mend a broken heart in *Persuasion* or Austen's narrator offering a panegyric to the novel form in *Northanger Abbey*.

With consumption comes choice. While choice is universal, the modern, Western concept of choice also has its roots in the eighteenth century when we first find the burgeoning of the marketplace and the marketplace of ideas. As much as humans—particularly in modern Western culture—wish for control over absolutely everything in their lives, there is very little we actually control. We cannot make a happy moment last forever. We never can control another person, nor should we try, though most of us do.

In other words, we are in a very similar place existentially as Austen's heroines are in a more literal way when it comes to choice and control. They must passively await the proposal, and their choices include how they're going to feel about that (anxiety, resignation, hope) and whether they say yes or no (though they still may be at the whim of their parents).

This limited choice and control for women were clear in Austen's culture and clear in her novels. It is less clear for modern Westerners, who, thanks to the British Enlightenment, generally see themselves as active and striving, in control of our own destinies. Ideas about the number of choices we make are dictated by the story our culture tells us about choice and control, as demonstrated by social psychologist Sheila Iyengar. Iyengar conducted a study asking American and Japanese college students to list the number of choices they had made the previous day. She found that the American students, as representatives of a culture focused more on the individual, thought of themselves as making 50 percent more choices than their Japanese counterparts, listing such things as hitting the snooze button on the alarm or brushing their teeth as choices (56–7). Iyengar's study shows that ideas about choice are connected to perspective and whether a culture is focused on community or the individual; it highlights American culture's desire to be in control. Everything is a choice, meaning I control what happens.

In reality, there is much in our lives that we do not choose. When we pretend otherwise and tightly grip control and outcomes, we create more suffering for ourselves and those around us. We can learn much about choice in studying Austen's heroines. From a Buddhist perspective, what we learn is that Austen's most popular heroine with modern audiences, Elizabeth Bennet, is the least enlightened whereas the less popular and more passive characters, Fanny Price and Anne Elliot, are enlightened.

Another appeal for modern readers is Austen's focus on the ordinary. We read about ordinary people living ordinary lives and grappling with ordinary problems. Our culture may be quite different from Austen's, yet our lives reflect this pattern of how day-to-day existence still carries with it the possibility of great suffering or anxiety. When we can recognize that everyone suffers, we cultivate compassion so that reading Austen demonstrates the awakening potential of narrative as we find compassion for characters living quiet lives.

Chapter One focuses on anxiety, which is the most prevalent form of suffering in our time according to the Dalai Lama. Anxiety is tied to evolution and narrative. Anxiety is an evolutionary adaptation since, in order to survive, our ancestors required fear to negotiate the hostile environment they faced. Anxiety operates as a kind of narrative. As elucidated by Michael Austin in *Useful Fictions*, we tell ourselves stories to determine if what we're facing is in fact dangerous or not, attributing a strange sound, for example, to something benign or to someone out to hurt us. Our ancestors told themselves a story about the rustle in the bush that determined their response, to flee if the narrative attributed the sound to a lion or to keep walking along if they thought that the sound was created by a bunny.

Because we live in far less dangerous times than our Pleistocene ancestors, we require far less anxiety than they did to survive.

Our happiness largely depends upon learning to alleviate unnecessary anxiety. We are no longer threatened regularly by natural predators, so human anxiety generally revolves around needing a sense of control. Humans wish to control what we can't, which makes us anxious. Anxiety comes from a gap between reality and the story we create about our ideal version of our lives. Novels can teach us how to negotiate anxiety by generating low-stakes anxiety. We identify with characters and their plights, causing us some unease, but our own survival is never at stake, allowing us to relax into narrative-induced anxiety.

While evolution generates anxiety to ensure survival, Buddhist psychology reduces anxiety to increase happiness via mindfulness. Chapter Two looks at narrative and anxiety from a Buddhist perspective. While our evolutionary impulses drive us to fear extinction, interbeing means that we cannot die. Buddhism, therefore, offers a way to break the cycle of suffering created by the vain hope that we can avoid pain and make pleasure permanent. Buddhist psychology makes clear that we are powerless to escape pain just as an Austen heroine is powerless to propose or to choose a career. What we can do is understand the Four Noble Truths: that suffering is inevitable, that we must discover the cause of our suffering, that we can end our suffering, and that we end it via the Noble Eightfold Path: Right View, Right Thinking, Right Speech, Right Action, Right Livelihood, Right Diligence, Right Mindfulness, and Right Concentration. In other words, Buddhism allows us to recognize the narrative, to detach from it, and to reframe in such a way that we do not increase our suffering through the endless narrative chatter of our evolutionary adaptation of anxiety.

Chapter Three analyzes Austen's most famous novel, *Pride and Prejudice*, a narrative dependent upon characters creating incorrect stories and miscommunicating throughout. Austen's best-known novel clearly establishes the suffering Buddhism has the potential to alleviate. The suffering arises from the three main poisons from which all afflictions arise: craving (or attachment), anger, and ignorance. The characters' deep belief in a separate self—their ignorance—leads to an attachment to an idea of who that self should be and anger when that vision is threatened. While it is one of Austen's most comedic works, underneath it rests an undercurrent of the same kind of daily suffering we all tend to inflict upon ourselves and others in our daily lives.

Chapter Four investigates experience from both a British Enlightenment and Buddhist enlightenment perspective. In spite of the privileging of experience during the British Enlightenment, the culture was still trapped by concepts that could create damaging stories. We can see this clearly through *Sense and Sensibility*'s Elinor and Marianne Dashwood, who fail at Right Thinking. Right Thinking requires being present, being sure, and rejecting habit energy. Elinor and Marianne, as the title suggests, are instead trapped by concepts. As the two heroines leave the familiar surroundings of their home due to their father's death, they are unable to grasp reality and instead force reality into a box. Viewing the world via the concepts of sense and sensibility respectively nearly costs Elinor her happiness and Marianne her life. More importantly, these concepts lead to great misunderstanding of true love as defined by Buddhism so that both characters suffer throughout the novel.

Chapter Five weaves together the evolutionary adaptation Theory of Mind with Buddhist compassion in *Emma*, the story of a pampered young woman who means no harm but whose misreading leads to a great deal of mis-writing when she scripts the lives of those around her with nearly disastrous consequences. Though our evolutionary propensity for story making by no means equals happiness, the happy ending is Austen's trademark. Fortunately, for Emma, Austen teaches her heroine empathy leading to compassion so that Emma gets her happy ending. Austen described Emma as "a heroine whom no one but myself will much like," but readers do like Emma because we share her faulty Theory of Mind and long for the happiness provided via compassion.

As with *Sense and Sensibility*, the characters of *Northanger Abbey* are trapped by concepts, but the novel delves more deeply into the root of these concepts through its focus on consumption, broadly defined, which I explore in Chapter Six. Austen sets much of the novel in Bath, a spa town with healing waters to consume and a shopper's paradise. From its long conversations on muslin to its defense of the novel, *Northanger Abbey* explores how what we consume can be wholesome or unwholesome, leading to happiness or to suffering. We all consume via our senses, our volition, and our own thoughts and feelings. To do so mindlessly is unwholesome and creates suffering—and, in the case of *Northanger Abbey*, comedy. Catherine falls prey to unmindful consumption in her reading of Gothic novels, but having escaped a conventional lady's education, she is a child of nature who, though naive, inches us closer to enlightenment through good volition.

Chapter Seven proves that, from a Buddhist perspective, Fanny Price is no longer "poor Fanny" as the seemingly passive main character of *Mansfield Park* is often labeled. Growing up as the poor relation in a house where she is often overlooked, Fanny learns to be quiet and observant and, by Western standards, an emotional punching bag. Viewed through Buddhism, though, Fanny becomes a budding *bodhisattva*, a compassionate being who achieves enlightenment in the service of others. To be a *bodhisattva*, one must cultivate deep listening, understanding, Right Diligence, and Right Livelihood (helping the unfortunate). Fanny successfully embodies *bodhicitta*, the awakened mind or the "mind of love." The seeming passivity that makes modern readers fail to appreciate Fanny exemplifies her ability to stop, the first step in achieving enlightenment, and to look deeply. Fanny's narrative of her own life does not require her to be its star. Instead she focuses on connection, or interbeing. Therefore, by the end of *Mansfield Park*, it is Fanny who brings healing and compassion to all of the other more active, striving characters who have created the suffering of the novel through focusing only on themselves.

Anne Elliot of *Persuasion* is the Buddha, a fully enlightened being, and is the subject of Chapter Eight. The external circumstances of Anne's life are extraordinarily painful. Anne faces spinsterhood and loss of income while enduring benign and at times cruel neglect from those around her. She is not valued or understood by anyone, even her supposed dearest friend Lady Russell who persuaded her to abandon the man she loves and her path to freedom. Yet Anne faces her suffering without denial, understands its source, and follows the Eightfold Path in such a manner as to never add to her own suffering. Her Theory of Mind rarely fails, so she does not exacerbate the difficult problems of her life via a dramatic narrative that puts her at the center of a victim drama. Anne gets her happy ending; more importantly, Anne has equanimity throughout. Her circumstances are painful, but she does not suffer unduly.

The Conclusion synthesizes the individual Buddhist analyses of Austen's novels and puts these ideas in context with the modern notion of bibliotherapy, the therapeutic use of literature for psychological issues.

# ONE

# Why Stories Matter
## *The Evolution and Narrative of Anxiety*

"Our minds are wired to create order, a cohesive narrative, and our stories are our anchors."
—Sharon Salzberg, *Real Love:*
*The Art of Mindful Connection*

"We were built by natural selection, and natural selection works to maximize genetic proliferation, period. In addition to not caring about the truth per se, it doesn't care about our long-term happiness."
—Robert Wright, *Why Buddhism Is True*

"Every day at Longhorn was now a day of anxiety."
—Jane Austen, *Pride and Prejudice*

The Buddha's first teachings were the Four Noble Truths. The first is that life inevitably involves suffering. The second is that we can discover the causes of suffering. The third is we can end our suffering. The fourth Noble Truth lays out the path to end suffering and is referred to as the Eightfold Path.

Some suffering is obvious: poverty, war, abuse, illness, and death. When the Buddha promised that we could end suffering, he did not mean that we could prevent painful things from happening, such as death. But the story we create about death can cause great suffering or not. The third Noble Truth means that we can change the story about death so that we do not suffer (as much, at least) from that death. As the Harry Potter series makes clear, it's a choice. We can fight death and create suffering for ourselves and others like Voldemort does, or we can see it as Dumbledore does in the first book

15

where he tells Harry, "to the well organized mind, death is but the next great adventure" (Rowling, *Sorcerer's Stone* 297). So pain, illness, and death are inevitable, but we can choose how much or little we suffer since much of suffering is reactionary and self-created through the stories we tell ourselves about events both big and small.

The stories we tell ourselves affect us powerfully, often in destructive and anxiety-producing ways. Because of this, many modern Buddhist intellectuals, including the Dalai Lama and Vietnamese monk Thich Nhat Hanh, believe that anxiety is the most prevalent form of suffering in the Western world. Anxiety is defined as "an emotion characterized by feelings of tension, worried thoughts and physical changes like increased blood pressure" (American Psychological Association). These "worried thoughts" are created by the monkey mind, the endless internal chatter narrating the events of our lives. There is simply what happens in life and then all of the narrative baggage we create around those events that can create anxiety. Everyone feels anxiety to some degree because it serves an important evolutionary purpose, but too much creates suffering—not just for ourselves but for society as a whole.

Modern science supports the claim that anxiety is the prevailing form of suffering in our time. It also documents the costs. Those with anxiety disorders typically have "recurring intrusive thoughts or concerns" and limit interactions because of worry. Physical symptoms of anxiety include rapid heartbeat, perspiring, trembling, and dizziness (APA). According to the Anxiety and Depression Association of America (ADAA), 40 million adults in the United States suffer from some form of an anxiety disorder, which is the most common mental illness in the U.S. affecting 18 percent of the population.

A study commissioned by the ADAA found that anxiety disorders cost the United States more than $42 billion a year, nearly a third of the $148 billion the U.S. spends on mental health.[1] More than half of these costs represent repeated health care visits since those with anxiety disorders visit doctors hoping for relief from physiological symptoms of anxiety that imitate symptoms of physical illness (ADAA). People with anxiety disorders are three to five times more likely to visit a doctor and six times more likely to be hospitalized for a psychiatric disorder than those who do not have an anxiety disorder (ADAA).

The financial cost represents not just an outlay of money to help treat what is generally recognized as a treatable problem but to alleviate symptoms not recognized as anxiety by those who have them. This is because the story those who suffer from anxiety produce to explain their physical discomfort leads them to search for a physiological disease rather than considering a psychological cause. For example, if someone experiences a panic attack, which is characterized by, among other symptoms, chest pains, she may interpret the event as a sign that she has heart disease and seek treatment for that rather than recognizing the panic attack as a manifestation of anxiety. It depends on the narrative that she creates. The physical sensation may be the same or similar for heart disease and for the panic attack; the pain is merely a physical sensation. The interpretation of that pain determines the course of treatment. Someone who is anxious and likely, therefore, to worry about health might be prone to interpret the symptoms as the more dangerous heart disease and spend considerable resources trying to cure a disease she does not have.

The cost of anxiety to the individual is high as well because long-term exposure to stress can cause physical illness and decrease quality of life. Stress and anxiety have demonstrably negative effects on our bodies. The brain must first create a story or narrative that a situation is cause for stress. Note that what may be stressful for one person may cause no stress for another. Once our brains signal to our bodies that there is stress, we release hormones that activate the adrenal glands to discharge cortisol, adrenaline, and noradrenaline, setting off the fight-or-flight response. This leads to increased heart rate, higher blood pressure, and faster breathing as well as a spike in glucose and fatty acids for available energy to act since our bodies now feel threatened and ready to respond to that threat.

This increase of bodily functions exacts a toll on our digestive and immune systems, which essentially shut down temporarily while blood flows away from the extremities to the core, and our ability to tolerate pain increases. This physiological response is evolutionarily adaptive; it prepares our bodies to face maximum damage and continue to function. Of course, it comes at a high cost, particularly if sustained. With our immune system compromised, we become more vulnerable to disease, including the common cold, something I witness among my college students every semester. Wounds and injuries also take longer to heal. With the body in a state of tension, sleep issues arise as well, which creates a domino negative effect to health since sleep is so important to fully functioning and impacts learning. Stress and anxiety are also linked to higher chances of heart disease.

Long-term exposure to the stress hormone hydrocortisone weakens the neurons of the hippocampus, the part of the brain associated with memory and learning, making it difficult to learn new information or recall what has been learned in the past. Stress hurts our ability to perform tasks since it decreases our ability to think and react quickly due to overtaxing our working memory, that is our ability to contain and manipulate information for a short period of time, such as the items on a list or phone numbers. Working memory is a central function of the mind and is connected with intelligence and basic sensory processes. Because working memory has a limited capacity, allowing anxiety to take over leaves inadequate space for working memory to do its job. Note that these problems are associated with anxiety and stress in general, not specifically with anxiety disorders. This is part of being human.

Therefore, we do not need to be diagnosed with an anxiety disorder to experience anxiety's deleterious effects, nor are all of the consequences physical. The Dalai Lama's coauthor for *The Art of Happiness*, physician Howard Cutler, reminds readers that all humans at some point will suffer from too much anxiety, undercutting our ability to be happy and interfering with accomplishing goals (509).

One way that anxiety undercuts our ability to accomplish goals is by reducing our self-confidence, as experiments conducted by business professors at Harvard and the University of Pennsylvania demonstrate. Because they have less confidence in themselves, those who suffer from anxiety are less likely to trust themselves so are more likely to seek advice and less able to determine whether the advice is good. They are prone to follow advice without evaluating whether it should be taken (Gino et al. 509). (Here, we might think of Anne Elliot in Austen's *Persuasion*.)

Anxiety also creates egocentrism: relying too heavily on our own perspective, assuming those around us see things the same way we do. Egocentrism produces the possibilities of isolation, conflict, and lack of empathy, making it hard to evaluate our situation and others around us correctly (Todd et al.). (Perhaps *Pride and Prejudice* comes to mind?) In situations that produce stress because we fear being evaluated, such as public speaking, anxiety often harms cognition and the ability to perform the task well—especially for those lacking expertise. With an already reduced working memory due to anxiety, anxious individuals waste even more working memory on worry and rumination rather than concentrating on accomplishing their goal (Brooks 1145). Anxiety also makes us risk aversive. (Fanny Price from *Mansfield Park* might relate.)

Yet just as the Buddha described suffering as inherent to living, anxiety also is necessary to life, serving an evolutionary purpose. Anxiety is a psychological adaptation that benefits the survival of our species. Anxiety would have been important for our ancestors because it makes us more vigilant toward potential threats around us and prepares us to avoid such threats, as previously noted when describing the fight or flight response. Unlike fear, which typically arises from a specific threat, anxiety is more diffuse, looking for sources of potential harm that may not be present. While fear narrows our attention, anxiety broadens attention to detect possible threats (Maner and Kenrick 120). Anxiety, then, like most adaptations, comes with a cost as it requires us to expend energy where danger may not be present.

Unlike fear, where our attention is narrowed in on a clear, present danger, anxiety rests on narrative, the stories we tell ourselves about our situation, which is, again, evolutionary in origin. Our ancestors encountered potentially dangerous stimuli that required interpretation, and they would not have survived if they had ignored every rustling sound from a bush. As Michael Austin explains in *Useful Fictions*, usually the sounds our ancestors heard were made by something harmless such as a bird or a bunny. But sometimes the rustling in the bush came from predator. Ignore the sound made by a predator and die.

Narrative determined response: Our ancestor hears a sound and tells himself that is a harmless bunny or bird. Or he tells himself it might be a lion. The narrative our ancestor told determined his next move. The bunny story means moving on calmly. The lion story means fight or flight. If he ignored that correct little tickling of anxiety, preferring calm over caution, he became lion food, and not only was he dead, but he was sacrificing his DNA, either by abandoning existing children he no longer could protect or by dying childless. But, of course, anxiety also must be mitigated. Decide every rustling of a bush means predator and our ancestor lives a life of extreme anxiety making him equally incapable of passing on his genes because he can't attract a mate or feed and protect his family.

Our ancestor's attention to possible dangers in the form of rustling bushes clearly was essential for survival given his environment. Those challenges led to our ancestors banding together, behaving as social animals dependent upon each other for survival. Human bonding created challenges as well because, as populations grew, access to resources became competitive. Scientists argue that navigating these social groups and environmental changes produced our powerful and oversized brains, larger than almost any species in relation to body weight.

From 800,000 to 200,000 years ago, human brains grew exponentially faster as our ancestors required better problem solving due to climate change, migration into new territories farther from the equator, and the dynamics of hierarchical social groups where the dominant members had better access to resources. As humans became ecologically dominant, they had to worry about being dominant within species with social interactions determining status (Geary 6–7).

Even the earliest modern humans, Cro-Magnon, organized coalitions and alliances within hierarchical groups (Keltner 63). Like us, our ancestors gained power within groups by navigating social situations well. Clearly those at the bottom of the pecking order were vulnerable but so were the dominant ones who had to maintain status at the top. Just like our modern social groups, socially dominant Cro-Magnons faced the vulnerability of having those with less power comment on their reputations (Keltner 63). For this reason, unlike other species, humans gain power not through physical strength but through emotional intelligence (Keltner xi). Power comes from understanding and managing our own emotions as well as successfully reading the emotions of others.

A number of adaptations flowed from the need to form and negotiate community, the most foundational of these being what scientists call our Theory of Mind, which, like anxiety, rests in narrative. Our Theory of Mind is what gives us the ability to read other people through reading and interpreting things such as body language and expression in order to attribute mood, motivation, truthfulness, etc., to others during social interactions and to predict future behavior.

We engage in this complex process of Theory of Mind on a constant basis but at an unconscious level. All of our encounters with fellow human beings require noticing smiles, frowns, furrowed foreheads, crossed arms, slow or fast-paced walking, tone of voice, eye contact, and more so that we can determine if someone is friendly, angry, threatening, romantically interested, or trustworthy. At a primal level, Theory of Mind serves the function of safety since it developed as an adaptation during the dangerous Pleistocene era. Still today, we use Theory of Mind as we traverse the sidewalk or parking lot to avoid becoming victims of crime.

Beyond this basic need for safety, our Theory of Mind is necessary to knit together our community, which depends upon reciprocity for success. Since not all members of a community can succeed all the time, community members must take turns helping each other. A system of reciprocity depends on the old adage "I'll scratch your back if you'll scratch mine." We see this across the animal kingdom among social creatures. For example, vampire bats share their nightly catch with fellow bats that may have been unsuccessful hunters that night, knowing that eventually every bat will encounter a bad hunting night and need help. The bat that refuses to share and eventually finds itself coming home without a meal ultimately starves since there is no bond of reciprocity obliging fellow bats to now share with it.[2] Bats, then, are engaging in complex behavior: identifying those bats that do not share, tracking that behavior, and responding accordingly.

Humans engage in reciprocal interactions all the time. We must evaluate whether the person with whom we are interacting is willing and capable of offering help and services in return since a successful social group depends upon the participation and cooperation of all members. Theory of Mind also allows for cheater detection, that is being able to recognize those who will not contribute to the community's good but rather attempt to freeload. Freeloaders benefit from community without contributing to it, like the vampire bat that enjoys the pleasures of community without contributing to fellow bats in need. My students complain of freeloaders all the time in the form of fellow classmates who are assigned to group projects and do little to nothing to help but still receive credit and a better grade than they deserve. Theory of Mind also allows us to predict who may undercut community via defection, taking advantage of community and then leaving.

Theory of Mind and its commensurate cheater detection were easier for our ancestors because archeological evidence demonstrates that, for most of history, humans lived in small communities of 50 to 150 people with many members of the group related to each other (Maner and Kenrick 123). Such intimacy produced ideal conditions for Theory of Mind with more opportunity to observe and communicate. Constant contact and interaction allowed for frequent opportunities to practice using Theory of Mind with the same set of people, which made it more reliable. In addition, evolution dictates the primal, unconscious need to carry forward our DNA, whether directly through reproduction or indirectly through cooperating with members of our family. Therefore, these smaller communities made largely of kin sharing DNA were more likely to consist of those who would reciprocate and cooperate given their common goal, making cheater detection less necessary and Theory of Mind more straightforward. Our ancestors needed that ease as the stakes for social rejection were very high. Being part of a community meant life or death; our ancestors generally lacked access to an alternate group if rejected by their primary social group. Solitude likely meant death in such a hostile environment.

Yet even in such evolutionarily beneficial circumstances, Theory of Mind is a complex process, requiring at an unconscious level the continuous tracking of who does what, when, and where. It also relies upon working memory, whose efficiency is jeopardized by anxiety, as already discussed (Ferguson 848). So our Theory of Mind is often wrong. Like anxiety, it is built upon narrative. Using Theory of Mind to understand others means being both a reader and writer of lived experience, as we make observations about others, ascribe motivation, predict behavior, and script our response accordingly. Yet we easily can misinterpret each other's actions and, consequently, intent.

For example, if we see someone yawn, we might assume that person is bored and not enjoying our company, leading us to feel rejected and resentful and then be rude to that person. However, the person may be yawning due to insomnia caused by personal distress so that the yawn has nothing to do with us, and, instead of feeling hurt, we should extend compassion. Since this hypothetical situation involves two people, it can lead either to an angry encounter or to the beginnings of a wonderful friendship as the person yawning becomes the recipient of either rudeness or kindness. Our narratives interact; all choices are dynamic with mine being affected by all those around me. As Douglas Kenrick, Norman P. Li, and Jonathan Butner argue "Not only does it take two to tango, but two rarely tango alone in a dark basement; instead, their carefully coordinated maneuvers are typically executed within a larger ballroom crowd who often change partners as they move in time to the same rhythms" (17). A good everyday example is driving, where each person's choice affects every other driver's choices with potentially dire consequences. The daily examples of road rage and accidents demonstrate just how hard Theory of Mind is in our modern culture.

As the driving example demonstrates, exercising our Theory of Mind is much more difficult for modern humans than it was for our ancestors. Generally, we no longer belong to small communities of 50 to 150 people, leading to a great deal of anonymity as we speed around in cars or walk on city streets. Our judgments of others as cheaters or cooperators in modern larger communities often depends on an indirect sort of reciprocity. While direct reciprocity allows us to track someone's immediate interactions with us, indirect reciprocity depends upon observing a history of someone helping others. In other words, we evaluate others based upon their reputation.

In fact, indirect reciprocity rests on reputation, so our acts of generosity "buy a reputation" that earns us a place within a cooperative social group (Pratto 54). This is why we are willing to pay the cost of buying a reputation. For instance, studies show that we are more willing to contribute to a charity if our donations are public since we are then seen publicly as generous, thereby building a reputation as someone who can and will help a worthy cause. If someone has a bad reputation, it is seen as fine not to help that person (Pratto 66).

Even as far back as the fourteenth century, Geoffrey Chaucer's *The Canterbury Tales* chronicled the difficulty of strangers thrown together and using Theory of Mind to read each other. In "The Pardoner's Tale," Chaucer explicitly connects reputation with how we hear the stories of others. The Pardoner tells his fellow pilgrims up front how he pulls scams and takes advantage of his listeners, essentially acknowledging his own bad reputation. But he then delivers such a profoundly true story about human nature that some pilgrims are seduced by his powerful storytelling anyway. Upon suddenly remembering who the storyteller is, they become quite angry with themselves for being pulled in rather than concentrating on the positive message.

Truth from the mouth of someone with a bad reputation produces anger and distrust. A more modern example that I share with my students is Jimmy Swaggart, a televangelist whose show was broadcast across more than 3,000 stations and cable systems at the height of his popularity and whose empire included the Jimmy Swaggart Bible College. In the late 1980s and early 1990s, however, Swaggart's empire came crashing down due to several scandals involving prostitutes. I ask students why this matters. If the Pardoner and Swaggart have good messages, why do we care how they behave in their private lives? The reason is that we are evolutionarily disposed to privilege reputation when judging credibility. The message and the messenger matter just as they did for Cro-Magnon man.

These examples also demonstrate how Theory of Mind does not necessarily protect us from cheaters. Chaucer's Pardoner temporarily manages to sway his audience, and Swaggart, though far less successful, still serves as an evangelical leader.

Cheating becomes even easier with migration and the possibility of reinventing the self. With migration, community members who are unwilling to cooperate and reciprocate can simply switch communities without their bad reputations following them (Nowak and Highfield 89). Eighteenth-century writers were experiencing this firsthand, and worries over these issues became the subject of some of the earliest novels, particularly those by Daniel Defoe, author of *Robinson Crusoe*, whose works often feature criminals moving from place to place avoiding their past misdoings. Such worries continue in modern society though we are more used to the idea of moving about. Think of the fictional example of Harold Hill from *The Music Man* who drifts from town to town promising to create boys' bands, taking money for musical instruments and leaving before anyone figures out the instruments will never arrive and the band will never play a note. A more disturbing real-life example would be Bob Evans, a serial killer who took the lives of six people over several decades, drifting across the United States and changing names as he moved. Such people are our modern lions.

The argument that the human brain grew rapidly as our ancestors negotiated hierarchical communities makes a great deal of sense, then. The ancestor facing a rustling sound in the bush formed a fairly straightforward narrative on his own. Social animals depend upon more complex narratives, tracking and remembering behavior in order to trust or not trust a fellow community member to reciprocate. More complex still is creating the narrative about the stranger whom one can know only through stories—through gossip, rumor, and hearsay that form a reputation for whether that person can be trusted. The brain power required to weave and unweave such stories required much more from our ancestors. Not only did humans have to learn to create reputations for themselves in order to secure a safe space within their community, they also had to evaluate the reputations of others. For this reason, Martin Nowak argues that "indirect reciprocity is the midwife of language and our big, powerful brain" (171). It is no wonder, then, that fictional works from *The Odyssey* to *Pride and Prejudice* to *Harry Potter* are universal as they feed our powerful brains' need to understand and generate stories.

While urbanization and these problems of reputation are centuries old, recent developments complicate things even further. Modern social media allow all of us to manipulate our reputations without the nefarious motivation of a serial killer or an evangelist wishing to separate his followers from their money. Social media expand our ideas of community exponentially. Facebook now has two billion community members. The average Facebook user has more than 300 Facebook friends, with "friends" being constructed very loosely from actual friends from our personal lives to friends of friends to total strangers. These friends are exposed to edited versions of ourselves; we get to craft our reputations more carefully. Facebook pages are a clear example of constructing narrative, our Facebook identities. To use Theory of Mind successfully, a Facebook user must apply the same kinds of critical thinking and reading skills one would bring to complex works of literature since Facebook pages consciously or unconsciously reflect an authorial attempt to create a persona in the same way an author tries to create a fictional character that reflects the complexity of a real person.

Social media also call attention to the complexity of social interactions with unspoken but important rules that affect reputation. My teen daughter has explained to me that she and her friends typically have a minimum of two Instagram accounts, one being the main account and the other spam. Some teens have three accounts, with the third being for only one's closest friends. For the main account, the user can post every other week or once a month but no more than a couple of times a week. More than that is considered annoying. The audience for this account may be public where anyone at all can see it, and only high-quality pictures of special events and friends should be posted. On the spam account, which includes actual friends, teens can post anything and as often as they want, including silly pictures and memes. If there is a third account, it is only for closest friends and includes more intimate material. Postings should occur late afternoon or evening since teens are more likely to be on their phones to see the posting and like it because the point is to get as many likes as possible.

When considering Kenrick et al.'s reference to the tango and the crowded ballroom, one can't help but marvel at how closely Instagram posting resembles the kind of intricate hierarchical social interactions present in an Austen novel where the characters had to participate in elaborate dances while engaging in witty repartee all while trying to evaluate if one's partner were worthy of further attention and perhaps a lifetime alliance. Arguably, Theory of Mind is more difficult for modern teens than for an Austen heroine in spite of our seemingly more casual society. Social media take to the extreme what has been true for centuries.

Given the importance of reputation and the complexity and fallibility of Theory of Mind, this adaptation can produce a lot of anxiety. Perhaps this is why the most prevalent anxiety disorder in the United States is social anxiety disorder. Social anxiety is specifically concerned with worry over humiliation or embarrassment in social situations out of fear of rejection or losing social status (Magee et al. 930). For this reason, social anxiety may serve an adaptive purpose, operating as a way to minimize the risk of negative evaluation from other members of the group in order to avoid social exclusion (Magee et al. 932).

While social rejection today may not carry the life-or-death consequences experienced by our Pleistocene ancestors, remember that adaptations operate at an unconscious level so that our primitive brains still calculate the cost disproportionately high. Our bodies still respond as if we might die from embarrassment, to use the cliché (Maner and Kenrick 125). There is a potential for a vicious cycle here. Our primitive brain emphasizes the need for a well-functioning Theory of Mind—reading the social situation well—but this may cause anxiety given the stakes of reading wrong. Such anxiety may, in fact, undercut successful deployment of Theory of Mind, creating the very negative evaluation that is feared and, hence, producing more anxiety.

Like anxiety in general, social anxiety produces egocentrism, occurring not only because someone has a distorted sense of self but because that individual exaggerates the extent to which others will be watching, judging, and evaluating her (Rector et al. 908). Such egocentric thinking makes us prone to read others incorrectly, assuming that we play a far greater role in their version of the interaction than may be true. Fearing evaluation and linking the uncomfortable physical sensations of anxiety with social interaction, those who suffer from social anxiety are likely to live smaller lives, limiting their social lives and perhaps feeling unable to pursue professional goals (Rector et al. 907).

Living more constricted lives as an attempt to control anxiety makes sense because anxiety arises from new or unpredictable situations over which someone feels a lack of control. In other words, there is a new story, and we are called to act in new ways. This feeling of powerlessness often creates a stress response, which we then interpret as a potentially damaging threat perhaps even to our lives given our unconscious overestimation of the stakes (Markle 25). For this reason, David Geary describes human behavior as an unconscious "evolved motivation to control" (4). This desire is so strong that we will engage in "magical thinking," in which we encounter situations so stressful that we create a narrative of control that defies logic simply to make ourselves feel better (Markle 19). Many people, for example, engage in a superstitious ritual to ensure a positive outcome: putting on that lucky shirt to make sure the right football team wins.

Austin describes an example from *Robinson Crusoe* powerfully demonstrating our need to understand. When Crusoe, after many years of isolation on his deserted island, discovers one footprint on the beach, he has no explanation and engages in a bit of magical thinking himself, wondering if his deserted island has been visited by the devil. When he later discovers cannibals, he is relieved. His desire for a rational story to explain the footprint is more powerful than the logical fear he should feel for his life as his island now has cannibals. Though scary, the cannibal narrative is less anxiety provoking because now the threat is concrete and real and something he might control.

Each of us differs in what we attempt to control and how much we attempt to control it. I've taken yoga classes where fellow students feel very anxious when yoga mats are not aligned. My yoga friends— by their own admission—have a vision of how our class should look; that straight linearity reinforces their calm, safe vision. I don't even notice others' yoga mats. I've gone skydiving with absolutely no fear. But getting lost—the mere idea of it—makes me anxious, much more so if I'm driving, so I push back against my anxiety by using GPS and leaving extra early if I have to go someplace new. The reality is I've rarely been lost, and I'm someone who has traveled a lot. (In fact,

I've been asked for directions in every foreign country I've visited, including in Asia and one time in Paris when I was hopelessly lost and holding a map.) My worry about getting lost is obviously about control and a diffuse worry over safety. I've lived in and traveled in cities known for dangerous neighborhoods. If I get lost, will I end up in a dangerous part of town? But it goes deeper than that since my anxiety generalizes to wherever I travel. Anxiety over yoga mats or getting lost rests completely in narratives. For someone like me who doesn't care about others' yoga mats, that situation is not capable of making me anxious. Others enjoy driving in new places and exploring. The same situation can produce anxiety or not for each individual depending on the story created by the person.

Anxiety is universal but also dependent upon cultural and personal narrative. In his work reconciling the cultural differences between Buddhism and modern Western culture, Harvey Aronson writes about Eastern versus Western interpretations of what Westerners call depression. In Eastern cultures, studies show that people create a story about physical symptoms complaining of exhaustion, inability to sleep, and headache among other symptoms and that the explanation for this condition is labeled *neurasthenia*, which means tired blood or frayed nerves. The Chinese participants of the study created a narrative for these symptoms that involved physiological causes. From the perspective of Westerners and modern psychology, a person feeling these same symptoms would be labeled as depressed, and the approach to cure this person would address psychological issues, which might include medication but would inevitably mean talk therapy to address emotions. So while the symptoms of anxiety affect all people, the stories we create lead to labeling physiological symptoms in ways that can make anxiety worse or better and suggest different ways to alleviate it.

This also means we can change the narrative about anxiety and even appreciate its benefits. Maybe that will make us less anxious about being anxious. Alison Wood Brooks notes that, though anxiety feels unpleasant, it can positively affect our behavior, for example motivating us to put in effort and prepare for a stressful event such as a performance if we know of it in advance (1145). The key is a moderate level of anxiety: too little, and individuals won't prepare, too much, and anxiety will mar the performance itself. So anxiety serves a purpose and when experienced at the appropriate level and context prepares us to avoid harm (Maner and Kenrick 120).

As with suffering in general, the third Noble Truth works here: We can alleviate our anxiety. We do this through attention to and understanding of narrative. Brooks' experiments demonstrate that the physiological symptoms of anxiety are very similar to those of excitement; if we choose to label the physical symptoms as excitement, we shift the narrative, and our working memory is no longer encumbered by anxiety. Rather, we are excited and ready to perform. Nothing has changed except for the explanation we offer ourselves.

Narratives and our approach to them matter for our health and well-being whether those narratives are the stories we tell about ourselves, the stories others tell about us, or the narratives created by authors that we then read. Austen understood and chronicled this, and Buddhism offers a way out of damaging narrative.

# Two

# A Buddhist Solution

"What wild imaginations one forms where dear self is concerned! How sure to be mistaken!"
—Jane Austen, *Persuasion*

"What makes us suffer is the way we think about what's happening."
—Pema Chödrön, *No Time to Lose*

"With your deluded mind, you make hell for yourself. With your true mind, you make paradise."
—Thich Nhat Hanh, *The Heart of the Buddha's Teaching*

Religion, philosophy, psychology, and, yes, Jane Austen share the belief that our perception of the world is limited and often in error. Based on our often flawed perceptions, we tell stories, and, when we do, we create narratives to explain the phenomena happening around us. The stories we tell ourselves about our daily lives and the people in them can create both happiness and suffering.

In psychology, talk therapy works because it teaches us to rethink the narratives we create about ourselves—to see ourselves and our situations in a way that allows for greater mental health and happiness. Similarly, Buddhism's Fourth Noble Truth lays out the ways to stop suffering—which sounds very much like the cognitive and behavioral changes modern psychology recommends, though going farther. We must change the way we think—the way we story our world, to use Zen teacher David Loy's phrase—and then change our behavior. In the same way that Marianne Dashwood must learn to see without the lens of sensibility or Emma Woodhouse without snobbishness and a desire to control, all humans must step back from their "very important stories," as Pema Chödrön calls them, in order to stop suffering.

The First Noble Truth posits that suffering is universal; much of that suffering comes from our stories. There are three levels of suffering. The first is the "suffering of suffering," which refers to physical and mental pain or discomfort. The second is the "suffering of change," which arises from wanting things to stay as they are and makes us uneasy due to the fear of change. The third and deepest form is the "ubiquitous suffering of conditioned existence," which rests on the false narrative of a unitary independent self (Wallace 40–1). While physical pain is an inherent part of nature, all other levels of suffering can be alleviated according to the Second Noble Truth. Since mental discomfort, anxiety over change, and the idea of an independent unitary self are all rooted in narratives, we can stop the suffering through changing the story. Mental health becomes an act of imagination in much the same way that the novels we read are products of imagination.

A fictional narrative, of course, has a point of view. A story is told from a perspective, whether a character tells her own story in the first person or an almost god-like narrator explains everything in an omniscient third-person voice. Each of us also creates personal narratives from a perspective, whether we are conscious of it or not. For example, I have constructed a narrative of myself as a middle-class American English professor living in Florida who is a single mother. These are facts, but they also are ideas about myself that color how I view events around me. They are part of the identity I've created for myself, and they affect how I present myself to the world and how I assume I'll be received by the world. When events don't conform to my idea about myself, I may feel threatened, which causes me to suffer. If the world does not accord me the treatment I expect due to my idea of myself, I, again, may feel defensive or threatened. Don't they know who I am?! Well, no, because all I am is a made-up story in my own head.

This is what Pema Chödrön means by "very important stories," which, when undercut by uncomfortable emotions, make us aware that we are not as in control of our lives as we like to pretend. To feel the discomfort of disappointment or embarrassment gives us a sense of groundlessness, a hint that the foundation we've created about ourselves and our place in life is only a story—because it is. Pema Chödrön argues that the realization that our story doesn't work to explain the world or ourselves is a "sort of death" (39), which we understandably resist. Therefore, a fearful response is perfectly natural as we "go into unknown territory" feeling our lack of control and power (*When Things Fall Apart* 40).

To return to the First Noble Truth, suffering is universal because this tendency toward narrative is universal. Evolutionary psychologists, for example, have long debated the purpose of fiction, which is universal across cultures and time. Is fiction itself an evolutionary adaptation or just a byproduct of an adaptation? Regardless of the answer, narrative is an inherent, powerful aspect of human existence. So is getting things wrong.

We are so often wrong because we story our lives from a wrong point of view or perspective. In his work connecting evolutionary psychology to Buddhism, Robert Wright correctly argues that "natural selection didn't design your mind to see the world clearly; it designed your mind to have perceptions and beliefs that would help take care of your genes" (33). Adaptations arose to carry forward our genes. Evolution doesn't care about personal happiness or clear perceptions as long as we have babies before we die.

One clear misperception shown by repeated experimentation is the idea of *beneffectance*, a term coined by Anthony Greenwald to explain how people strive to present themselves as beneficial and effective to others, which also becomes how they see themselves. Beneffectance makes evolutionary sense because cooperation was so important to our ancestors as social animals and is still for us today. We need good reputations in order to gain trust and status within our social group, and our social group is what kept us alive in the Pleistocene era. Where misperception comes into play is that we tend to delude ourselves about the degree to which we are beneficial and effective.

We do this frequently. Wright cites one study of 50 drivers who described themselves as "expert" drivers, though all 50 had been in a recent car accident, and two-thirds of them had been cited as guilty for the accident (83). In addition, people tend to see themselves as morally above average. "This is an especially important piece of self-flattery, because it helps fuel the self-righteousness that starts and sustains conflicts, ranging from quarrels to wars" (Wright 85). In other words, our self-deluding narratives may serve us evolutionarily, but they have potentially negative social consequences from more car accidents because drivers fail to assess their abilities to global conflict.

Importantly, perspective comes not merely from evolutionary

adaptations but also from culture. We have cultural narratives, and cultures shape our personal narratives. As part of an ongoing series of dialogues between Western scientists and the Dalai Lama, Owen Flanagan, professor of psychology and philosophy, described studies demonstrating that Americans share "positive illusions" about themselves; they believe that they and their loved ones are smarter and better looking than others, and they judge their own musical or speech performances as better than others' (Goleman 294). While such thinking may increase personal self-esteem, a positive from a Western viewpoint, it creates division and hierarchy—things to be avoided according to Buddhism.

The contrast between Eastern and Western medicine provides an excellent example of how different lenses determine what we see and how we interpret what we see. Ted J. Kaptchuck, in his book about Chinese medicine, *The Web That Has No Weaver*, proclaims that the Chinese could not produce an Aristotle because Eastern thought is not based on binaries or dialectical thinking, that is not on either/or propositions. Or as Aristotle himself put it: "There is a principle in things, about which we cannot be deceived but must always, on the contrary recognize the truth—viz. that the same thing cannot at one and the same time be and not be, or admit any other similar pair of opposites" (qtd. in Kaptchuck 139). Rather thinking that two opposites can both be true, Western scientific thought rests on the notion of experiment-driven data proving *the* discoverable truth.

In Western medicine, such thinking leads to symptoms being traced back to a cause, which creates a diagnosis and then a cure. In Chinese medicine, which is based on the theory of yin and yang, the only constant is change.[1] Evaluations of patients are holistic, with no separation of psychology from the physical body, and with an emphasis on change and patterns. This means that, within the framework of Chinese medicine, two patients seeing the same doctor with the same symptoms may receive different treatments. The goal is not a labeled diagnosis but a cure that restores balance and harmony. Eastern and Western medicine have different narratives of how the universe and, consequently, of how the body works, leading to different ways of thinking, diagnosing, and treatment.

The same cultural perspective colors treatment of what Western medicine would describe as psychological issues, as Daniel Johnson and Lisa Johnson found in their survey of studies on stress. Western biomedical, psychiatric, and behavioral medicine approaches emphasize specific treatments predicated upon a precise diagnosis to alleviate stress. In contrast, mindfulness, which has its roots in Eastern philosophy and religion, is a practice proven effective in treating stress in general, whatever the cause of the stress. Importantly, stress is an excellent example of how narratives can cause suffering as happy events such as a wedding or graduation can cause just as much stress as events that we would consider negative such as being fired can. What these events share is how the person experiencing them stories them and whether the person feels out of control. As with the discussion of anxiety in Chapter One, it all depends on perspective; what may stress one person will cause no stress for another.

Western and Eastern cultures tend to approach ideas of well-being differently because they are predicated on different ideas about the individual. The "independent self" of Western society sees him or herself as separate and distinct from others, including family, friends, and colleagues. More typical of Asian cultures is the idea of the "interdependent self," where people view the self as interconnected, defined by social relationships, and operating within a social context. In presenting her research to the Dalai Lama on the independent versus interdependent self, psychologist Jeanne Tsai notes the consequences of these differing mindsets (Goleman 241). Those operating from an independent-self perspective tend to be more sensation seeking, quicker to become emotional, and more prone to strong emotions. Those in an interdependent-self framework consider more carefully how their actions and emotions affect others so tend to be more even keeled, toning down their own emotions for the sake of others.

All of this matters because once "people lock onto a vision of reality that appeals to them, they tend to hold their views as being uniquely true. According to Buddhism, this is a fundamental delusion" (Wallace xi). The worldview we adopt determines our values, which "in turn strongly influence our way of life. In our pursuit of happiness, we devote our time and energy to that which we value" (Wallace 36).

The Dalai Lama and Thich Nhat Hanh have both written about this problem for modern capitalistic culture. Our economic system and technology heighten the anxiety inherent to human existence. The Dalai Lama has noted that citizens of poorer countries suffer more physical pain but appear less anxious than those living in developed first-world nations because of how these cultures value materialism. Materialism leaves people with "anxiety, discontent, frustration, uncertainty and depression" as they concentrate on wanting more (*Essential* 9). Thich Nhat Hanh shares the same observation saying the anxiety from those in developed countries comes from their constant thinking and their lifestyles (*Heart* 217). The narrative of materialism—that stuff will make us happy—leads to great suffering.

In addition to materialism, science, the dominant Western worldview to explain the world, offers both answers and anxiety in its storying of reality. The Dalai Lama argues that Western science has taught us to feel even more anxious in the face of uncertainty than we are prone to by our human condition. Westerners believe "everything can and must be explained and accounted for. But when you encounter phenomena that you cannot account for, then there's a kind of tension created; it's almost a feeling of agony" (*Art* 63).

Differing cultural values and perspectives affect our self-esteem as well. When first meeting with Western scholars, the Dalai Lama was shocked to learn about the idea of low self-esteem. Mark Epstein recounts the Dalai Lama approaching each Westerner in the room, asking, "Do you have this? Do you have this?", and as each person nodded yes, the Dalai Lama shook his head incredulously. In Tibet, with its emphasis on interdependence, self-esteem is fostered from an early age and positive self-esteem simply a given. In the more independent Western materialistic culture, we are left feeling more isolated and alienated and hence more prone to low self-esteem.

While these cultural differences change the appearance of suffering, we once again must come back to the First Noble Truth and the universality of suffering: East, West, across all times. The discussion of cultural differences corresponds to the Second Noble Truth: that we must find the causes of suffering. Beyond these specific cultural examples, though, Buddhism recognizes underlying universal causes of suffering. Degrees and manifestations of suffering may differ, but the root causes are ignorance and attachment.

Suffering comes from ignorance about emptiness and about interbeing, to use Thich Nhat Hanh's phrase. The two terms are related. Interbeing refers to the idea that everything and everyone in existence are connected and interdependent. Thich Nhat Hanh uses a tree to explain the term. He argues that, when looking at the tree, one is seeing not just the tree and its obvious component parts of branches and leaves but all the elements necessary to produce it, including, for example, the sky, sun, and clouds necessary to provide carbon dioxide, light, and rain. It's not that these elements helped to nurture the tree so that it could grow but that they are an inherent part of the tree. They "interare." There is no independent tree but rather something we label a tree that is made up of interdependent aggregate parts such as seeds, water, sunlight, minerals, soil, etc. If someone planted the tree, then that person's labor is also part of the tree. An attempt to remove all of these elements of the tree (sky, sun, labor, etc.) to get to its inherent nature as tree will fail; there is no independent entity of tree. This is emptiness, the idea that we cannot locate any separate independent entity—no essential tree, just something we label a tree that exists due to its aggregate parts.

The same is true of the self. There is no separate independent entity that we can point to as a self. "I" is a fiction. Rather, every person consists of aggregate parts in the same fashion that is true of a tree. There is no core essence to which we can point and declare "that is the self," a part that truly defines the self as the self.

Science supports the Buddhist idea of emptiness. Empirical research by psychologists and neuroscientists demonstrates "that there is no independent self in the mind, the brain, or anywhere else inside or outside the body" (Wallace 26). David Barash argues from an evolutionary perspective that the ideas of emptiness and interdependence make scientific and logical sense, pointing to ecosystems, the connection between organisms and their environment, and our genetic connections tying us to our families. Our bodies themselves prove the point given that we have 10 times as many foreign cells in our bodies as we do those with our genetic signature; 100 trillion cells, most of which are in our intestines, are microbes from different genomes not produced by our own bodies (Barash 57). The self-proclaimed self hosts much that is not the self.

Obviously, there are practical concerns here. Buddhism does not require that we renounce our identities and try to live our daily lives as a non-self. Buddhists recognize that the self as a concept is an essential aspect of everyday reality. In the same way that we label a tree a tree so that we can talk about it, I identify myself as Kathryn. The problem comes when I get attached to this idea or concept and fail to recognize Kathryn as a concept, as a convenient idea necessary to operate in this world. I must move beyond "Kathryn" and everyday reality to reach the ultimate level of reality where I recognize emptiness so that "seeming entities break down into their constituent processes" (Goleman 93). And "seeming entities" includes you and me.

Recognizing emptiness matters because it is the key to nirvana, that is freedom from ignorance. When we cling to the fiction of self without recognizing it as a fiction, we create all kinds of suffering. Again, the First Noble Truth makes clear this is universal. "We are all engaged in a futile struggle to maintain ourselves in our own image" (Goleman 44). Trapped by ignorance, "we build stories on stories, and the problem with the stories begins at their foundation" (Wright 152). Ignorance of emptiness means that all of our stories will be ones that force us into other mistakes: clinging to the impermanent as permanent and attachment.

Acknowledging emptiness allows us to accept impermanence. As with interbeing or interdependence, science supports the Buddhist belief in impermanence. Everything and everyone are in flux. Everything is in motion. Barash writes, "there is simply no life that is based on steady-state, fixed, and frozen relations with its surrounding." Organisms are alive because they "are open to the rest of the world, from which they derive energy in order to continue. Permanence is a death sentence" (61).

Yet, stuck in ignorance, most of us act as if we were a stable permanent self. A Harvard study found that people generally acknowledged how much they had changed in the past but tended to grossly underestimate how much they will change in the future. The participants saw their current identity, no matter what their age, as a stable one, a sort of end game that previous change had brought them to permanently. However, the evidence—their own reading of their own lives as filled with change—predicts that they will continue to change. The participants created a narrative of stable identity destined to create suffering because it will make them resistant to change as they cling to their rooted ideas of themselves. They refuse to embrace the wisdom of impermanence. But the Buddha taught that "we cannot sustain the illusion of our self-sufficiency. We are all subject to decay, old age, and death, to disappointment, loss, and disease" (Epstein 44).

When we fail to recognize emptiness, we instead over-identify with our idea of "I" and all of our passing emotions and moods, taking a fleeting thought or feeling and labeling it as an inherent part of who we are in ways that are painful. "From a Buddhist perspective, one's perceptions, emotions, thoughts, ideas, mental images and other experiences are not oneself. Therefore, it is delusional to make such judgements about oneself, as an independent agent, based on transient mental events and processes. The resulting reification of oneself as 'abnormal,' 'bad,' and 'worthless,' is likewise misguided and results in needless suffering" (Wallace 53). Even identifying positive aspects of the "self" in delusional ways, such as that American tendency to see ourselves as above average, produces suffering, for we then become attached to the impermanent, wanting it to last and creating unease within as we dread losing the wonderful feeling of fill-in-blank here of whatever makes you so happy you can't stand the idea of losing that feeling.

And this is how suffering builds. Ignorance of emptiness leads us to believe there is a self who needs protecting, so now we have to keep away the things that might harm us or that we simply don't like, and we must attract and keep those things that give us pleasure. We develop aversion and craving—forms of attachment based upon a fictive self, all of which will only create unease, which is another way of translating *dukkha*, the Sanskrit word more often translated as suffering. "A wide range of mental afflictions involving craving and hostility arise from three fundamental misperceptions: grasping onto impermanent phenomena as unchanging and enduring, regarding phenomena that are by nature unsatisfying as true sources of well-being, and viewing impersonal things and events as 'I' and 'mine'" (Wallace 132).

By clinging to the concept of an essential self and seeing the body as me, myself, and I, we get caught up in dualistic thinking. Life becomes me versus them, me against the rest of the world, or simply me, me, me. I am the subject, and everything else the object. Dualistic thinking leads to judgment, evaluating everything and everyone as good or bad, pleasurable or unpleasurable, and desirable or undesirable. Wright argues that, from an evolutionary perspective, humans are "automatic evaluators. We tend to assign adjectives to nouns, whether consciously or unconsciously, explicitly or implicitly" (161). We've evolved to evaluate because our information processing is designed for the spreading of our genes, so we assess for optimal conditions. Importantly, those judgments provoke feelings to motivate us to act in optimal ways that benefit our genes.

A simple example from evolution is the evolved preference for sweets. Because sweet food tends to be safe and non-poisonous, our ancestors evolved a preference for sweetness. Eating sweets produced a pleasurable eating experience. Since we prefer pleasure to pain, our ancestors ate sweets and were, thereby, more prone to eating safe food. However, in our modern times, most of us still have this adaptation and seek the pleasure of sweets to our detriment. For our ancestors, the sweet was a healthy piece of fruit. For us, the sweet might involve fruit, but that fruit often is part of a pie, donut, or pastry—and not so healthy for us anymore. The feeling of pleasure tied to the judgment of what we enjoy eating can lead to health problems as we overindulge. This is only one example of how those things that give us pleasure can ultimately contribute to our suffering.

From a Buddhist perspective, pleasure undercuts enlightenment because it reinforces the ignorance of impermanence as we constantly search for the one person or thing that will ultimately make us feel complete and content. Yet pleasure is always temporary. "Pleasure exhausts itself in the enjoying, just like a candle that burns down and disappears" (Ricard qtd. in Goleman 85). And pleasure is unreliable; something that gives us great pleasure once often fails to do so again. This is why I've only been skydiving one time. The experience gave me incredible pleasure. Knowing that I'll never recapture that feeling again, I haven't tried.

Note, there is nothing inherently wrong with pleasure or desire. The Buddha rejected extreme asceticism as the path to enlightenment, arguing for balance. Focusing only on pleasure or rejecting all pleasures of life reinforces "the fiction of a self" (Epstein 91). The pursuit of pleasure leads down the path of craving and attachment. Extreme asceticism focuses us on aversion (and craving, I'm sure). Both are examples of dualism, seeking out or avoiding seemingly external sources of pleasure. Neither can lead to enlightenment because they block an understanding of emptiness. Instead, the Buddha taught the Middle Way, or balance. Only the Middle Way can enlighten us, whereas pleasure temporarily alleviates, at a superficial level, "our ground state of suffering" (Epstein 160). Our modern culture seduces us with many opportunities to mask our suffering with temporary pleasures rather than addressing its root cause.

All of this adds up to distorted perspective and false narratives guaranteed to continue the cycle of suffering. For example, because we find someone attractive when we are first dating and find his company pleasurable, we are likely to exaggerate those qualities that we like and dismiss those we don't. This unfairly objectifies the person we're dating, raises unreasonable expectations, and inevitably negates any possibility of unconditional love—since he is now the object of our affection rather than the subject whom we love. We become attached to that image we've created and become angry with the actual person for not living up to that image.

Even if we are not guilty of such projection, we may cling to our idea of that person as who he was when we first loved him so that when he inevitably changes, we feel betrayed. Our object of pleasure then becomes an object of aversion. Because we have labeled that person as key to our happiness, we now suffer greatly and, obviously, impose suffering upon the person to whom we were initially attracted. Here is the domino effect of narrative: The fictive self creates the object of attraction, a storybook romance partner, and when that character fails to follow the script, we are guaranteed an unhappy ending.

Fortunately, the Third Noble Truth means we can change the script and write a happy ending. This is due to Buddhism's ideas about how we generate knowledge and know the world. Buddhist epistemology rests on the notion that our processing of information comes in two steps. When we first see physical phenomena, this is pure perception without any sort of label, just a visual cognition. The second step is to label or identify what we see, which is a mental cognition that rests on previous experience. When we recognize that our visual cognition has no concepts because pure physical perception and that all thoughts stemming from that moment are concepts, we see that we are narrating our lives, that life is an "ongoing construction of reality" (Goleman 321).

The Dalai Lama describes this awareness of ourselves as narrators of our own lives as like knowing we are wearing sunglasses. The awareness of the distorted color we are seeing through tinted glasses allows us to recognize that what we are seeing is not true (Epstein 73). With this recognition, we can disrupt narrative so that we are no longer trapped by it. The ability to identify narrative but not identify *with* narrative allows us to break old, unhealthy patterns so that we can respond to the moment rather than to habitual thinking. We learn to be in the moment, not in our minds. That moment between nonconceptual and conceptual cognition is a door we can walk through and leave suffering behind.

Being in the moment directly, no longer trapped by dualism, allows us to drop judgment. The Venerable Kusalacitto explains that we can recognize the two-step process of sense and mental cognitions through cultivating mindfulness and awareness. These habits allow us to register color or sound as color or sound without also deciding that the color is revolting or the sound melodic. The color is green, not putrid green. The sound is music, not the best song The Beatles ever played. "When you act like this, your mind will stay very calm. No negative emotion that could harm you will come to you" (qtd. in Goleman 170). The mind can relax, not worrying over how the sensation may revolt or please and, therefore, must be avoided or sought after. As Wright explains, "To perceive emptiness is to perceive raw sensory data without doing what we're naturally inclined to do: build a theory about what is at the heart of the data and then encapsulate that theory in a sense of essence" (148).

The key difference, then, between Western talk therapy and Buddhism is that the Buddhist aim is not to replace an unhealthy narrative with a healthier one but to rid ourselves of narrative altogether. As psychologist and Buddhist practitioner Mark Epstein writes, "The crumbling of the false self occurs through awareness of its manifestations, not through the substitution of some underlying 'truer' personality. The ability to become aware of self-representations without creating new ones is, psychologically speaking, a great relief" (73). The relief flows from the releasing of the narrative that produced ignorance of emptiness and impermanence. The Buddha taught:

> All worry about the self is vain; the ego is like a mirage, and all tribulations that touch it will pass away. They will vanish like a nightmare when the sleeper awakes.
> He who has awakened is freed from fear; he has become Buddha; he knows the vanity of all his cares, his ambitions, and also of his pains [qtd. in Epstein 47].

To release the narrative of the false self, the independent self, is to lose all need for anxiety—as there is no longer a self that needs protection (Epstein 45).

With the removal of ignorance, we can access an ever-present purified mind, and we do so through the Fourth Noble Truth, which lays out the Eightfold Path: Right View, Right Thinking, Right Mindfulness, Right Speech, Right Action, Right Diligence, Right Concentration, and Right Livelihood.[2] Not surprisingly given the centrality of interbeing, the path is not linear where one masters the first step and progressively moves to the next. Rather, all parts "interare" and should be practiced simultaneously. In fact, Thich Nhat Hanh's ordering of the path here is different from how it is listed in other sources, which emphasizes its nonlinearity. And, of course, the language here is a translation, so, while Thich Nhat Hanh uses the language "View," others translate that as "Understanding." The key, though, is the word Right. Right is defined contextually, not doctrinally. With the Buddhist emphasis on the primacy of experience, Thich Nhat Hanh explains, "right and wrong are neither moral judgments nor arbitrary standards imposed from the outside. Through our own awareness, we discover what is beneficial ('right')" (*Heart* 11). Right is not solipsistic, though, as what is right must be of benefit to all, given emptiness and interconnectedness.

Right View, first and foremost, is a deep understanding of the Four Noble Truths. It means no longer being caught by concepts so that we can see things as they truly are, which is why merely knowing the Four Noble Truths at an intellectual level is inadequate, for "Buddhism is not a collection of views. It is a practice to help us to eliminate wrong views" (Thich Nhat Hanh, *Heart* 56). Deep understanding means practicing the *Dharma*—the Buddha's teachings. Right View ties directly to the issue of perspective. Knowing that we are prone to error due to our conceptual thinking, we must treat our perceptions with skepticism, release concepts, and "touch 'things-in-themselves,'" which allows us to recognize how our concepts are the consequence of wrong perceptions (Thich Nhat Hanh, *Living Buddha, Living Christ* 254). Because the mind is inherently pure, and everyone inherently capable of enlightenment, Right View can't be taught; it's intuitive and cultivated through mindfulness.

Right Thinking means understanding things as they are, which can be difficult because our bodies and minds are often not doing the same thing. Thich Nhat Hanh has quipped in response to Descartes' famous "I think, therefore I am," that I think therefore, I am not here (*Heart* 59). Right Thinking means not living in our heads and recognizing that much of our thinking is not necessary. Thich Nhat Hanh lays out four practices of Right Thinking. First, he advises asking, "Are you sure?" He even recommends creating a sign with those words and displaying it prominently to avoid the domino effect of wrong perceptions causing wrong thinking and, thereby, causing suffering. He also suggests asking, "What am I doing?" By this, he means be present. If washing dishes, be present with washing dishes, not making to-do lists for the next day. Third, he offers the greeting,

"Hello, Habit Energy," as a reminder that we tend to stick unthinkingly to habits, even those that do us harm, and respond habitually rather than to the present. Recognizing and accepting without guilt our habitual responses undercuts their power. Lastly, we should awaken *bodhicitta*, defined as the "mind of love," that is the desire for personal enlightenment for the purpose of helping others.

Right Mindfulness is traditionally taught seventh in the Eightfold Path, but Thich Nhat Hanh highlights it early, seeing it as the heart of the Buddha's teaching. His doing so underscores how the path is not a consecutive linear progression. Buddhist psychology states that we are always placing our attention somewhere; Right Mindfulness means placing our attention in the present moment without judgment. The Four Foundations of mindfulness practice are body, feelings, mind, and phenomena. With each, the goal is to be present without evaluation.

Mindfulness of the body allows for insight into impermanence, emptiness, and interbeing. By recognizing the body as constituted of parts (32 in traditional Buddhism), we become aware that the body is not a solid, unitary entity but is made up of teeth, nails, bones, etc. Such recognition moves us away from notions of "my body" and towards the knowledge that each of us is merely a physical being (like Thich Nhat Hanh's tree) made up of constituent parts working together and shifting and changing with each moment. Seeing the impermanence of body helps us to realize it cannot be a source of permanent happiness.

Mindfulness of feelings means being present to whatever feelings arise without being caught by them. Buddhist psychology divides feelings into pleasant, unpleasant, and neutral feelings. By being present to a feeling and labeling it, we can recognize that feelings are impermanent and that we are not defined by them; they are not inherent to an identity. Right Mindfulness leads to understanding that any feeling is temporary and not "my feeling" but rather "a feeling" and, therefore, not a source of lasting happiness.

Mindfulness of the mind is similar in that we can trace the train of our thought, recognizing thoughts as fleeting and not becoming trapped by our "very important stories." All thoughts come from external information via the senses or from internal mental formations. Some mental formations are wholesome, some unwholesome, and, as discussed with the term Right, these categories are contextual. For example, guilt can be wholesome if we have genuinely hurt someone as it will lead us to rectify our error and ask forgiveness. However, a false sense of guilt born of emotional abuse or shame is unwholesome and unhealthy.

Mindfulness of phenomena refers to where we place our attention. Anger, for example, does not arise spontaneously. An object or event of some kind creates that anger. The object or event could be external, perhaps getting cut off in traffic, or internal, a memory of, well, being cut off in traffic. Right Mindfulness requires focusing attention on the *dharma*, referring not just to the teachings of the Buddha, but to internal insight and understanding that ultimately allow for genuine understanding of interdependence.

Right Speech is less difficult to understand in that it simply means telling the truth consistently without cruelty or exaggeration. However, even Right Speech is contextual. The Buddha was said to have the gift of modifying how he explained his teachings to his audience to best meet their needs so that he did not teach the same way all of the time; rather, he gauged what his listeners were ready to hear and how they would best hear it. The foundation of Right Speech, therefore, is deep listening and once again requires true presence and egolessness that allows us to understand each person and how best to relay our message to her.

Right Action refers to mindfully practicing nonviolence to ourselves and others and is closely connected to Thich Nhat Hanh's teachings of what he calls the Five Mindfulness Trainings: reverence for life, living in a manner that promotes social justice without taking from others, sexual responsibility, Right Speech, and mindful consumption. Nonviolence to the self means showing ourselves kindness and compassion first since without that we cannot share those qualities with others. Mindful consumption is broadly defined as not only literal food but how we feed all of our senses. We should not consume material harmful to ourselves such as violent imagery.

Right Diligence means directing effort toward the right goals. In other words, put energy into what alleviates suffering and leads to happiness.

Right Concentration refers to single-mindedly focusing attention on the object of concentration, such as the breath during meditation. Concentration is an active faculty of steadily holding attention on one object without distraction or interruption. Mindfulness, which is used in partnership with concentration, allows us to notice when our concentration has wavered. So, for example, as we concentrate steadfastly on the breath during meditation, our monkey mind will start to wander, and it is mindfulness that will allow us to notice we are no longer steadily attentive and bring us back to the moment so that we can begin concentration again. Right Concentration is wholesome, with attention focused on what will bring enlightenment, for it is possible to be concentrated on an object that brings suffering as would be the case, for example, with an obsession, maybe with that fruit pie mentioned earlier. Concentration is a tool of focus, bringing attention where it is needed, but mindfulness allows for an understanding of what is being seen.

Right Livelihood is defined as work that does not compromise the ideals of love and compassion.

Through practicing the Eightfold Path, genuine happiness can be achieved rather than transitory sensual pleasure. Unlike pleasure, which appears to come from external sources, happiness is "a deep sense of fulfillment, accompanied by a sense of peace and a host of positive qualities such as altruism" (Ricard qtd. in Goleman 85). Happiness is not dependent upon our circumstances but on our perspective. As Wallace states, "hedonic pleasure is something we seem to get from the world, whereas genuine happiness results from what we bring to the world" (105).

Happiness comes from attentional, cognitive, emotional, and conative balance, which Buddhists define as cultivating a sincere desire for what will lead to our own and others' well-being. Ignorance of impermanence and emptiness makes balance impossible as we put our attention in the wrong places thanks to craving and attachment. When we have balance—or equilibrium—happiness is possible no matter the conditions of life. When the mind is out of balance, we experience anxiety, depression, and a general unease. We cannot be happy no matter what the conditions of our life. When not in balance, we often turn to pleasures to distract us, but this is not happiness.

The Dalai Lama has shared the story of a Tibetan monk once imprisoned by the Chinese for 18 years who said, after his release, that he had at times been in danger. The Dalai Lama expected the monk to recount stories of torture, but the monk explained there were occasions when he was in danger of losing compassion for his captors. The monk understood that his happiness depended not upon his living conditions or sensual pleasure but upon his own state of mind.

While Austen's heroines have more freedom than a monk imprisoned by the Chinese, they experience their own limited choices due to patriarchal enclosures. Perhaps it is because Austen personally faced the limitations of being a brilliant writer when writing by women was denigrated that she understood and represented so clearly the importance of a balanced mind for happiness rather than circumstances. Austen is also the first of the English novelists to capture how the monkey mind works through her use of the narrative method of free indirect discourse. Her narrative style depicts realistically how our minds work in terms of misperception and how we create our "very important stories" in such a way as to create our own suffering as well.

# THREE

## *Pride and Prejudice* and Poison

"Heaven forbid!—That would be the greatest misfortune of all!—To find a man agreeable whom one is determined to hate!"
                    —Jane Austen, *Pride and Prejudice*

"The Buddha taught 'some kind of humiliation awaits us all.' No matter what we do, he taught, we cannot sustain the illusion of our self-sufficiency. We are all subject to decay, old age, and death, to disappointment, loss, and disease. We are all engaged in a futile struggle to maintain ourselves in our own image."
                    —Mark Epstein, *Thoughts Without a Thinker:*
                    *Psychotherapy from a Buddhist Perspective*

"I often say, 'To be or not to be, that is no longer the question. The question is one of interbeing.'"
                    —Thich Nhat Hanh, *The Other Shore*

Austen's most popular novel originally had the title *First Impressions*, which may help explain its popularity. While most of us do not inhabit small English villages, we all face the problems created by first impressions, both in making good ones and in trying to read others correctly when we meet them. Problems arise because our attempts to make good first impressions can lead to social anxiety and because there is so much at stake in reading others well. We often do not. The characters of *Pride and Prejudice* certainly do not. The novel is a study in getting things wrong and offers an opportunity to explore how much suffering this causes. The suffering arises from the three main poisons from which all afflictions arise: craving (or attachment), anger, and ignorance.

Austen famously begins her novel with "It is a truth universally acknowledged." A Buddhist would end the sentence differently from Austen's quip on men and marriage, pointing to the three poisons as the universal cause of suffering. Certainly, Austen's work is a comedy, and we get the standard Austen happy ending. However, there is great suffering within the pages of *Pride and Prejudice*—exactly the kind of suffering to which we are all most prone. This is not the suffering of *War and Peace*. Austen's characters suffer on what appears to be a smaller scale. But their suffering occurs daily, with its own high stakes.

While the stakes are not life and death for the Bennet family, they are high enough; the family estate has been entailed to a male relative because Mr. and Mrs. Bennet produced no male heir and five daughters, whose fortunes will not amount to much when their father dies. In addition to the economic worries, the Bennet household is an unhappy one, with Mrs. Bennet complaining incessantly of her nerves as she schemes to get her daughters married, and Mr. Bennet using his acerbic wit to insult everyone. Each of the girls has a character flaw that leads to more suffering. In typical Austen fashion, strangers bring everything to a head. The arrival of Mr. Bingley, Mr. Darcy, Mr. Collins, and Mr. Wickham provides the possibility of suitors and produces opportunities for travel that, in the end, result in all four men married—three to Bennet daughters, two happily so.

But, within the seemingly lighthearted romance plot, we find deceit, anger, fear, manipulation, sexual misconduct, and jealousy—in addition to pride and prejudice. When Charlotte Brontë accused Austen of being "only shrewd and observant," lacking Romantic flare, she seems not to have noticed so much passion simmering beneath the surface—all stemming from the three poisons.

Within Buddhism, the first of the poisons, ignorance, refers to a failure to understand emptiness, interconnectedness, and impermanence. Ignorance rests upon a false sense of individualism, the belief that there is an essential self that needs protecting. Buddhism challenges us to find any inherent essential aspect that we can point to as the self, arguing instead for emptiness, the notion that no such entity exists but that our use of the words *I, me, myself,* and *individual* are merely ways for us to navigate the world but not ultimate truth. Rather, each of us is a manifestation, a "coming together of many causes and conditions" (Thich Nhat Hanh, *Other* 114), called *interdependent co-arising.*

The doctrine is more easily understood with the example of a rainbow. A rainbow exists because of the reflection, refraction, and dispersal of light in water droplets that result in visible colors in an arc in a section of the sky opposite the sun. The rainbow depends on specific weather conditions to manifest, and since those weather conditions will shift, rainbows are temporary sights of beauty. Rainbows, therefore, perfectly exemplify emptiness, interconnectedness, and impermanence. Buddhists argue that people share these same qualities—that we are manifestations just like a rainbow.

The best teaching about emptiness and the freedom that comes from recognizing it is found in "The Heart Sutra." The *bodhisattva*, or awakened one, Avalokiteśvara explains his insight that "the five *Skandhas* are equally empty/and with this realization he overcame all ill-being" (30). Like the components and conditions that make up a rainbow, people are made up of the five *skandhas*: body, feelings, perceptions, mental formations, and consciousness. None of these components is an essential self; each is interdependent and co-arising and only at this moment because at any given moment, my body, feelings, etc., change.

Buddhism completely rejects the notion of an autonomous essential self because such a notion inevitably leads to suffering. Thirteenth-century Zen master Eihei Dōgen "taught that enlightenment is just intimacy with all things" (Levitt, *Other* 11). In other words, enlightenment or nirvana comes from recognizing the interconnectedness of all beings, of all elements, of all.

Science appears to confirm Buddhism in this. In discussing connections between evolution and Buddhism, we share 99 percent of our genes with other humans, 98 percent with chimps, and 92 percent with mammals overall (Barash 86). Barash refers to this as "the fact of connectedness" (90). Research supports the Buddhist notion that we carry our ancestors within us as well, not merely at the level of DNA. Through measuring levels of respiratory sinus arrhythmia (RSA), a marker of physical and mental health, scientists found a mother's history of stress and trauma affects the amount of RSA she will pass on to her infant. This study goes beyond the inevitable connection a woman shares with her child while pregnant. It finds that a woman who suffered childhood abuse would pass on biological markers of that trauma to her infant as part of giving birth (Gray).

The ignorance of connectedness creates craving and anger. Seeing ourselves as a separate entity attaches us to those things that give us pleasure, causing us to seek them out rather than focusing on those things that will bring genuine happiness—things that lead us to enlightenment benefit all. Connected to the image of ourselves as separate entities is a belief in permanence. We build a "fixed image of self" that must be protected, which leads to "craving for security wherever it can be found" (Epstein 59). When we are denied those things that we crave, particularly those that reinforce a (false) sense of security, we become angry and blame. "Because of our craving, the Buddha is saying, we want things to be understandable. We reduce, concretize, or substantialize experiences or feelings, which are, in their very nature, fleeting or evanescent. In doing so, we define ourselves by our moods and by our thoughts" (Epstein 77). Doing so only reinforces ignorance and leads to more craving and ignorance.

While the three poisons are universal, Austen's historical context is ripe for their exploration, as the historical Enlightenment is often seen as the rise of the individual. As noted previously, in a forum discussion between scientists and the Dalai Lama, Jeanne Tsai explained that Western culture "views the self as separate from others, including parents, siblings, coworkers, friends. Such people view the self as being comprised of values, beliefs—internal attributes" (qtd. in Goleman 241). This contrasts with the interdependent self in Asia where the idea is of a "self as connected with others, as very much part of a social context" and defined by social relationships (241). Austen's novels capture Enlightenment ideas, including this growing sense of the Western ideology of the separate self.

Yet hers is a transitional period in which traditional European ideas of community still held sway and share in common the description Tsai attributes to Asian ideas of the self. Published 62 years before Austen began writing what she then called First Impressions, Alexander Pope's "Essay on Man" reflects the connectedness previously explained by Buddhism and now proposed by science.

> And, if each system in gradation roll
> Alike essential to th' amazing whole,
> The least confusion but in one, not all
> That system only, but the whole must fall.

Austen knew Pope's work, and her own emphasis on life in a country village shows her interest in connectedness, her recognition of how the actions of one affect so many around him while simultaneously capturing this nascent notion of the independent self.

Eighteenth-century thinkers recognized the dangers attending the Western view of the autonomous individual. One of the period's best-known writers, Samuel Johnson, sounds surprisingly similar to a Vietnamese monk of the twentieth and twenty-first centuries. Thich Nhat Hanh, in a gloss of his translation of "The Heart Sutra," notes that belief in "a separate self" makes us "worry about our position, our status, and what people think of us" (104). Johnson's 1749 "Vanity of Human Wishes" treats exactly this subject, warning his readers that with wealth comes worry over theft and losing one's money; with power comes fear of violence; with long life comes decay and needing care from others who may only wish for our death and their inheritance. Johnson writes:

> Yet still the gen'ral Cry the Skies assails
> And Gain and Grandeur load the tainted Gales;
> Few know the toiling Statesman's Fear or Care,
> Th' insidious Rival and the gaping Heir.

His point is that we suffer from all of the so-called blessings that we constantly yearn and pray for; we are anxious to gain these things and more anxious to lose them once we have them because there is a sense of threat from others. Modernist writers reacting to the atrocities of World War I, such as James Joyce, saw the cost of the emphasis on separation rather than connection and called it "existential loneliness," the idea that, not only can we never truly understand others, but we likely cannot even understand ourselves. In his collection *Dubliners*, Joyce populates each story with characters who attempt to connect but who cannot and instead find themselves paralyzed by feelings of alienation and loneliness.

Recognizing this cultural split between East and West when it comes to perceptions of connection or strong individualism, Henry Aronson, like Tsai, notes the "social warmth" in Asia versus the Western "emphasis on individuation." This Western emphasis requires creating a bridge between individuals. The bridge consists of attempting to find similarities between ourselves and others through conversation (16). This brings us back to first impressions since, without an assumed sense of connection, we each must work to impress others that we are worth knowing and trusting.

Sociolinguist Deborah Tannen has done extensive work on the way that conversation operates as social glue. Though her work is based on modern studies, the principles operate across cultures so seem apt for discussing conversation across time. Tannen notes that conversation can, of course, bring people together, but it can, and often does, unintentionally destroy the bridge it is meant to create. Tannen's findings concern different conversation styles, for example between men and women. Girls and women rely heavily upon conversation to bond and look for sameness between each other. Boys and men, on the other hand, bond through activities and are more overtly competitive in their talk. Women interrupt each other with sounds meant to show understanding and connection while making eye contact. Men hear such interruptions as rudeness. The Western solution to connection, therefore, is precarious—something that Austen explores in all of her work and particularly in *Pride and Prejudice* with its emphasis on competition rather than connection.

The novel emphasizes lack from the beginning, with Mrs. Bennet seeing Bingley's arrival as an opportunity for her daughters and a competition with the other local families, as there are not enough suitors for the area's eligible young women. She tells Mr. Bennet, "Only think what an establishment it would be for one of them. Sir William and Lady Lucas are determined to go, merely on that account" (4). Immediately, relationships between people are described as competing for limited resources, with people objectified for their money and status. The goal is not only to find a marriage partner, but also to secure a means of support, since the ladies, to retain their social standing, must marry well.

The theme of deficit and competition creates the central conflict of the novel upon Bingley's introduction to Meryton society. When it is rumored that Mr. Bingley will bring 12 ladies and seven gentlemen to the ball, "The girls grieved over the number of ladies" as competitors for partners (7). Fortunately, Mr. Bingley only brings two ladies—his sisters—and another eligible bachelor, one with an income even larger than his own. But the deficit economy continues, as there are still not enough male partners for dancing so that the ladies must continue to compete.

Of course, this sets the stage for bad first impressions, as Mr. Darcy stubbornly refuses to dance with anyone but Bingley's sisters. With rumors of his great fortune, the

> gentlemen pronounced him to be a fine figure of a man. The ladies declared he was much handsomer than Mr. Bingley, and he was looked at with great admiration for about half the evening, till his manners gave a disgust which turned the tide of his popularity, for he was discovered to be proud, to be above his company, and above being pleased; and not all his large estate in

Derbyshire could then save him from having a most forbidding, disagreeable countenance, and being unworthy to be compared with his friend [8].

It does not take much to go from object of admiration to disgust upon first encounters, and this negative idea of Mr. Darcy persists in Meryton and Longbourn throughout the novel. Once made, the impression sticks. Here is an example of treating the impermanent, a single moment of time, as permanent, taking Mr. Darcy's behavior on this one occasion as an inherent part of his character.

Mr. Darcy brings much of this on himself. While his refusal to dance is antisocial, his rejection of Elizabeth is blatantly rude—an act Austen's original readers would connect to morality and ethics (Scheuermann 107). When Bingley urges him to dance, pointing to Elizabeth as an eligible partner, Darcy replies loudly enough to be heard, "She is tolerable, but not handsome enough to tempt me, and I am in no humour at present to give consequence to young ladies who are slighted by other men" (9). Beyond insulting Elizabeth's beauty, Darcy characterizes her as a loser in the competition for male attention—a high-stakes competition that Elizabeth particularly feels thanks to her nagging, fearful mother who creates an atmosphere of constant anxiety at home.

Mrs. Bennet flip-flops between ecstasy over her matchmaking schemes and catastrophic personal pain when they appear to fail. She demonstrates how "hope and fear is a feeling with two sides. As long as there's one, there's always the other.... Hope and fear come from feeling that we lack something; they come from a sense of poverty" (Pema Chödrön, *When Things Fall Apart* 88). Even without the financial and insistent pressure of the marriage market, the Dalai Lama argues that the Western notion of "endless pursuit of romantic love" "cannot be seen as a positive thing" but something "that is based on fantasy, unattainable, and therefore may be a source of frustration" (*Art of Happiness* 234). Romantic attachment under these circumstances creates poisonous craving.

The novel is replete with examples of conditions in which the three poisons are most likely to thrive. The result for Elizabeth is her famous prejudice against Mr. Darcy. She continually misreads him because she is so attached to her first impression, which wounded her pride. Even as she describes the scene with her telltale sparkling wit, she admits, "I could easily forgive his pride, if he had not mortified mine" (14). Notably, she says this to Charlotte Lucas, the "old maid" of the novel who has little to recommend her in the competitive marriage market and so must marry a fool or not marry at all.

Elizabeth has other choices here. She could opt for mindfulness, which would allow her to see how her perspective has been formed, so that she would not cling to it and continue to generate suffering. The Buddhist scholar Robert Thurman argues that "the best time to observe the self clearly is when we are in a state of injured innocence, when we have been insulted and think, 'How could she do this to me? I don't deserve to be treated that way.' It is in this state, he says, that the 'hard nut' of the self is best found" (qtd. in Epstein 211). The rejection that Elizabeth experiences is an opportunity to question the idea of there being a separate individual self and to be open to the idea of interconnectedness.

This kind of openness requires great courage: "The only reason that we don't open our hearts and minds to other people is that they trigger confusion in us that we don't feel brave enough or sane enough to deal with. To the degree that we look clearly and compassionately at ourselves, we feel confident and fearless about looking into someone else's eyes" (Pema Chödrön, *When Things Fall Apart* 153). Openness feels like vulnerability within a Western framework, a difficult feeling in a competitive environment. Instead, Elizabeth gets trapped by her emotions in a "refractory period" (Epstein 148) feeling hurt and unable to process new information. Rather, she sees everything through the lens of that hurt and thereby becomes biased. From a Buddhist perspective, emotions become destructive as soon as they disrupt the mind's equilibrium (Goleman 157), which is certainly true of Elizabeth after Darcy's slight. Proof of her clinging to that moment comes at Rosings months later, when she brings it up to Colonel Fitzwilliam. Though she speaks in a lightly joking tone, the fact that she is still operating from that one moment is evident.

In this, she shares much in common with Darcy, who holds the advantage of being aware that he has this fault and recognizing it as a fault. He confesses to Elizabeth, "My temper would perhaps be called resentful—My good opinion once lost is lost for ever" (40). Even as Elizabeth responds, "That is a failing indeed!", close examination would show her that her own resentment has led to her having a grudge against Mr. Darcy. Pema Chödrön notes that when we are in pain or unease—in other words, suffering—blaming is a typical method of trying to escape those feelings (*When Things Fall Apart* 159–60). Holding a grudge and blaming mean forming a narrative in which we get to be the victim and hold no responsibility for our own discomfort. In this way, blame can become a destructive emotion that obscures reality. "With a destructive emotion, there will always be a gap between the way things appear and the ways things are" (Goleman 75). This is a kind of attachment because it "means clinging to one's way of perceiving things" (Goleman 78). Elizabeth is not wrong in viewing Darcy's actions as rude at the initial dance, but she fails to consider it as an action, a moment in time, and stubbornly views all of his further actions and all that she hears about him through the lens of that moment.

This clearly is the case, for Elizabeth largely reads others well. With the initial exception of her father, whom she admires more than she ought, she has a clear understanding of her family, recognizing her mother as histrionic and unwilling to listen to reason, her sisters Kitty and Lydia as silly flirts, her sister Mary as pretentious, and Jane as too willing to believe the best of everyone. She immediately suspects Mr. Collins of being an obsequious fool before he even arrives. After her father reads Mr. Collins' letter, Elizabeth is "chiefly struck with his extraordinary deference" and responds aloud, "He must be an oddity, I think.... Can he be a sensible man?" (44). Of course, she fails to predict Charlotte's engagement to Mr. Collins in spite of Charlotte openly expressing her cynical views on marriage, and she even finds herself disappointed in her friend. Here, though, she is willing to forgive. But the combination of a scarcity viewpoint and her personal grudge undercut her powers of observation, leaving her open to deception.[1]

Nowhere is this clearer than in the introduction of the pleasure-seeking adventurer who represents the dangers of a culture too focused on the individual: George Wickham. Austen's introduction of Wickham and his immediate encounter with Darcy place Elizabeth in a realistic position we all encounter since the "narrative veil" leaves her to read body language and draw her own conclusions (Williams 204). She must fill in the gaps in an effort to understand the odd meeting she witnesses between Wickham and Darcy, as must we as readers, for the narrator tells us, "Both changed colour, one looked white, the other red" (50). We are left to imagine who turned which color and also what the change in color signifies. Elizabeth "makes her judgment of the two men based on their 'countenances,' or her 'first impressions' of them. In the description of the changing colors of Darcy and Wickham, the conflict of the novel is presented in miniature" (Williams 208). The conflict is yet more complicated by the veil Elizabeth has drawn for herself, that of her grudge toward Darcy.

That conflict must then be resolved via conversation—that Western mode of making connection, and a tool that fails repeatedly in the novel.[2] This particular conversation fails because it must take place with Wickham, a great violator of Right Speech who gossips, distorts, and lies. Elizabeth is vulnerable to Wickham's lies thanks to a burgeoning attachment. Later, Elizabeth will recognize that Wickham shares far too much personal information during their first conversation, but, at the time, she takes his confidence as a flattering interest in herself—the use of conversation to create an intimate bond. Her discussion with Jane afterward proves how her bias prevents her from listening to Wickham with discernment. When Jane responds with gentle skepticism, saying it is hard to know what to believe, Elizabeth responds, "I beg your pardon;—one knows exactly what to think" (59).[3] But this is false. Jane is right, though partially for the wrong reasons, since her view reflects her predilection to see only the best in everyone. Wickham's story, as Elizabeth notes, contains persuasive details, but there is no corroborating evidence. Elizabeth sees what she wants to see, declaring "there was truth in his looks" (59).

Thanks to the blindness that she herself will acknowledge later, Elizabeth is shocked by Darcy's proposal in what becomes a scene full of anger as each—operating from an individualistic perspective—feels attacked. Believing himself to be conferring a favor and lowering himself, Darcy makes his offer in an offending manner. When Elizabeth rejects him, Darcy defends his style of proposal by proclaiming "disguise of every sort is my abhorrence. Nor am I ashamed of the feelings I related. They were natural and just. Could you expect me to rejoice in the inferiority of your connections?" (127). Though he is Wickham's opposite here since he is nothing but forthright, Darcy also violates Right Speech, for "honesty without kindness, humor, and goodheartedness can be just mean" (Pema Chödrön, *When Things Fall Apart* 151).

Yet we are to believe Elizabeth when she proclaims, "You could not have made me the offer of your hand in any possible way that would have tempted me to accept it" as she acknowledges "from the very first moment I may almost say, of my acquaintance with you, your manners impressing me with the fullest belief of your arrogance, your conceit, and your selfish disdain of the feelings of others, were such as to form that ground-work of disapprobation, on which succeeding events have built so immoveable a dislike" (127–8). Here is genuine insight as Elizabeth traces her anger back to that initial dance, though we readers recognize the full repercussions while Elizabeth does not—yet. Notably, her own anger and wounded pride lead her to speak as disdainfully and rudely to Darcy as he has to her. Within a Buddhist framework (and, really within a Christian one), Elizabeth's retort is wrong. While we may understand it and even cheer her on for retaliating against the pompous Mr. Darcy, her response only creates more distance, disdain, and anger.

Darcy's letter the next day seemingly lifts the veil, allowing Elizabeth at long last to see clearly and move beyond the grudge that she has been so consistently nurturing. She acknowledges, "Pleased with the preference of one, and offended by the neglect of the other, on the very beginning of our acquaintance, I have courted prepossession and ignorance" (137). Elizabeth has failed at the reciprocal part of Right Speech, which is deep listening. Reflecting upon her conversation with Wickham, Elizabeth realizes that much of what he told her was true in terms of his family's relationship with the Darcys, hence his sense of credibility, but she now sees her own blindness. Rather than hearing Wickham, she used the opportunity to justify her own hurt feelings. Only after Darcy's letter does she recognize how she has ignored the evidence in front of her of Darcy's character, as someone esteemed by his friends and who has never demonstrated irreligious or unethical behavior. With Darcy's letter, "how differently did everything appear" (136). What the letter allows our quick heroine is time, the ability to read and reread the letter, avoiding her faulty listening skills.[4]

However, beyond the credible recitation of facts, Elizabeth is swayed still by attachment. Just as she believed Wickham because it fed her ego, she is doing so again by feeling flattered by Darcy's proposal. Darcy's letter explains that, while inferior family connections might be objectionable, it is the behavior of Elizabeth's parents and three younger sisters that caused him to intervene between Mr. Bingley and Jane. He points to Mrs. Bennet's "total want of propriety so frequently, so almost uniformly betrayed by herself, by your three younger sisters, and occasionally even by your father" and, importantly immediately writes, "Pardon me—It pains me to offend you" (130–1). Darcy already demonstrates a better understanding of Right

Speech, the importance of tailoring one's words to the listener. He continues with "let it give you consolation to consider that, to have conducted yourself so as to avoid any share of the like censure, is praise no less generally bestowed on you and your eldest sister, than it is honourable to the sense and disposition of both" (131). In other words, he admires Elizabeth and Jane for their ability to rise above the rude conduct of the rest of the family. Even as he honestly shares his potentially hurtful opinion, he now does so, tempering it with kindness and praise.

Austen makes clear that Elizabeth's willingness to change perspective comes from lifting of the grudge that had made her feel less desirable—and which she had attempted to assuage, first through attraction to Mr. Wickham, and then to Darcy's cousin. The narrator tells the reader, "The compliment to herself and her sister, was not unfelt" (137), and the blame for problems can now shift to her own family whose behavior "merited reproach" making "her sense of shame severe" (137). Austen's word choice here echoes her description of Elizabeth's feelings at the Netherfield ball, where she "blushed and blushed again with shame and vexation" (68). Darcy's letter is only telling her what she has already felt for herself and has "soothed" her, that has flattered her.

From this, Elizabeth has an epiphany, proclaiming, "Till this moment, I never knew myself" (137). But the realization points not to overcoming ignorance but, as Austen makes obvious through her word choice, an understanding of herself—as a separate individual. The epiphany comes midway through the novel, meaning there is more to learn and more exploration of how these characters continue to operate on a model of Western individualism that creates conflict.

Even with the person she trusts most and shares her most intimate feelings, she experiences a sense of separation. When Elizabeth finally has time alone with Jane, she unburdens herself at last about Darcy's proposal and his story of Wickham. "The tumult of Elizabeth's mind was allayed by this conversation." Here, we see the potential for conversation to alleviate suffering. However, Elizabeth has withheld information, not telling Jane about Darcy's role in keeping her apart from Bingley so that "there was still something lurking behind" (148). Our narrative voice here feels so blended with Elizabeth's that it is difficult to tell if the reason behind her failure to disclose—prudence—is one we are to approve of or not. What we can know with confidence is that a disquiet still exists for Elizabeth and that full and open conversation with the person dearest to her is not happening.

Less subtly, Elizabeth's conversation with her father is a complete failure when she attempts to persuade him not to allow Lydia to go to Brighton. We do not hear Elizabeth's initial words directly, getting a gloss from the narrator instead, but our narrator tells us that Mr. Bennet "heard her attentively" (151). When he nonetheless dismisses her concern, she responds more passionately, explaining how the actions of one sister carry great consequences for all. She tells him that Kitty will be sure to see Lydia as a model, mimicking her flirtatiousness and vanity, concluding with "Oh! my dear father, can you suppose it possible that they will not be censored and despised wherever they are known, and that their sisters will not be often involved in the disgrace?" Mr. Bennet sees "that her whole heart was in the subject," but he fails to act, pronouncing that Lydia's visit to Brighton will allow her to learn "her own insignificance" at little expense to himself (152).

This key conversation along with the first two proposals Elizabeth receives fail because their purpose is to control rather than connect. At their foundation, they rest upon ignorance and attachment: seeing the other person as separate and desiring something from her or him. Though dissimilar in style, both Mr. Collins and Darcy propose to Elizabeth with no doubt of being accepted and, consequently, with no understanding of their listener. Mr. Collins dwells chiefly upon his own value as a spouse thanks to his patroness Lady Catherine and his future ownership of Longbourn; he begins by saying he will list his reasons for marrying before being "run away by my feelings," but his language reflects only feelings of self-importance and entitlement. He cares nothing for Elizabeth, which the narrator has previously told us and which he proves by proposing to Charlotte just days later. His proposal amounts to an egotistical speech so that he fails to hear Elizabeth when she repeatedly and clearly refuses his offer.

Though of a milder degree—because there are no true feelings of love—Mr. Collins' proposal, like Darcy's, results in anger, the third poison. Both Mr. Collins and Darcy violate the principle of Right Speech articulated by the Venerable Vangisa who responded to the Buddha's teaching with the following verses: "Speak only endearing speech, / speech that is welcomed" ("Subhasita Sutta"). This does not mean only tell people what they want to hear, but it points to talking to people in such a manner that they can hear. Elizabeth wants neither man's proposal. With Mr. Collins, Elizabeth knows what is coming and wishes to escape, but her mother insists that she stay and listen to him. Knowing it would be best to get it over with, she vacillates between "distress and diversion" (72). As the conversation proceeds and Mr. Collins refuses to listen to her response, distress takes precedence with Elizabeth speaking with "warmth" and finally silenced, leaving the room with the resolution that she will "apply to her father" to speak for her. The narrator takes us to Mr. Collins and Mrs. Bennet after this, leaving the reader to imagine Elizabeth's anger and frustration at being forced to entertain a proposal she does not want and silenced by egotism that fails to consider what she wants at all. At all levels, the proposal violates Right Speech leaving everyone involved angry.

The use of words to dominate becomes particularly clear when employed for wit rather than communication. Mr. Bennet speaks primarily in this mode, even with his distressed favorite daughter when she attempts to persuade him not to let Lydia go to Brighton. All of his communication with Mrs. Bennet uses wit to distance and denigrate her. From the very first page, he lies to Mrs. Bennet, telling her that he will not visit Bingley when he moves into Netherfield; his sole reason is to tease and vex her. When he continues his teasing, not admitting he has already visited Bingley, he baits his daughter Mary, saying to her, "for you are a young lady of deep reflection I know, and read great books and make extracts" (6). When Mary does not know how to respond, he quickly dismisses her, returning the conversation to Bingley. Later, Mr. Bennet will publicly humiliate Mary at the Netherfield ball—but with wit—rebuking her for playing at the piano too long. When the women arrive home after the first assembly where they meet Bingley, Mr. Bennet has stayed up on purpose to hear about it in hopes "that all his wife's views on the stranger would be disappointed." He wishes to hear Mrs. Bennet has been made unhappy. When she, instead, enthusiastically praises Bingley, he interrupts her repeatedly and impatiently. He does not listen. And his preference is not to listen at all rather hiding in his library than in engaging with his family.

Mrs. Bennet, obviously, is annoying, clueless, and attention seeking, so the reader's sympathy rests with the understandably taxed Mr. Bennet. However, Mr. Bennet's choice of sarcasm and silence exacerbates every bad quality of Mrs. Bennet and his daughters. Austen on more than one occasion comments in her work that a rational, good spouse has the potential to improve the other spouse. She notes that Fanny Price would have brought out the best in Henry Crawford, for example. While we are to read it ironically when Mrs. Bennet exclaims, "You have no compassion on my poor nerves" (4), since she is once again being histrionic, she is also right: Mr. Bennet lacks compassion and uses his words to exert power rather than create intimacy as conversation is supposed to do in a culture focused on the individual. He craves a rational partner, which he cannot have thanks to his own choice of spouse, and, failing that, he craves solitude. Unable to achieve either, he operates from aggression and anger, leaving his daughters vulnerable to the poor instruction they receive from their mother and to the predatory actions of Wickham.

Even Mary, whose story occurs on the outskirts of the main plot, suffers from Mr. Bennet's thoughtless comments, for the ending tells us that "no longer mortified by comparison between her sisters' beauty and her own" Mary develops more as a person. While the narrator points to her sisters' beauty as the cause, understanding that Mary has felt mortification takes us back to Mr. Bennet's unkindness and the way that such dismissive, rude comments must have contributed to Mary's insecurity. Rather than conversation meant to connect, Mr. Bennet uses conversation to create distance and reinforce the sense of a separate self and isolation that causes great suffering.

The same can be said of Caroline Bingley. With the women set up as competing, notions of connection are hard to nurture, and there is an undercurrent of anger as a result.[5] Miss Bingley correctly sees Elizabeth as competition for Darcy long before Elizabeth sees this for herself. When they are all thrown together at Netherfield thanks to Jane's illness, the narrator uses the word *jealous* more than once to describe Caroline Bingley's feelings. This leads her to insult Elizabeth to Darcy, teasing him by saying that, when he marries Elizabeth, she hopes he will cure Mrs. Bennet of her loquaciousness, the younger daughters of running after officers, and Elizabeth herself of "that little something bordering on conceit and impertinence" (36). Later, clearly blinded by jealousy, Miss Bingley "in the imprudence of anger took the first opportunity of saying with sneering civility, 'Pray, Miss Eliza are the ___shire militia removed from Meryton? That must be a great loss for your family'" (174). Sneering civility is an oxymoron if ever there was one, but constrained by expectations of proper behavior for a lady, Caroline covers her aggressive attack with a veneer of civility that does nothing to blunt her pointed criticism.

The narrator guides our response to ensure we see this, telling us that Elizabeth must exert "herself vigorously to repel the ill-natured attack" (174). Significantly, the comment aimed only at Elizabeth strikes others in the room though unintentionally with Darcy showing a "heightened complexion" and his sister "overcome with confusion, and unable to lift up her eyes"—recognizing the veiled reference to Wickham with whom she had attempted to elope before Darcy's intervention. They all recover, but Georgiana "not enough to be able to speak any more" (175), meaning that Georgiana can no longer participate in conversation, cutting her off from everyone else in the room. Like the proposals and Mr. Bennet's interaction with his family, Caroline Bingley's attempt to exert power creates harm and a sense of separation.

Caroline is only one of the angry women in the novel who uses her words to wound rather than communicate. Equally seeing Elizabeth as a threat, Lady Catherine dismisses and denigrates her throughout, culminating in the full-scale attack at Longbourn toward the end of the novel. When Elizabeth visits Charlotte, Lady Catherine calls attention to her inferior rank by inviting her to practice piano at Rosings—but in a servant's quarters, announcing, "She would be in nobody's way, you know, in that part of the house." Darcy "looked a little ashamed of his aunt's ill breeding" (115). Given her snobbish view of Elizabeth and her desire for Darcy to marry her own daughter, Lady Catherine's ill breeding becomes more aggressive when she confronts Elizabeth in the belief that she is engaged to Darcy. After accusing Elizabeth of "arts and allurement" and "inferior birth," Lady Catherine exclaims, "Are the shades of Pemberley to be thus polluted?" (231, 233). Lady Catherine's anger represents the most insidious ignorance of interconnectedness, rigidly ascribing to a class hierarchy that, in her eyes, makes Elizabeth ineligible to be Darcy's wife with no concern for either of their feelings about the matter.

But Elizabeth is not merely a victim of angry women; she is an angry woman herself, perhaps at least in part because of the angry women who are so prone to marginalize her due to her social status. Her social circumstances and education leave her highly vulnerable to ignorance, craving, and anger. Within a culture that emphasizes the individual and hierarchy, Elizabeth lacks the resources to control her destiny, particularly in the deficit economy Austen creates. Elizabeth must marry. Her choices include the fool, Mr. Collins, or the rude snob, Darcy.

Her angry response to Charlotte's engagement to Mr. Collins demonstrates how strongly she abhors marriage as commerce. She tells Jane, "You shall not defend her, though it is Charlotte Lucas. You shall not, for the sake of one individual, change the meaning of principle and integrity, nor endeavour to persuade yourself or me, that selfishness is prudence, and insensibility of danger, security for happiness" (91). The narrator refers more than once to the distance Charlotte's engagement creates between the two good friends, and Elizabeth's comment to Jane proves how negatively she judges Charlotte's actions. It reads almost like a personal betrayal, not because Charlotte has engaged herself to the man who had mere days before proposed to her, but because Elizabeth's opinion of Charlotte has changed so drastically as to see her violating her integrity and behaving selfishly. Perhaps Tannen's ideas about sameness bonding female friendships applies here, with Elizabeth feeling that the foundation for her friendship with Charlotte is gone. It might be that some of her anger comes from being made to question her own judgment of Charlotte as a friend.

Her inclinations point her toward Wickham, who, fortunately for her, has no serious intentions toward her, or to Colonel Fitzwilliam, who pointedly explains to her that as a second son he must marry for money. And there is Darcy, too rude to marry upon first proposal, and whom she must wait and hope for afterward when she grows to love him, since her culture does not allow her to express her feelings for him or to propose herself.

The mashup version of the novel, *Pride and Prejudice and Zombies*, picks up brilliantly on the anger Elizabeth feels in the original, making her a formidable zombie hunter who relishes watching zombies burn, kills with pleasure, and even engages in cannibalism. After vanquishing a ninja, she eats his heart. The adaptation takes to extreme the dangers facing the Bennet family and the cost of anger.

In the adaptation, Elizabeth follows in her father's footsteps, becoming an adept zombie hunter, and in the original, she also wields the same weapon as her father: wit. When describing the initial negative encounter with Darcy, she does so wittily though subsequent happenings show that the moment was hurtful. Like her father, therefore, she uses wit as a means to cover or even ameliorate personal pain. She also uses wit to make light of the serious in her conversations with Jane to the point where Jane mildly reproves her, saying, "My dearest sister, now be serious. I want to talk very seriously" when Elizabeth shares the news of her engagement to Darcy. Joan Klingel Ray argues that Mr. Bennet, "for all his wonderful witticisms, is just plain grumpy, readily irritable, as Elizabeth is around Darcy" (34). Elizabeth recognizes this herself when Darcy proposes, noting that she has abused him "abominably to your face" (239). Elizabeth is primarily referring to the first angry proposal, but, throughout her interactions with Darcy, she has often been rude. She quips with Charlotte at the Netherfield ball that "if I do not begin by being impertinent myself, I shall soon grow afraid of him" (17).[6]

Austen was correct in describing Elizabeth as "delightful," and she clearly is Austen's most beloved and enduring heroine. Her wit is part of that delight. Yet it is her very wit that points to her lack of enlightenment. Michał Bajerski's study of wit found a correlation between emotional intelligence and wit, with those who have higher emotional intelligence using wit less often due to the understanding that irony has the possibility of being heard negatively and critically. Bajerski postulates that those with higher emotional intelligence are more comfortable communicating directly. We might link this back to our deficit economy in the novel. Tannen observes that women are more inclined to communicate indirectly; this cannot mean, of course, that women demonstrate less emotional intelligence. Rather, a patriarchal culture that strips women of their powers and emphasizes individualism teaches women to communicate indirectly— something we see repeatedly in the novel both in terms of waiting for that next proposal or, in Elizabeth's case, defensively via wit.

Austen, of course, is famous for her style of free indirect discourse and use of wit. Carole Moses argues that "Elizabeth's wit defines theme as the novel develops a critique on the worth of an ironic worldview" (156). Moses notes that the narrator's voice blurs with Elizabeth's. When we get into Elizabeth's head, we hear her thoughts in her voice. This makes it difficult for us to determine if we are engaging in Elizabeth's misperceptions about what has been happening or listening to the narrator tell us the "reality" of the situation since the voices merge so seamlessly at times. Similarly, Austen uses Mr. Bennet and narration to lead "her readers into a trap. We share in Mr. Bennet's ironic vision and laugh along with him at the follies and inconsistencies of his relatives and neighbors, but suddenly we find ourselves uncomfortable with his irresponsible and insensitive behavior" (Auerbach 163). Emily Auerbach reads the overall message as "[b]e on guard ... against humor that divides, pains, or destroys" (164).

Buddhism takes this warning one step farther, arguing against division itself, against the model of civilization that emphasizes the individual in *Pride and Prejudice*. The novel produces the requisite happy ending, with Elizabeth and Darcy married and living close by the married Bingley and Jane. All loose ends are nicely tied up along with some just deserts. Yet this is a happy ending within cultural conventions. The happiness—or nirvana—of enlightenment is not achieved. Elizabeth masters the rules of the game that she is playing, but she never sees that it is a game that ultimately has no winners. "When we are able to see that the nature of all things is our own true nature, we become free" (Thich Nhat Hanh, *The Other Shore* 101). Elizabeth has her happy ending, not happiness. She is not free.

# FOUR

# *Sense and Sensibility* and Love

"The Buddha is a teacher of love. True love."
—Thich Nhat Hanh, "Does Buddhism
Support Romantic Love?"

"I feel no sentiment of approbation inferior to love."
—Jane Austen, *Sense and Sensibility*

With Buddhism's focus being suffering and the cure for suffering, love inevitably is central to the teachings. One only needs to listen to contemporary music to know that love brings great suffering and happiness. Of course, love is the main topic of Austen's novels with plots revolving around the suffering of a main couple leading to their ultimate happy ending of marriage. More so than any of Austen's novels, *Sense and Sensibility* explores love in all its forms and the suffering that comes from failing at true love due to being trapped by concepts.

The underlying problem of *Sense and Sensibility*, like *Pride and Prejudice*, has its roots in inheritance—or lack thereof—with the Dashwood family displaced from their home by a half-brother and his greedy wife, Fanny. Before leaving, Elinor, oldest of three sisters, meets Fanny's brother Edward with whom there is immediate attraction but who is destined for greater things and a richer wife by his controlling mother. Nineteen-year-old Elinor, her sisters, and mother remove to the cottage of a distant relative, Sir John Middleton. There, sixteen-year-old Marianne, the middle sister, meets Colonel Brandon, a man in his thirties (who quietly but desperately falls in love with her) and the romantic and handsome Willoughby who steals her heart. Elinor learns from the vicious Lucy Steele of her secret engagement to Edward, Willoughby woos but never commits to Marianne and later leaves her unceremoniously, and the sisters change locales once again, this time to London with Mrs. Jennings, the mother of Lady Middleton. Eventually, as more secrets come out, particularly as Marianne learns of Willoughby's engagement, suffering comes in great measure with Elinor constantly thrown into Lucy's company and Marianne becoming deathly ill. All ends well, of course, with Lucy breaking the engagement to marry Edward's younger brother in order to follow the money, Elinor and Edward reuniting, and Marianne accepting Colonel Brandon's proposal.

Most literary critics approach the novel from the paradigm set by the title, exploring the concepts of sense and sensibility and resting their arguments on which concept Austen endorses.

While the eighteenth century is often called the Age of Reason, sensibility took a central role as the century began to wind down. Sensibility meant the outward show of inward moral worth through emotional display—a marked sensitivity that proved good character. Many eighteenth-century novelists employed swooning and crying to demonstrate the morality of characters. Yet sensibility was the subject of some debate given the still-strong ideal of reason—or sense—and the ability to fake emotion, making such displays unreliable proof of goodness.

In her introduction to the novel, Kathleen James-Cavan points to this as a problem with sensibility. She speculates that the title *Sense and Sensibility* may come from an allegorical 1799 essay in *The Lady's Monthly Museum*. The essay personifies "'Sense' as the male offspring of 'Genius' and 'Learning' who must contend with the temptations of 'Susceptibility' for the favours [*sic*] of the fair 'Sensibility,' which descended from 'Modesty' and 'Truth'" (12). The allegory labels "Susceptibility" as excessively and inauthentically indulging in emotion. The problem is being dramatic and faking feelings.

So *Sense and Sensibility* is usually viewed as either a conservative critique of sensibility and an endorsement of sense or as an argument that sensibility must be tempered by effort in order to avoid self-indulgence. Put another way, be like Elinor, the disciplined character who represents the perspective of sense, a view endorsed by Austen's contemporaries. An anonymous review of the novel from 1812 notes that Elinor possesses "great good sense, with a proper quantity of sensibility" (qtd. in Watson n.p.).

From a Buddhist perspective, though, the primacy of sense or sensibility (or a mixture of the two) is the wrong question. Both *sense* and *sensibility* are concepts, and concepts always lead to wrong perceptions and, thereby, to suffering. For Elinor gets it wrong too, and what she gets wrong so profoundly—as do all the characters—is true love.

Buddhism defines true love explicitly. The *brahma-viharas*, as they are called in Pali, the language of the Buddha, translate as "heavenly" "abode" or "home." We can develop the four aspects of true love—*metta* (loving-kindness), *karuna* (compassion), *mudita* (sympathetic joy), and *upekkha* (equanimity)—through the practice of the *brahma-viharas* (Salzberg 1–2).

Of course, love is a universal idea with many definitions as well as a biological universal. Like much in evolution, love comes at a cost. Anthropologist Helen Fisher has done extensive research on love, including studies that placed subjects into MRIs. When shown pictures of their romantic partners, parts of the brain associated with dopamine, a neurotransmitter connected with pleasure, were activated. Two regions of the brain showed the most activity, the caudate nucleus, where reward detection and expectation are processed, and the ventral tegmental, also associated with rewards, focused attention, and pleasure. The ventral tegmental is part of the primitive brain, unlike the hippocampus, which is more logical. This means that our primitive brains light up with chemicals that produce the same effect as euphoria-inducing drugs. When we are falling in love, the stress hormone cortisol increases while decreasing serotonin, whose function is to regulate our sense of well-being and happiness. These fluctuations in cortisol and serotonin lead to the obsession characteristic of falling in love. Adding to the chemical cocktail are oxytocin and vasopressin, hormones released during pregnancy, nursing, and attachment between mother and child. And if that weren't enough, the neural pathway that regulates negative emotions becomes deactivated, so our ability to engage in critical thinking is reduced. Given the overwhelming nature of biological love, it's no wonder that every culture has made it a subject of art and found it necessary to conceptualize love in order to understand it.

In Western literature, we can go back to antiquity for innumerable examples, from Greek tragedy where Medea kills her own children for revenge against Jason, the love of her life, to the Roman poet Ovid's *Metamorphosis* describing the god Apollo's love of Daphne. The early Italian Renaissance writer, Petrarch, would pick up Ovid's themes and tropes in describing the unrequited love he felt for

Laura. Petrarch created love poetry standards of entrapping eyes and hair that would make their way into the English Renaissance sonnets of Shakespeare and his peers. Certainly, love was the subject of most novels during the time that Austen was writing. Early novels often followed the adventures of rogues, but as the genre developed, romance took center stage.

Love literature often reflects the biological discomfort all humans are prone to when falling in love. The great works of literature describe the combination of pleasure and pain. Perhaps the best know is Petrarch who saw Laura in church on Easter and who spent his life loving and writing about her from afar. Love is delightful anguish from Petrarch's perspective:

> Bitter tears pour down my face
> with an anguished storm of sighing,
> when my eyes chance to turn on you
> through whom alone I am lost from the world [Sonnet 17]

Even as Petrarch laments his bitter tears, he blesses the day that he met Laura. He didn't know about brain chemistry, but he must have felt that chemical cocktail of pleasure and pain.

From a Buddhist perspective, this is not true love. When love contains the four elements of loving-kindness, compassion, joy, and equanimity, it is wholesome, to use Thich Nhat Hanh's language. Love brings happiness to both parties, not anguish.

Loving-kindness starts with the self. The traditional *metta* meditation includes phrases along the lines of "May I be (or feel) safe. May I be happy. May I be healthy. May I live with ease." These same phrases are then extended out to a mentor, a neutral person, someone who is sometimes called a troublemaker, and finally to the world at large. The idea is to generate an energy of love and kindness that produces a sense of connection with others. Loving-kindness, therefore, shares nothing with the craving passion described by Petrarch or the English sonneteers. Craving is unwholesome; it is a form of suffering. *Metta*, rather, is open and totally accepting, what we generally mean in Western culture when we say unconditional love: freely given and not hinging on certain behaviors. The other parts of true love spring from loving-kindness.

Compassion builds on metta and on the First Noble Truth, for to feel compassion, we must acknowledge without fear the omnipresence of suffering for all beings, including ourselves. We must, in fact, be open to suffering, something that modern culture certainly doesn't encourage and that we are not inherently prone toward doing. Like metta, compassion must begin with the self since to blame ourselves and carry guilt and shame shuts us down rather than leaving us open.

Joy refers to the ability to rejoice in the happiness and success of others rather than to feel envy. Often when someone we know—or even love—succeeds, we feel threatened rather than truly happy as if happiness were in limited supply and there's now less of it for us. The joy belonging to true love genuinely celebrates the happiness of others.

Equanimity is certainly not something associated with the crazy-making biological cocktail nor the vengeful Medea and love-sick Petrarch. Yet true love requires calm that comes from letting go and not attempting to control. Equanimity grows with the acceptance of impermanence and simply being with things as they are in the moment.

The wholesome true love of Buddhism is not present in *Sense and Sensibility*. Rather, caught by concepts—whether that be sense and/or sensibility or even love—the characters proclaim love but build boundaries. The problem is not the particular concepts found in the title but concepts as a framework for good living.

The best elucidation of the problem of concepts can be found in the sutra called *The Diamond That Cuts through Illusion*, a dialogue between the Buddha and his student Subhuti at the monastery in Anathapindika's park recorded perhaps in the first century B.C.E. The sutra is one of the central teachings of the Mahayana tradition of Buddhism. The Buddha tells Subhuti that "this sutra should be called The Diamond that Cuts through Illusion because it has the capacity to cut through all illusions and afflictions and bring us to the shore of liberation" (14). The illusions are concepts, and concepts create afflictions.

The goal laid out in *The Diamond Sutra* is signlessness. We have to use language in order to communicate. We can't, as another eighteenth-century writer, Jonathan Swift, pokes fun of in *Gulliver's Travels*, carry around every possible object we might need to refer to on a daily basis. If I need to communicate the thing we call chair, I can't pull one out of my pocket. But I also need to recognize there isn't anything inherently chair about chair. In fact, when I say the word chair, a very different picture of chair can pop up for listeners.

Maybe it's the green one that I meditate on that my stepmom gave me. Or perhaps it's the blue plastic IKEA one that's part of my dining room set. As for the word chair, there's nothing fixed about it as a sign for the physical object of chair. If I were in Spain and talking about a chair, I'd say la silla. This is all pretty obvious, but we walk around in our daily lives trusting in those signs and not necessarily giving them much thought. Yet "where there is sign, there is illusion" (Thich Nhat Hanh, *Diamond* 57) and deception.

When it comes to chair, that might not be a particularly big deal, but when I use a word—or sign—to indicate a concept, it might lead to all sorts of communication problems or divisiveness. For example, the words liberal and conservative might mean very different things to people, and they are labels that can make people dislike each other without having a single personal encounter.

We need words and concepts to communicate, but we are prone to understanding things in relationship to their opposites. Someone is alive because she is not dead. Someone is present because she's not absent. In the twentieth century, French theorist Jacques Derrida would introduce the theory of deconstruction calling these binary oppositions, but the Buddha was there centuries before to note that these opposing pairs presented problems. One term is clearly preferable. I love my mother, so I want her alive. I love my daughter, so I want her present. Dualism leads to judgment and discrimination because we crave or attach ourselves to one idea or sign and reject and avoid the other. This leads to affliction and away from true love as we tend to prioritize the concept over the person.

Such dualism is what signlessness seeks to disrupt, for "Buddhas are called Buddhas because they are free of ideas" (Thich Nhat Hanh *Diamond* 18). Of course, humans function via ideas. I'm currently using ideas and concepts to explain escaping from the deception of signs as representatives of ideas. In his commentary on *The Diamond Sutra*, Thich Nhat Hanh acknowledges that the Buddha sees a rose exactly as we all do. "But before he says the rose is a rose, the Buddha has seen that the rose is not a rose" (55). The Buddha recognizes the "non-rose elements" that make up the rose (the sunshine, water, soil, etc.), so he simultaneously sees the rose is a rose and not a rose, rejecting dualism and thereby able to use the sign—"rose"—without producing suffering. Thich Nhat Hanh writes that when "we perceive things, we generally use the sword of conceptualization to cut reality into pieces," but the Buddha is not trapped by concepts, avoids delusion, and rejects ignorance (55). He experiences reality and escapes suffering because he is not enslaved by signs (or words or concepts). Concepts concretize, but reality is like a flowing river.

To live thusly is to have an awakened mind—*bodhicitta*—sometimes translated as the mind of love. Nondualism allows for true love because true love rests upon genuine connection, no longer seeing the self as a separate entity unconsciously addicted to a chemical cocktail designed to help the species survive. Sharon Salzberg explains how Western notions of love generally refer to passion, which depends upon a sense of separation from others since passion denotes longing, craving, and desiring met expectations. The word passion, she explains, has its roots in the Greek word for suffering. Dualism and separation equal suffering.

Recognizing connection, on the other hand, allows the achievement of loving-kindness, compassion, joy, and equanimity. Trapped by concepts, the characters of *Sense and Sensibility* fail to do this. Though the stated central themes of Austen's novel may be sense and sensibility, the book is clearly concerned with what makes one happy with the word happy appearing 136 times and the word happiness 73. Austen uses the word love, or the variation beloved, 108 times. Attached to concepts, the characters define love as attachment and fail at the Second Noble Truth, never seeing the true cause of their suffering.

All of the characters are trapped by concepts but not only by sense and sensibility as many aspire to power and wealth, a false perspective of happiness that Austen exposes from the first page of the novel. Rather than leaving his estate unencumbered to his legal heir, Henry Dashwood, the nameless owner of Norland operates on the patriarchal and unfair principles of primogeniture, making sure that the estate stays within the male line. He creates a will that leaves Henry's wife and daughters with little to live on as the estate goes to Henry's son from a previous marriage: Mr. John Dashwood, who doesn't need the increase in wealth.

Immediately, there is failure at Right View, Right Diligence, and loving-kindness with characters perceiving incorrectly, misdirecting energy, and lacking love. Shortly after Henry Dashwood inherits, he falls fatally ill. On his deathbed, Henry asks his son John to care for his half-sisters without specifying the terms. Austen doesn't allow us to hear their conversation, but the narrator assures us that John Dashwood "promised to do everything in his power to make them comfortable" (43). For several days, the idea of giving his sisters £1,000 apiece "warmed his heart," at his own generosity, though he could clearly afford more. However, his wife, "more narrow-minded and selfish" than he, vetoes his intention, arguing that to "take three thousand pounds from the fortune of their dear little boy would be impoverishing him to the most dreadful degree" (46). After all, "what possible claim could the Miss Dashwoods, who were related to him only by half blood, which she considered as no relationship at all, have on his generosity to so large an amount. It was very well known that no affection was ever supposed to exist between the children of any man by different marriages" (46). John is easily persuaded given that he has been treating his sisters and stepmother with "as much kindness as he could feel toward anybody beyond himself, his wife, and their child" (46).

Because John and Fanny define happiness through wealth and power, that is where they apply their energy, and rather than keeping his promise to his father, John easily justifies his lack of support for his sisters by narrowly defining his family so as not to include them. Austen captures the conversation that follows where Fanny easily persuades John to no more than "such kind of neighbourly acts" as offering assistance when the Dashwood women should leave what had been their home so that he and Fanny can take possession.

Rather than, as with a loving-kindness practice, extending wishes for well-being to all beings, John and Fanny prioritize their own immediate family of three, leaving his sisters and stepmother to fend for themselves while willingly accepting gifts for themselves. When he and Fanny go to London, Fanny's mother gives them £200; he tells Elinor, "extremely acceptable it is, for we must live at great expense while we are here." He then pauses for Elinor's "assent and compassion" (242) before detailing all of the expenses he's endured since inheriting a great estate. These expenses include a dinner party where "the servants were numerous, and everything bespoke the Mistress's inclination for shew, and the Master's ability to support it" (249). In his book on true love, Thich Nhat Hanh extends the definition of equanimity to argue that it has no boundaries and must be inclusive. John and Fanny, with their focus on power and wealth, fail at four aspects of true love.

Austen's narrator makes clear that John is no villain in spite of the numerous instances of his focus on wealth. Rather, he is misguided, so driven by desire for wealth and power that he is blindly selfish. Perhaps the only aspect of love that John appears close to achieving is joy, for he wishes very much for his sisters to marry well, but, alas, the wish is only to appease his own conscience in not offering brotherly love or support.

His myopic focus on wealth and immediate family is encouraged by Fanny, which is unsurprising given her own family. While Mrs. Ferrars, her mother, is generous with her £200 gift, she is stingy with her love and has taught her daughter to feel the same. Upon perceiving that Edward esteems Elinor, Fanny becomes "uneasy" and quickly "uncivil," taking "the first opportunity of affronting her mother-in-law on the occasion, talking to her so expressively of her brother's great expectations, of Mrs. Ferrars' resolution that both of her sons should marry well, and of the danger attending any young woman who attempted to *draw him in*" that she gets her wish, offending Mrs. Dashwood so thoroughly that she and her daughters move as soon as possible rather than being given the time and space they need to grieve.

When in London, Fanny's rudeness and selfish behavior continue. She excludes Elinor and Marianne from her society as much as possible. This is truly an unkind act that extends beyond the personal hurtfulness of ignoring family, for there are material consequences given Elinor and Marianne's status as young single women who would benefit from introductions to likely suitors. Eventually, Fanny's pride requires her to include Elinor and Marianne when an acquaintance visits while the sisters are present. Her conscience justifies her incivility to the sisters, but she cares deeply about the opinion of others so that she feels forced to include Elinor and Marianne when the acquaintance later extends an invitation to them. The narrator with a bit of bite offers insight into Fanny's motivation, telling the reader that "while the imaginations of other people will carry them away to form wrong judgements of our conduct, and to decide on it by slight appearances, ones' happiness must in some measure be always at the mercy of chance" (263). Because Fanny's actions are dictated from selfishness, power—that is wrong notions of happiness—and not love, her happiness, indeed, is out of her control, as she learns much to her chagrin not long after when favoring Edward's secret fiancé in order to avoid offering appropriate hospitality to her own extended family.

Said fiancé must be secret, though, for Fanny is a mere shadow of her controlling mother who has parented two selfish children in her own image fixated on society and wealth and a third, Edward, who disappoints her thanks to his compassion and honor. Mrs. Ferrars openly slights Elinor upon meeting her and, cluelessly like her daughter, distinguishes Edward's secret fiancé in her efforts to belittle Elinor. Upon learning of the secret engagement and finding her son pliable to neither bribe nor threat to end it, Mrs. Ferrars disinherits her oldest son in favor of the younger, a rude, undeserving dandy who shares her unwholesome values.

It is likely the withholding and conditional nature of Mrs. Ferrars's love that made Edward vulnerable to the machinations of Lucy in the first place. Edward, himself, recognizes that his upbringing has been deleterious to his happiness and without attention to his own ideas of what would make him happy. He tells Mrs. Dashwood, "It has been, and is, and probably will always be a heavy misfortune to me, that I have had no necessary business to engage me, no profession, to give me employment, or afford me anything like independence ... and the nicety of my friends [has] made me what I am, an idle, helpless being" (132). As an older son bound to inherit a large fortune, Edward needs no profession, but he wishes for a sense of purpose, preferring to have one and of all professions, preferring the church. His mother and sister, though, wish "to see him distinguished—as—they hardly knew what. They wanted him to make a fine figure in the world in some manner or other" (53). But, for Edward, "all his wishes centered in domestic comfort and the quiet of private life" (54). Young, inexperienced, lacking any sense of worth from his own family, Edward is an easy target for the mercenary Lucy Steele. There is no true love within the Ferrars family.

While the Ferrars family is extreme, it's not the exception in lacking true love. Sir John Middleton, who offers the use of his cottage to the Dashwoods, shows familial generosity in doing so to a distant relation. However, we soon learn that the Middletons themselves fail to offer each other true love or happiness though Sir John operates from "kindness" and a "good heart" (70). With little in common, Sir John and Lady Middleton gather visitors around them as much as possible; "It was necessary to the happiness of both; for however dissimilar in temper and outward behaviour, they strongly resembled each other in that total want of talent and taste which confined their employments, unconnected with such as society produced, within a very narrow compass" (69). Sir John simultaneously operates from a good heart and to avoid the company of his own wife when asking the Dashwoods to stay and insisting on frequent visits from the cottage to Barton Park.

This theme is reinforced by Lady Middleton's sister, Mrs. Palmer, who repeatedly refers to her husband as "my love" while Mr. Palmer offers such sneering rudeness in return that Austen uses the words *scolding* and *abusive* to describe his behavior. Elinor reads Mr. Palmer as purposely behaving with incivility as "a wish of distinction," resulting in "his contemptuous treatment of everybody, and his general abuse of everything before him" (141). Mrs. Palmer chooses not to see this, laughing that "sometimes he won't speak to me for half a day together, and then he comes out with something so droll" with droll clearly meaning insulting (142). With Right Speech and deep listening an essential component of true love, the Palmers miss the mark. Mrs. Palmer declares to Elinor that she could have married Colonel Brandon if she'd chosen, though he never made a single overture to her, but her mother, Mrs. Jennings, declared the match beneath her. The implication is that her marriage to Mr. Palmer was one made for social position and wealth with no true love to start or forming after the marriage.

While Mrs. Dashwood and her daughters escape the traps of false love presented by wealth, power, and societal expectations, they nonetheless struggle with true love as well thanks to being trapped by equally powerful concepts: the sense and sensibility of the title.

With or without the Buddhist framework, one can see immediately that Mrs. Dashwood's perceptions are skewed by sensibility. When discussing Edward with Elinor early in the book, Mrs. Dashwood proclaims that she loves Edward solely for being unlike his sister and because she feels "no sentiment of approbation inferior to love" (54). After her bold declaration of love, Mrs. Dashwood "now took pains to get acquainted with him," indicating her lack of sincerity even as her declaration is sincere. With her perspective skewed by sensibility and an addiction to love as passion, she fails to offer her daughters guidance or consider the ramifications of their love interests. For while Edward is heir to a large fortune, that fortune, other than "a trifling sum," is completely under the control of his mother who would not (and later does not) approve of a match with Elinor (53). While Austen's happiest marriages are never mercenary, her novels offer warnings about marrying only for love with no money. Mrs. Dashwood is failing in her parental duties by encouraging a match that likely will not happen or would put Elinor into a necessitous life.

Austen uses the revelation of Edward's engagement with Lucy to make this point. Upon learning of Edward's disinheritance, Mrs. Jennings speculates on what the future holds for the couple: "they will wait a twelvemonth, and finding no good comes of it, will set down upon a curacy of fifty pounds a-year, with the interest of his two thousand pounds, and what little matter Mr. Steele and Mr. Pratt can give her,—Then they will have a child every year! And Lord help 'em! how poor they will be!" (289). Elinor escapes this fate thanks to Colonel Brandon's intervention, but she and Edward do end up settling on much less than Edward's expectations thanks to his mother—something Elinor's mother should be considering, especially given Elinor's own pragmatic personality. Elinor reveals exactly that when talking to Marianne at the end of the novel about her life with Willoughby if she had married him. Knowing his personality, his desire for an expensive lifestyle, and his lack of funds, Elinor tells Marianne "that your marriage must have involved you in many certain troubles and disappointments ... you must have been always poor" (354).

In this way, though with better intentions, Mrs. Dashwood shares in common with Mrs. Ferrars an inability to see her own child due to seeing her through the lens of concepts. Valuing her perspective of sensibility, Mrs. Dashwood dismisses Elinor in language that could be construed as hurtful when they later discuss Willoughby's behavior toward Marianne. Convinced of her interpretation of events that support a belief in passionate romantic love, Mrs. Dashwood tells Elinor, "I have explained it to myself in the most satisfactory way;—but you, Elinor, who love to doubt where you can—it will not satisfy you" (110). She then exclaims, "Oh! Elinor, how incomprehensible are your feelings! You had rather take evil upon credit than good" (111). To be understood is a universal human need, and the sense of being understood immediately allows us to feel connected and to suffer less. Mrs. Dashwood's words indicate not only a lack of understanding her daughter but also her phrasing increases that distance with her accusation that Elinor enjoys doubting and is extraordinarily cynical. And, of course, Mrs. Dashwood is wrong about Elinor and about Willoughby. Her confidence in her own perspective—blocked by concepts—blinds her to the truth on more than one occasion.

Yet Mrs. Dashwood depends exactly on that: love. With faith that her love for Marianne is guide enough, she does nothing to intervene as Marianne recklessly pursues a relationship with Willoughby. Upon

Willoughby leaving with Marianne pining, Elinor urges her mother to talk to Marianne and discover the source of her suffering. Appearances point to an engagement between the two, but Marianne has never been open with her family about the relationship. Mrs. Dashwood objects to Elinor's supplication by telling her, "I know Marianne's heart; I know that she dearly loves me, and that I shall not be the last to whom the affair is made known" (116). But Mrs. Dashwood's confidence is misplaced. There is no doubt that she loves her children, but she fails to know them, and her confidence in "romantic delicacy" prevents her from recognizing the truth.

Her romantic viewpoint fails her in reading Willoughby as well since his behavior points to the classic romantic hero. Once again in dispute with Elinor, Mrs. Dashwood proclaims, "Has not his behavior to Marianne and to all of us, for at least the last fortnight, declared that he loved and considered her as his future wife, and that he felt for us the attachment of the nearest relation?" (112). Yet romance does not equate with love and can disguise nefarious intentions rather than emotional commitment.

Marianne mirrors her mother in suffering from an inability to see clearly thanks to sensibility. In fact, thanks to sensibility, Marianne wishes only for a mirror, which is what leaves her vulnerable to Willoughby. She explains to Mrs. Dashwood that "I could not be happy with a man whose taste did not in every point coincide with my own. He must enter into all my feelings; the same books, the same music must charm us both" (55). Austen mirrors this language to emphasize how Marianne desires someone who shares all of her own tastes and passion. As she and Willoughby become acquainted, the narrator shares, "Their *taste* was strikingly alike. The *same books*, the same passages were idolized by each" (emphasis added 83). Equating similarity of tastes—which can be faked—with the qualities of a moral, committed man puts Marianne in harm's way.

And it creates more boundaries. With different motivation, Marianne initially treats Edward in the same fashion as his family, dismissing him thanks to his shy diffidence. While claiming to love and appreciate him, she tells her mother how short Edward falls of her own notion of a romantic partner: "there is something wanting—his figure is not striking; it has none of that grace which I would expect in the man who could seriously attach my sister. His eyes want all that spirit, that fire, which at once announce virtue and intelligence. And besides all this, I am afraid, mama, he has no real taste"

(55). Marianne's sentimental markers of virtue obviously lead to her suffering, for when she meets Willoughby, she rests her entire faith and affection on similarity in taste and his dashing good looks, not being attentive to actual experience as Willoughby's behavior clearly belies an unkind, secretive nature.

Elinor sees both this and how Willoughby shares her sister's less admirable qualities. While not fully appreciating the scoundrel Willoughby is, she sees his propensity "in which he strongly resembled and peculiarly delighted her sister, of saying too much what he thought on every occasion, without attention to persons or circumstances" (84). Marianne's neglect of proper manners is peppered throughout the book, from her refusal to participate in polite conversation to complete inattention to those around her. While Willoughby clearly knows how to charm, "he was a lover; his attentions were wholly Marianne's, and a far less agreeable man might have been more generally pleasing" (90). Austen never endorses sycophantic politeness. (For proof, see *Pride and Prejudice*'s Mr. Collins.) However, there's a meanness to Marianne and Willoughby's exclusion of others. When Elinor references "saying too much ... without attention to persons," examples move beyond the speech of a lover to his beloved in company. Marianne and Willoughby engage in spiteful speech at times especially in reference to Colonel Brandon who, in contrast, "was on every occasion mindful of the feelings of others" (95).

Though it sounds more admirable to center life around love rather than wealth and power as the Ferrars family does, Mrs. Dashwood and Marianne's approach is equally unwholesome. As with their addiction to sensibility, not recognizing it as a mindset or concept, they misdefine happiness. Marianne confuses pleasure for happiness, as can be seen in her relationship with Willoughby. Pleasure is that temporary jolt of good feeling, like what we might feel from eating chocolate and which can be produced by the chemical cocktail of love. Happiness refers to a state that is wholesome and beneficial to all, such as the good feeling one might have offering deep listening to a friend.

With her misunderstanding of these two terms, Marianne uses her sensibility in making moral judgments, claiming that she knows she is right because she would feel it if she were wrong. After an unchaperoned tour with Willoughby of his aunt's estate, she defends herself against Elinor's charges of wrongdoing by explaining, "if there had been any real impropriety in what I did, I should have been sensible of it at the time, for we always know when we are acting wrong, and with such a conviction I could have had no pleasure" (102). The key term here is *pleasure*, as we are quite capable of finding pleasure in wrong, hence the cliché guilty pleasure. Marianne, in fact, is wrong by societal standards to tour the estate, since she and Willoughby are not engaged and because it's an intrusion on the hospitality of the absent Mrs. Smith, who later will disinherit Willoughby upon learning of his true character.

Buddhism, with its endorsement of trusting to personal experience, may appear similar to Marianne's claim of experiential knowledge of morality. After all, Thich Nhat Hanh writes, "because of mindfulness, when something is right, we know it's right, and when something is wrong, we know it's wrong" (*Heart* 56). But Marianne is mindlessly caught by concepts, not mindful. Her pleasure in Willoughby's company creates a lack of connection and care. Marianne, while claiming great love and even sacrificing herself on sensibility's altar of love, does not feel love. Marianne's deceptive happiness literally harms her to the point of near death.

Ultimately, Marianne lacks loving-kindness for herself. Thich Nhat Hanh proclaims, "If you do not give right attention to the one you love, it is a kind of killing" (*Heart* 65). Marianne eventually sees this, telling Elinor that her illness allowed time for reflection: "I saw in my own behaviour, since the beginning of our acquaintance with him last autumn, nothing but a series of imprudence towards myself, and want of kindness to others. I saw that my own feelings had prepared my sufferings" (350). Such understanding from a teen is admirable indeed, but Marianne's intended plan of reformation demonstrates her continued immaturity as she declares she will devote herself entirely to her sisters and mother and check any remembrance of Willoughby "by religion, by reason, by constant employment" (351). This is immediately followed by "If…" showing her lack of resolve. Once again, we find a character with a good heart who will struggle to live up to unrealistic goals.

That Marianne has escaped false love is reinforced by Willoughby's apology to Elinor during Marianne's illness, which rather than excusing him highlights his narcissism. Upon arriving at the residence of the Palmers, he uses a "voice of command rather than supplication" to insist that Elinor listen to him as he narrates his own story in an attempt to make her "hate [him] one degree less" (325–6). This demonstrates that his visit is more about himself than about alleviating the feelings of the Dashwood sisters. He goes on to explain he couldn't marry Marianne due to his lack of fortune and to blame Colonel Brandon's young ward for their affair, which resulted in her pregnancy: "I do not mean to justify myself, but at the same time cannot leave you to suppose that I have nothing to urge—that because she was injured she was irreproachable, and because *I* was a *libertine, she* must be a saint" (emphasis in original 329). Saint or not, she is merely 17 to Willoughby's more worldly 25 and must bear the cost of the transgression within her own body, a cost he could have alleviated by marrying her, which would have prevented his aunt from disinheriting him. Willoughby's last words to Elinor are that he now will live in dread of hearing that Marianne is married, for "she will be gained by someone else" (338). Even as his rejection has caused her to suffer to the point of near death, he cannot find joy in her finding true love for herself with someone else.

That someone else whom Willoughby rightly dreads is Colonel Brandon, the unexpected husband more than double Marianne's age. For some readers, this match feels unsuitable for that very reason and for the differences in their temperament. Others rejoice that the long-suffering and kind Brandon at last finds happiness. The key to deciding is understanding if this relationship is one of true love or if the Colonel, like the other characters, is trapped by concepts.

While admirable in many ways, Brandon is trapped by his past. When relaying his story to Elinor, he reminds her of his previous comment that Marianne puts him in mind of someone from his past: "That same warmth of heart, the same eagerness of fancy and spirits" (225). Brandon's tale of the lost Eliza, his near relation and an orphan forced into an unhappy marriage with his older brother though in love with him, explains his being from first introduction "silent and grave." Though some of this comes from the epilogue to Eliza's story—Willoughby's seduction of Eliza's daughter—there is no sense that Brandon's demeanor has changed significantly. His gravity seems to be of long standing and made him "an absolute old bachelor" (71). As he is relaying the story so many years later, he refers to "this gloom—even now the recollection of what I suffered—" (226) and clearly is still suffering. Again, granted, the news of Willoughby's seduction and the consequences are fresh, but clearly Brandon has failed to move on and find happiness from a very young age when he lost Eliza. While this perhaps does not mar his affection for

Marianne, his admission that it comes from her resemblance to his lost love leaves room for doubt that he loves Marianne for Marianne but rather is using the relationship to rewrite the story of his doomed first love.

Like Colonel Brandon, Elinor appears to embody the sense concept of our title. And, like Brandon, Elinor's harmful clinging to concepts is less clear in comparison to Marianne. In fact, many literary critics believe she represents (to make a Buddhist pun) the middle way, showing the necessary balance between sense and sensibility. She is not governed purely by the mind, showing real and deep feeling, but she does not allow her feelings to govern her either, appearing to demonstrate self-discipline and effort. But while Elinor does not sink under her misery as Marianne does, she is not happy, nor is she genuinely calm. Rather, like Brandon, Elinor exhibits stoicism, an appearance of calm that opens her to charges of inauthenticity and that, thereby, parallels her to the novel's great hypocrite, Lucy Steele.

Austen describes Elinor's response to learning the news of Edward and Lucy's engagement through language of concealment, not as genuine acceptance. Elinor's immediate response is to hide her feelings:

> She thought she could even now, under the first smart of the heavy blow, command herself enough to guard every suspicion of the truth from her mother and sisters. And so well was she able to answer her own expectations, that when she joined them at dinner only two hours after she had first suffered from the extinction of all her dearest hopes, no one would have supposed from the appearance of the sisters, that Elinor was mourning in secret over obstacles which must divide her forever from the object of her love [166–7].

Austen's language is telling, including in this short passage the words *guard*, *suspicion*, *truth*, *appearance*, and *secret*. No one, of course, would expect Elinor to be happy at such a moment, but the language adds up to her being absolutely disingenuous, not governed by sense to produce calm but rather concealing her suffering and thereby cutting herself off from those she loves best.

Yet one can hardly blame Elinor as those who love her best struggle so much to demonstrate true love. Elinor senses this, leading to an emotional separation from her mother that predates their physical separation upon visiting London. She hides her feelings, believing "she was stronger alone, and her own good sense so well supported her, that her firmness was unshaken, her appearance of cheerfulness as invariable, as with regrets so poignant and so fresh, it was possible for them to be" (167). Keeping up appearances, though, is hardly facing up to and coping with suffering.

Within a few paragraphs of describing Elinor's response to Lucy's revelation, Austen describes Elinor's desire to encounter Lucy again to demonstrate her "calmness in conversing" (167) and attain the "comfort of endeavoring to convince Lucy that her heart was unwounded" (168). Her heart is wounded, but "she did not mistrust her own ability of going through a repetition of particulars with composure" (168) if given the opportunity to talk with Lucy again.

Elinor proceeds to create that opportunity by pretending she wishes to help Lucy with the basket she is creating for Lady Middleton's daughter immediately after Lucy's clearly feigned joy to complete the project. In this way, Austen connects the two characters' acting skills, in the process degrading Elinor. As Elinor answers "with a smile, which concealed very agitated feelings," she blushes "for the insincerity of Edward's future wife" (175). Though I tell my students no clichés, this is pot calling kettle black. Obviously, there is a hugely important difference between Elinor and Lucy in terms of motivation. Lucy is, to use modern parlance, a mean girl, and her attempts at concealment are purposely hurtful. However, both Elinor and Lucy here are managing their public personas in an egotistical way; both are going for the power play, and neither is interested in genuine communication, a trend that continues for Elinor.

Austen describes a later conversation between Elinor and Colonel Brandon as carried on in a "calm kind of way, with very little interest on either side," so that "they continued to talk, both of them out of spirits, and the thoughts of both engaged elsewhere" (187). Having chosen stoicism and the veneer of calm, Elinor finds herself cut off from all those around her, leading to mild resentment on her part. When Mrs. Dashwood effuses joyfully over Marianne's recovery from her illness, proclaiming that she's the happiest woman in the world, "Elinor could not hear the declaration, nor witness its proofs without sometimes wondering whether her mother ever recollected Edward. But Mrs. Dashwood, trusting to the temperate account of her own disappointment which Elinor had sent her, was led away by the exuberance of her joy" (341). Elinor's own reassurance over her calm acceptance of Edward's engagement leaves her feeling misunderstood, but she is, herself, responsible for creating that misunderstanding through false reassurance. Thich Nhat Hanh warns that "if you keep your suffering to yourself, it might grow bigger every day" (*Heart* 38), which proves true for Elinor as her silence creates the suffering of distance from others.

So while critics often point to Elinor's effort as Austen's endorsement of her approach to problems, she lacks the Buddhist sense of discipline that brings genuine happiness. Many conflate Zen Buddhism with stoicism, believing that Buddhist practices lead to a lack of emotion. However, this is untrue. As Pema Chödrön defines it, discipline means not trying to escape reality, but to be here now, and to be here now may mean experiencing great anger, fear, or anxiety, but the point is to experience it and let it go (*When Things Fall Apart* 199). No matter what the present moment may be, as Salzberg writes, "being fully in the present is the source of ... happiness. We open to our own experience, and inevitably that opens us to others" (17). Elinor, given her lack of connection, fails to exhibit discipline since to do so would open her to others, not shut her down, and this, in turn, closes her off from the opportunity for real happiness, "which at heart is a yearning for union, for overcoming our feelings of separateness" (Salzberg 21). To be truly present and open to happiness, as Chödrön writes, "we are giving up control altogether and letting concepts and ideals fall apart" (63). Elinor fails at this, choosing rather to control the perceptions of those around her, dividing herself from love and happiness thanks to her concept of sense, or, as I'm calling it, stoicism.

Some characters in the novel are hard-hearted and selfish, not loving because of that (Lucy, Willoughby, Fanny, and Mrs. Ferrars), but many of the characters fail at love in spite of good hearts. Austen explicitly tells us Sir John has a "good heart," and John Dashwood, though being "cold hearted," "might even have been made amiable himself" if he had married a kinder woman (43). The intent to love and be kind is clearly shared among the other characters. Even busybody matchmaker Mrs. Jennings has "active good-nature" (346). But they fail nonetheless with Mrs. Dashwood, for example, coming to realize that "she had been unjust, inattentive, nay, almost unkind, to her Elinor" (359). The first necessary step to share true love is the intention, and these good-hearted characters share that. However, they lack the ability. They are unskillful. This causes suffering, for "to love without knowing *how* to love wounds the person we love" (Thich Nhat Hanh, *Love* 30, emphasis in original).

The three jewels of Buddhism are the Buddha, the *dharma*,

and the sangha. The Buddha is a jewel because we all have the same capacity to reach enlightenment just as the Buddha did. Everyone has Buddha nature and can call upon that for support. The *dharma* refers to the teachings, such as *The Diamond Sutra*. The sangha is the group that supports each other in the practice. This is what the characters lack in *Sense and Sensibility*. Ironically, their desire for the concept of love and their addiction to the chemical cocktail of love block them off from the true love they could find with each other as a *sangha*. Boundaries and secrets—all coming from concepts— prevent the characters from offering each other deep listening and encouragement to reach toward enlightenment. They get their happy ending thanks to Austen, but they have more to learn as enlightened beings.

# FIVE

# The Secret to the Happy Ending

## Compassion in Jane Austen's Emma

"You have no compassion on my poor nerves."
—Jane Austen, *Pride and Prejudice*

"With compassion in our heart, every thought, word,
and deed can bring about a miracle."
—Thich Nhat Hanh, *The Heart
of the Buddha's Teaching*

When Jane Austen began writing *Emma* (published in 1815), she declared, "I am going to take a heroine whom no one but myself will much like." *Emma's* enduring popularity as novel and movie adaptations (nine thus far, including pop culture favorite *Clueless*) proved Austen wrong.[1] Most readers likely do find the character Emma frustrating, but we also find her endearing because she is so very similar to us in getting things wrong and in attempting unsuccessfully to control life. Emma, the character, demonstrates how faulty our personal narratives can be, and *Emma*, the novel, is a study of the consequential suffering. Of course, unmitigated suffering is not an option for Austen, known for her comedies, so she provides the requisite happy ending and points to the cure: empathy leading to compassion and, ultimately, happiness.

*Emma* opens with the marriage of Emma's governess, leaving our 20-year-old heroine as mistress of the house since her mother is long dead and her married sister lives in London. Said house is considered one of the most important estates in the neighborhood, securing Emma's position as the woman with the highest status in the village of Highbury despite her youth and inexperience. Austen makes clear that Emma has received inadequate guidance, with her governess Miss Taylor, now Mrs. Weston, being more led than leading, and her father, Mr. Woodhouse, suffering from hypochondria and needing tending rather than offering any. Instead, the two adults in Emma's life offer little direction, seeing Emma as nearly perfect and in need of no guidance, which proves false. Emma proceeds to engage in matchmaking schemes that go awry thanks to her misreading of her new friend Harriet Smith's value on the marriage market, to being blind to Mr. Elton's interest in herself, and to misunderstanding new-comer Frank Churchill, Mr. Weston's son, and the returned Jane Fairfax who are, we learn at the end of the novel, secretly engaged. The only one to see Emma clearly and offer guidance is the aptly named Mr. Knightley, whom Emma will eventually marry.

The novel's central plot revolves around Emma's inability to read others, causing her to script narratives around false premises accordingly. Before exploring her misreadings, though, I will give Emma a bit of a defense. When reading those whom she loves and knows well, Emma does okay by herself. Mr. Knightley teases Emma for taking any credit in helping along the marriage of Miss Taylor to Mr. Weston, accusing her of pride in making "a lucky guess" when Emma explains she years earlier suspected an attraction. Emma retorts "a lucky guess is never merely luck" (13). Of course, she's right. She has not merely guessed, but based upon the behavior of Miss Taylor and Mr. Weston, Emma has successfully read the situation, for our narrator assures us that Mr. Weston had wanted to marry Miss Taylor for a while but had waited to propose until he had bought the estate of Randalls. She reads her father perfectly at the small gatherings at their home and to the great advantage of her father's guests. Given his own supposed sensitive constitution, Mr. Woodhouse protects his guests from most of the best dishes being served at meals. On one occasion, Emma helps Mrs. Bates and Mrs. Goddard to "large slices of cake and full glasses of wine," suspecting that Mr. Woodhouse has prevented them from eating the "plentiful dinner" she had provided (177). Emma knows her father's predilection and sees to the needs of her guests while protecting her father's feelings, in other words understanding all those around her.

Her understanding demonstrates the ability to empathize well under specific circumstances, that is when interacting within the small circle of Highbury and particularly within her own family, which makes common and evolutionary sense. In typical fashion, Austen introduces strangers to tax our heroine's abilities: a student at the boarding school, Harriet Smith; the clergyman, Mr. Elton, who has been in Highbury less than two years; Jane Fairfax, niece and granddaughter of long-time residents who has been absent much of her life; and Frank Churchill, son of Mr. Weston from his previous marriage known only by name and reputation.

One explanation for Emma's struggle to empathize outside her familiar circle is evolution because evolution privileges our genes, our families. "Our evolutionary background makes it hard to identify with outsiders. We've evolved to hate our enemies, to ignore people we barely know, and to distrust anybody who doesn't look like us. Even if we are largely cooperative within our communities, we become almost a different animal in our treatment of strangers" (de Waal n.p.). But Buddhism argues that humans can become enlightened and move beyond evolution—in Emma's case, learn compassion.

The complicating addition of new people to read demonstrates that Emma lacks empathy, a main ingredient of compassion. While Theory of Mind, discussed in Chapters One and Two, "refers to our ability to represent other people's mental states such as beliefs, knowledge, and intentions," empathy "encompasses our ability to be sensitive to and vicariously experience other people's feelings and to create working models of emotional states" (Reniers et al. 50). Empathy offers the evolutionary advantage of a stronger family bond, hence it being an adaptation and why it makes sense for Emma to have empathy for her father most of all even though her own strong health differentiates her so clearly from his hypochondriac worries. A key ingredient of empathy, because it is the tracking of others' emotions, is differentiating our own feelings from those of others, so perhaps the contrast in health from her father works to Emma's advantage; she is unlikely to crave gruel like her worrying father. Like Theory of Mind, then, empathy requires perspective taking, distinguishing our own experience from another's, while "at the same time we are vicariously affected by the other's. This process culminates in a cognitive appraisal of the other's behavior and situation: We adopt the other's perspective" (de Waal n.p.). Thus, empathy is a daily unconscious exercise of great complexity.

The unsuccessful exercise of empathy often comes from not successfully moving beyond our own perspective. Failure at perspective-taking is called *attribution bias* where, as social psychologist Ellen Langer notes, "we presume that our own behavior makes sense and that any well-adjusted person would act in a similar way" (151). With attribution bias, our narrative rests upon our own egocentric beliefs and perspective. This tendency toward ascribing our own motivations to others is heightened by anxiety because anxiety forces us to focus on potential threats and protecting the self, increasing our "reliance on egocentric self-knowledge when trying to understand others' differing perceptual and conceptual perspectives" (Todd et al. 385). Egocentrism also creates rigid thinking that undercuts flexibility in coping and explaining life events (Fresco et al.), which also would make tracking and perspective-taking difficult.

From a Western perspective, developing empathy skills has many benefits. Empathy "enhances emotional well-being, interpersonal relationships, and life success" (Wei et al. 195). Because empathy generally leads to prosocial behavior, it generates gratitude and positive personal responses from others in the community, leading to happiness because of greater connections and the empathetic person sensing her own kindness (Wei et al. 196). Adam Smith also notes from an evolutionary framework that empathy can enhance inclusive fitness directly since empathy arose as an adaptation to make parents more responsive to infants and indirectly as it leads to "friends who are reliable reciprocators" (4). Ultimately, empathy leads to morality (de Waal n.p.).

Mr. Woodhouse embodies all of the qualities that undercut successful empathy.[2] Austen introduces him as "a nervous man, easily depressed, fond of everybody that he was used to, and hating to part with them; hating change of every kind" (9). This disposition creates an egocentric worldview for Mr. Woodhouse where he fails to read anyone correctly and, thereby, models for Emma a highly dysfunctional approach to living, one of control and egocentrism.

Seeing Mrs. Weston's marriage as the source of unwanted change in his own life, Mr. Woodhouse refers to her as "poor Miss Taylor" throughout the novel, despite her increase in wealth and status via a happy marriage created out of affection. Austen, through her characteristic free indirect discourse, does not leave her reader to guess at this, telling us from Mr. Woodhouse's "habits of gentle selfishness and of being never able to suppose that other people could feel differently from himself, he was very much disposed to think Miss Taylor had done as sad a thing for herself as for them, and would have been a great deal happier if she had spent all the rest of her life at Hartfield" (9).

Examples of Mr. Woodhouse's lack of empathy abound in the novel; there truly is no point throughout the entire book when he gets something right. One example will suffice. When awaiting a visit from his daughter Isabella and her husband, Mr. Woodhouse complains of his son-in-law, John Knightley, being "too rough" with his sons and of their uncle, Mr. Knightley, tossing them in the air "in a very frightful way!" Emma attempts to explain, noting her father's egocentrism by telling him that John Knightley "appears too rough to you ... because you are so very gentle yourself; but if you could compare him with other papas, you would not think him rough." She also points out that the children love their uncle tossing them in the air and clamor for turns. Mr. Woodhouse responds, "I cannot understand it," which is clearly the case because he would not parent in the same active style nor enjoy roughhousing (69–70).

Mr. Woodhouse's egocentrism prevents his ability to enter into the pleasure of others, nor can he understand their pain so focused is he on his own script. When Mr. Knightley unexpectedly leaves for London, Mr. Woodhouse is deeply disturbed because of its impromptu nature and because Mr. Knightley chooses to go on horseback. To distract him, Emma shares the sad news that Jane Fairfax has found a place as governess and must leave soon, a matter of great import and a decision so painful to Jane that it makes her ill. The distraction works for "it supplied a very useful check,—interested, without disturbing him. He had long made up his mind to Jane Fairfax's going out as governess, and could talk of it cheerfully, but Mr. Knightley's going to London had been an unexpected blow" (318). Mr. Woodhouse's rigid thinking leaves no room for spontaneity and blocks empathy, let alone compassion.

Mr. Woodhouse copes with his poor empathy through rigidly controlling his social network not only in terms of whom he will see but also where and how. He rarely goes more than half a mile from his own front door, and, on the few occasions he does, he requires a great deal of personal attention. When he goes to Mr. Knightley's nearby estate for a strawberry picking party, he stays inside with either Mrs. Weston or Emma tending to him. His preference is to invite a limited number of guests—all middle-aged or older women—to his own home for afternoon visits. He is able to function fine within this carefully scripted life. *The Way of the* Bodhisattva describes the approach to life that Mr. Woodhouse exhibits. In his most famous passage, Shantideva writes:

To cover all the earth with sheets of hide—
Where could such amounts of skin be found?
But simply wrap some leather round your feet,
And it's as if the whole earth had been covered! [5.13].

We are all prone to trying to make the world bend to our whims and will, just like Mr. Woodhouse, but we are better off putting on a pair of shoes and traveling the path in front of us.

There are decided repercussions for those around Mr. Woodhouse beyond his female guests whose health he protects by stingily offering up refreshments while arguing for the healthfulness of gruel. At the most basic level, his daughters have lived sheltered lives within the bounds of Hartfield, narrowing their exposure to society and potential mates. Isabella has married the younger brother, Mr. John Knightley, and, when the novel opens, Emma has no suitors. Isabella has inherited her father's personality and tendency toward hypochondria and subsequent anxiety. No Theory of Mind is required as Austen's narrator introduces Isabella: "She was not a woman of strong understanding or any quickness; and, with this resemblance of her father, she inherited also much of his constitution; was delicate in her own health, over-careful of that of her children, [and] had many fears and many nerves" (79). Isabella's long conversations with her father comparing health advice from medical caregivers annoy her husband and increase her father's anxiety. Isabella has fully adopted her father's perspective; unable to imagine a different way to view the world, she sees it as her father does to her own detriment and, one assumes, to her children's.

While not so thoroughly trapped by an inability to engage in perspective taking as her sister, Emma also struggles with Right View from the Eightfold Path that leads to enlightenment. Right View requires seeing things as they are, not from a false perspective, and it necessarily means not being trapped by egocentrism. When Thich Nhat Hanh urges his readers to ask, "Are you sure?", the answer clearly will be no if the reader lacks empathy. Unfortunately, Emma's answer is always yes when it should often be no.

From a Buddhist perspective, empathy is a central component of compassion that ideally extends to all, not merely to those we love, indeed not merely to those we know. Compassion "is more than simply feeling for another—empathy—but a concerned, heartfelt caring, wanting to do something to relieve the person's suffering. And that holds whether the being involved is oneself, someone else, or an animal" (Goleman 61). Compassion is one of four central components of genuine love, which consists of: *maitri* (loving-kindness), *mudita* (joy), *upeksha* (equanimity), and *karuna* (compassion).

Such deeply felt connection for others depends upon a worldview that is more communal rather than focused on the individual and hierarchy. It must move beyond the kind of egocentric perspective Emma learns from her father. Emma, thereby, works from a double disadvantage given a family and societal education that taught her to think primarily of herself and her superior status within her culture.

Both the narrator and Mr. Knightley note this lack in Emma's education. The narrator tells the reader immediately after describing Miss Taylor's leniency as governess that the "real evils indeed of Emma's situation were the power of having rather too much her own way, and a disposition to think a little too well of herself," but notes that the "danger" is "unperceived" (7). When Mr. Knightley shares with Mrs. Weston his concern over Emma's friendship with Harriet, Mrs. Weston responds that it will be good for Emma as she wishes to improve Harriet's education and, hence, will read more herself. Mr. Knightley expresses his skepticism by saying, "Emma has been meaning to read more ever since she was twelve years old. I have seen a great many lists of her drawing up at various times of books that she meant to read regularly through," which, of course, she never does (32). Austen intuitively knew that literature develops empathy. One study found a clear connection between reading about social interactions that required Theory of Mind to understand and the development of empathy, exactly the skill set created by the novel *Emma* and that Emma as eponymous heroine lacks (Wallentin et al.).

Emma's cultural biases appear quite clearly in her quick dismissal of Robert Martin as an appropriate suitor for her new friend Harriet. Harriet, though of mysterious patrimony, appears to Emma to be a gentleman's daughter given her placement at Mrs. Goddard's school and continued maintenance there as a boarder. When Emma first meets her, Harriet already has formed an attachment to Robert Martin, a farmer, via her friendship with his sisters at school. Emma is blind to how advantageous this match is for Harriet. Emma fails to see this because she fails to see Robert Martin entirely, which she admits to Harriet without recognizing the cost of her blindness. After Harriet tells Emma that Mr. Martin has passed Emma often in Highbury, Emma retorts:

That may be—and I may have seen him fifty times, but without having any idea of his name. A young farmer, whether on horseback or on foot, is the very last sort of person to raise my curiosity. The yeomanry are precisely the order of people with whom I feel I can have nothing to do. A degree or two lower, and a creditable appearance might interest me; I might hope to be useful to their families in some way or other. But a farmer can need none of my help, and is therefore in one sense as much above my notice as in every other he is below it [26–7].

Austen's contemporary, the poet John Keats, wrote in a letter that "if a sparrow come before my Window I take part in its existence and pick about the gravel" (Keats 200). But poor Emma fails to see a neighbor and man respected by others. Here is a lack of empathy and hence compassion to the extreme.

Even Emma's professed friendship with Harriet comes from egocentrism. Her first meeting with Harriet leads to a description of Harriet as if she were a doll to play with: "a very pretty girl, and her beauty happened to be of a sort which Emma particularly admired. She was short, plump and fair, with a fine bloom, blue eyes, light hair, regular features, and a look of great sweetness." Perhaps more importantly, Emma is taken with her manners "shewing so proper and becoming a deference, seeming so pleasantly grateful for being admitted to Hartfield, and so artlessly impressed by the appearance of everything in so a superior a style to what she had been used to" (21). Emma's interest in Harriet arises primarily from Emma's own sense of superiority and Harriet's recognition of her own inferiority. Harriet presents herself as a willing project and an even more willing flatterer.

While Emma has cast Harriet in a role of unpolished foundling in her script, she has taken on the role of mentor, once again to flatter herself. Linda Zionkowski discusses the social obligation of older women to advise and mentor younger women so that "Emma's desire to advise and direct is not a fault peculiar to her; rather, her assumption of a mentor's authority signifies her compliance with the duties for women enjoined by her culture" (230). Emma never sees Harriet clearly because she assumes a part and because she lacks the necessary life experience to play the part of mentor adequately.

In a literal sense, Emma's artwork serves as evidence that she struggles with perspective and Right View. The skills for portraiture require a correct reading of body language, facial expressions, and perspective. Emma's art consists of a series of incomplete portraits of only her family members and her governess. Once again, we are reminded that Emma focuses only on her family. As with her refusal to give adequate attention to Mr. Martin, Emma's incomplete pictures show a limited scope and lack of effort, which Austen makes explicit: "steadiness had always been wanting; and in nothing had she approached the degree of excellence which she would have been glad to command, and ought not to have failed of" (39). Put into Buddhist language, Emma lacks Right Diligence, putting forth effort into what is worthy of time and effort.

Rather, Emma chooses ill-conceived matchmaking over developing her talent. She abandons each piece due to lack of perseverance, an unwillingness to find self-reward from effort and instead searching for reward in the praise of others. This she receives amply from Harriet and Mr. Elton when she shares the incomplete portraits, pointing again to the lack of truthful feedback in her education. When Harriet's portrait is finished, it reflects precisely the problem that Emma has when reading her friend and her situation: Emma has improved her rather than capture her likeness accurately because she is using the portrait as an excuse to bring Mr. Elton and Harriet together as part of her matchmaking scheme. Mrs. Weston, rarely one to criticize anything Emma does, after praising the portrait, tells Mr. Elton that "Miss Smith has not those eye-brows and eye-lashes. It is the fault of her face that she has them not," and Mr. Knightley correctly claims that Emma has made Harriet too tall, which "Emma knew she had, but would not own" (41). Emma deliberately creates a false artistic perspective when it comes to Harriet, refusing to see her correctly in order to cast her as the heroine to Mr. Elton's hero in a false script created for her own ego.

When feeling contrition after Mr. Elton declares his "love" for her, Emma recognizes her egocentrism, and readers get a hint of the potential dangers of operating in the world this way. Emma's blindness came from a script of her own making where her friend is more beautiful and better born than reality and where a man of Mr. Elton's status would wish to be with someone of Harriet's dubious background. Emma sees this for herself the day after Mr. Elton's harsh comments where he explains he would never lower himself, realizing "she had taken up the idea, she supposed, and made everything bend to it" (112), in much the same way her father has made the world around him bend to his own needs.

In fact, the scene where Mr. Elton declares himself points to another cost of Mr. Woodhouse's self-centeredness. Everyone is gathered at Randalls, Mr. Weston's estate, when unnecessary alarm is raised about a snowstorm. While great attention is paid to Mr. Woodhouse's worry over a safe return home and Isabella concentrates only on returning to her children, Emma is left unchaperoned and alone with Mr. Elton in the second carriage where "the door was to be lawfully shut on them." The language is typically Austen mild, but the "lawfully shut" screams volumes about the potentially inappropriate nature of this unchaperoned ride, and Austen also lets her readers know that Mr. Elton "had been drinking too much of Mr. Weston's good wine." Nothing, of course, happens beyond Mr. Elton's declarations of love, but the language is subtle and telling with Emma's "hand seized" and Mr. Elton "making violent love to her" (108). In reading Austen, readers don't fear for Emma's safety, but there are hints enough here that there are dangers in this carriage ride that an observant, empathetic father would have prevented.

Though recognizing her egocentrism, Emma lacks compassion, concentrating largely on own her feelings. Emma's primary emotion is offense that Mr. Elton should presume to think himself worthy of her. She notes with disgust his rejection of Harriet due to inferior rank while simultaneously not seeing for herself that Emma's rank puts her far out of his reach. "Perhaps it was not fair to expect him to feel how very much he was her inferior in talent, and all of the elegance of mind. The very want of such equality might prevent his perception of it; but he must know that in fortune and consequence she was greatly his superior" (113). She is capable of entering into Mr. Elton's feelings, correctly surmising that he never loved her but wished to advance in life via marriage. However, her empathy in no way extends to compassion; while she considers how hard it will be for Harriet to be running into him in the future, she gives no thought to Mr. Elton's feelings of humiliation. While Mr. Elton is certainly not set up by Austen for the reader to feel pity, from a Buddhist perspective, Emma and we should feel compassion.

As for Harriet, while Emma goes to great lengths to show kindness through distracting Harriet, she realizes that she cannot enter into Harriet's experience as she is "an indifferent judge of such matters in general" (119). She is not capable of fulfilling the role she set for herself as mentor and fails in genuine empathy, which from a Buddhist perspective requires three parts: "beginning with shared feeling, then feeling combined with understanding, and lastly, feeling combined with both understanding and the sense of a need to act, to become engaged, on behalf of those who are suffering" (Barash 146).

Rather than listening to Harriet, Emma chooses to distract, another marker that she lacks compassion. Mark Epstein explains that "the name of the Chinese representation of compassion, the Buddhist 'goddess' Kuan Yin, literally means 'observer' (kuan) of 'sounds' (yin). We practice meditation when we listen to the feelings of another: to their pain, their distress, and their suffering" (xvi). Here, and on an important later occasion, Emma fails to listen. More importantly, she still congratulates herself on separating Harriet from Robert Martin: "There I was quite right. That was well done of me" (114). This further proves her inability to see what is best for Harriet as she continues failing to see Robert Martin at all. In fact, where Emma seems to feel the most worry is in distressing her father should he find out, once again showing that her empathy and compassion are still limited to family.

This approach will cost Emma later as, following conventions of appropriate mentor behavior, she refuses to let Harriet confide in her fully when Harriet explains she has a new attachment. Emma assumes that Harriet means Frank Churchill and forbids further discussion, saying, "Let no name ever pass our lips" (283). After greatly admiring Harriet's calm response to Frank and Jane's engagement, Emma learns her mistake, discovering that Harriet's love interest is Mr. Knightley, which at last awakens Emma to her own love for Mr. Knightley.

Yet even as she fails in her interactions with Harriet, she does try. We can see a clear contrast in Emma's interactions with Jane Fairfax, a woman her own age who is more socially suited to be Emma's friend than Harriet but with whom Emma fails to connect. Jane's parents died young, leaving her to the remaining family of a grandmother and aunt—Mrs. and Miss Bates—who live in genteel poverty. Jane, though, is rescued at a young age by a friend of her father who raises her with his own daughter, thereby allowing her to move in society, though always with the understanding that her fate is life as a governess given her lack of personal fortune.

Both Harriet and Jane deserve Emma's compassion, not merely in the Buddhist sense for all beings, but because both women suffer from their low positions in an English social hierarchy due to unfortunate circumstances over which they have no control. Because they are women, they cannot make their own fortune in the world. They must marry well. Neither is likely to do so, Harriet because of her unknown patrimony and Jane due to her parents' deaths leaving her in poverty. But Emma only chooses to help Harriet (though unskillfully).

Whereas Harriet feeds Emma's egocentrism, Jane, though of inferior social standing, challenges Emma's sense of herself as the most accomplished young lady in Highbury. She is competition. Her beauty is of a more elegant strain, like Emma's, and she exhibits superior skill in ladylike accomplishments in comparison to Emma. With Jane's arrival in Highbury, Emma now perceives for herself the "danger" of an unsupervised education, for when she fairly compares herself to Jane Fairfax, she comes up short. When asked to play piano and sing at the Coles' party, Emma "knew the limitations of her own powers too well to attempt more than she could perform with credit; she wanted neither taste nor spirit," but like her reading, Emma has not exerted herself through practice. When she finishes, Jane plays, and Emma "never could attempt to conceal from herself" that Jane's performance "was infinitely superior to her own" (188). The next day, "she did unfeignedly and unequivocally regret the inferiority of her own playing and singing. She did most heartily grieve over the idleness of her childhood—and sat down and practised for an hour and a half" (191). Harriet, arriving as Emma plays, praises her thoroughly, including the compliment that Emma performs better than Jane. Harriet, due to reinforcing Emma's desired self-image, wins Emma's favor rather than Jane who, though not perceived as a rival, reminds Emma of her personal failings.

In truth, Emma's real failing is in Right Mindfulness. Mindfulness refers to awareness of a person's body, feelings, mind, and objects of the mind (things she perceives). Emma fails to be aware of her own mind, that is mindfulness of the mind (*chitta samskara*). She lacks an understanding of how she forms her own ideas and thoughts. Sankhāra, or mental formations, refers to Buddhist notions of where thoughts come from. Within each person is store consciousness, not exactly the same as Western ideas of the unconscious, but similar in that we are not aware of it at a conscious level. When a seed in store consciousness is touched, it manifests into mind consciousness as a mental formation.

A formation is anything made up of parts so that, for example as discussed in Chapter Two, a tree is a formation consisting of earth, sun, rain, etc. A mental formation is the coming together of a seed in store consciousness and whatever may touch the seed; that combination then creates an idea or reaction. For example, the seeds of happiness and parental love are present in store consciousness. The act of a mother witnessing her child do something thoughtful and kind will touch those seeds, and she will feel happiness and love about and toward her child at the level of mind consciousness. While these are healthy feelings, all mental formations are impermanent so have the potential to cause suffering if we cling to them rather than recognizing their impermanence. With our mother, she might quickly turn to anxiety or sadness if she starts to wish for this beautiful moment with her child to last forever; if she, rather than embracing the moment, starts grieving over her child growing older and leaving.

Some mental formations, such as the mother's love, are wholesome, but others are unwholesome. Something is wholesome if it brings happiness and enlightenment to all. A wholesome mental formation in some contexts is unwholesome in others. As with the use of the word *Right* for the various parts of the Eightfold Path, it is contextual. To hearken back to Chapter One's discussion of anxiety, anxiety is an evolutionary adaptation that can serve us well, for example helping us to perform better in a piano recital. However, anxiety also can become a debilitating disorder and is, in that context, unwholesome. Unwholesome mental formations are called *kleshas* or sometimes obscurations because they lead us away from enlightenment and happiness. The basic unwholesome mental formations are "greed, hatred, ignorance, pride, doubt, and views" and the secondary *kleshas* arising from them are "anger, malice, hypocrisy, malevolence, jealousy, selfishness, deception, guile, unwholesome excitement," etc. (Thich Nhat Hanh, *Heart* 74).

Mindfulness of the mind means to notice the mental formations, not to judge them or ourselves. If practicing mindfulness of the mind, I can become aware of anger toward a friend who canceled plans again, but I do so without negatively judging myself for feeling that anger. I do not add a sense of guilt for feeling anger on top of the anger. Rather, noticing the mental formation as impermanent and not an inherent part of self means being able to step back and make the decision to nurture it or not. The mother feeling happiness and love for her child can water that seed. When I feel anger toward my friend, I can notice the anger, not let it take over, and allow it to go back into store consciousness. What may complicate the process is what is stored in seed consciousness comes from a collective unconscious—that is, seeds planted by ancestors and culture that may feel so natural that we are not prone to noticing them. Since mental formations color our perceptions, this mindfulness is crucial to individual happiness and to all with whom we come in contact as the mental formations affect how we see the world.

Emma's lack of mindfulness has resulted in nurturing the seeds of egocentrism modeled by her father and the seeds of superiority created by a culture that privileges her as the daughter of a landowner, as compared to the other women in the novel who lack a privileged place in society merely through accident of birth. Through the basic *klesha* of pride and the secondary *klesha* of envy, Emma's obscured perceptions block her empathy, deny compassion to those who deserve it, and create unhappiness for more than just herself.

That brings us back to Jane, for Emma's interactions with her awaken the seed of envy though she is incapable of seeing this. When Jane returns to Highbury, Emma, acknowledging her injustice in not liking Jane, attempts a fresh start only to almost immediately revert back to dislike, finding Jane "disgustingly" and "suspiciously reserved" (140) and deciding that, as Jane appears more and more withholding during conversation, she "could not forgive her" (141). Her lack of empathy leads her to misread Jane throughout the novel, though to Emma's credit this is true of every character in the novel except for the perceptive Mr. Knightley who has vague misgivings.

Those vague misgivings come from the other stranger introduced to Highbury: Frank Churchill, who shares Emma's egocentric approach to life and predilection for script writing but who operates purely from personal gain and lacks any empathy at all. A key difference is that while Emma feels empathy within her small circle, especially for family, Frank makes no effort as a son, at long last visiting his father only as a pretense to see Jane, to whom he is secretly engaged. Having been raised by a controlling and hypochondriac guardian himself, Frank lacks empathy and controls the scene around him to hide his engagement or risk being disinherited. Whereas Emma creates narratives unconsciously, failing at mindfulness of the mind, Frank purposely deceives in order to cover his affection for Jane and to spend more time with her.

For example, Frank, though really a stranger, emphasizes his insider status as Mr. Weston's son to dupe those around him more thoroughly. Upon first arriving and touring Highbury, Frank shows uncommon interest in the Crown and then upon passing Ford's (the local shop) exclaims, "pray let us go in, but that I may prove myself to belong to the place, to be a true citizen of Highbury" (166). Later, when learning of Frank's engagement, the reader can make the connection that the Crown is opposite the Bates' home where Jane is staying and that Frank's sudden interest in Ford's comes just as Emma begins to question him about his previous acquaintanceship with Jane in London when she was still with her guardian, Colonel Campbell.

More heinously, Frank successfully uses his public flirtations with Emma to throw others—including Emma—off the scent, leading Emma into bad behavior in violation of Right Speech. He not only denigrates Jane to Emma but also encourages Emma to ascribe Jane's visit and behavior to love for Mr. Dixon. Because of Emma's own envy and her egocentric belief that she is perceptive, she is quick to catch Frank's hints and engages in gossip with him about Jane.

One source of gossip starts with Frank's gift to Jane of the pianoforte, a gift that shows little thoughtfulness, as it creates a great stir among Highbury with speculation about who could have sent it. Most assume it came from Jane's former guardian, Colonel Campbell, though everyone is curious as to why he did not send warning that the gift was coming or a letter of explanation. Trying to throw others off the scent, Frank encourages Emma's idea that it could come from Colonel Campbell's daughter, Mrs. Dixon, or even her husband, Mr. Dixon. The passage demonstrates how Frank plays Emma in that there is so little attribution. For more than a page, Austen makes no attempt to differentiate Frank's comments from Emma's. One must carefully follow the conversation to see who is speaking, giving the sense that Frank is leading Emma on. In the meantime, Emma, encouraged by Frank, makes false accusations of a potential love interest between Mr. Dixon and Jane that could damage Jane's reputation.

All of this comes to a head at the pleasure outing to Box Hill. The outing results in Frank, feeling slighted by Jane, flirting too outrageously with Emma and offering a veiled insult to Jane. As he had first met Jane in a public, social setting, his comment is personally stinging when he says, "as to any real knowledge of a person's disposition that Bath, or any public place, can give—it is all nothing; there can be no knowledge," implying his own mistaken reading of Jane as a desirable mate. He concludes his jibe with "[h]ow many a man has committed himself on a short acquaintance, and rued it all the rest of his life!" (307). Due to his inability to empathize, Frank is unable to enter into Jane's feelings as she languishes at her grandmother and aunt's, keeps their engagement secret, suffers while watching Frank flirt, and deals with Mrs. Elton's push to get her a governess position. His Theory of Mind is excellent as his manipulation of all those around him demonstrates, but his lack of empathy nearly loses him his fiancé as Jane takes a job as a governess after the Box Hill incident.

However, the breakthrough for Emma's education in empathy comes at Box Hill where even as she appears to enjoy Frank's flirtations, she "laughed because she was disappointed" (304). This is our helpful narrator, not Emma's own insight, yet it shows Emma sensing the tension of the moment, aware that all is not right. With the edginess of the mood created by the always discontented Eltons and by Frank's flirting, Emma herself becomes edgy and, in an attempt at wit, makes a cutting remark to the loquacious but kind Miss Bates. Emma, again, is clueless until Mr. Knightley strongly remonstrates her privately, asking, "How could you be so unfeeling to Miss Bates? How could you be so insolent in your wit to a woman of her character, age, and situation?" (309). Mr. Knightley's reference to feeling is telling, and his reference to situation means not only Miss Bates' genteel poverty but also her status as a single woman or, put crudely, an "old maid." Emma, throughout the novel, affirms strongly that she will never marry due to her loyalty to her father. Harriet, upon hearing this proclamation earlier in the novel, proclaims, "But then, to be an old maid at last, like Miss Bates!" (73) to which Emma responds after several unkind comments about Miss Bates, "between *us,* I am convinced there never can be any likeness, except in being unmarried" (emphasis in original 73). With her egocentrism and lack of empathy, Emma cannot enter into the experience of Miss Bates, a woman with whom she has little in common.

After the incident on Box Hill, however, Emma, still recognizing Miss Bates for the chatterbox that she undeniably is, sees the connection between them, which Austen couches in emotional terms. Emma recognizes the "brutal" and "cruel" nature of her joke and "felt it at her heart." As she rides away from Box Hill, she "felt the tears running down her cheeks almost all the way home, without being at any trouble to check them, extraordinary as they were" (310). Austen hints here at newly-awakened emotion in Emma as well as a new understanding of perspective as Emma contemplates the day later that evening. "How it might be considered by the rest of the party, she could not tell. They, all in their different homes, and their different

ways, might be looking back on it with pleasure" (311). Unlike her
father, Emma appreciates that others have experienced the same day
as she but may have done so quite differently and thereby produce
very different narratives.

In contrition for her rudeness, Emma visits Miss Bates early the
next day only to find that Jane refuses to see her though she catches
a glimpse of Jane "looking extremely ill" (312). Rather than taking
offense, as she likely would have done in the past, Emma again has
an emotional response. The narrator tells us, "Her heart had been
long growing kinder towards Jane; and this picture of her present
sufferings acted as a cure of every former ungenerous suspicion, and
left her nothing but pity" (313). Austen's continued use of emotive
language emphasizes the increase in empathy that Emma feels, and
her kindness persists in spite of Jane rebuffing her attempts to help,
which Austen describes with even more emotive language such as
"sympathy," "consideration," and "regret" (320). Emma, from this
incident, comes to know herself and others better; she has become
more mindful, no longer nurtures the seeds of pride and envy, and
learns compassion. She goes from not seeing Mr. Martin at all to
feeling compassion toward Miss Bates, immediately feeling contrition and repenting through active courtesy (Right Action) the next
day. So while the Box Hill scene's immediate consequence is to create animosity and separation, it ultimately serves as the foundation
of empathy that allows Emma to feel compassion.

We readers can see the parallel between Frank and Emma, and
she does also. Toward the end of the novel, when all secrets are
revealed, Emma tells Frank, "I am sure it was a source of high enter-
tainment to you, to feel that you were taking us all in.—Perhaps I am
readier to suspect, because, to tell you the truth, I think it might have
been some amusement to myself in the same situation. I think there
is a little likeness between us" (391). Emma recognizes here that both
of them have lacked empathy in their dealings with others during
the course of previous events. She acknowledges both the actual
costs—her embarrassment over sly innuendos about Jane and Mr.
Dixon, which Frank encouraged—and the potential costs of this lack
of empathy; she asks Mrs. Weston upon learning of Frank's engagement to Jane, "What right had he to endeavour to please, as he certainly did—to distinguish any one young woman with persevering
attention, as he certainly did—while he really belonged to another?—
how could he tell what mischief he might be doing?" (326). Mr. and

Mrs. Weston clearly feared exactly this in breaking the news—that Emma had become attached to Frank and would be devastated by his engagement—proving Emma correct in her assessment of Frank's actions. Frank's letter confessing his engagement shows his blindness to the potential damage to Emma, saying it never occurred to him that she might become attached.

In Frank's case, Mr. Knightley correctly surmises that he is simply a lucky man, not a deserving one who has learned anything. His aunt dies, and, with that obstacle removed, he now can marry Jane. Fortunately, for him, Emma did not fall in love with him. Jane forgives him. However, he has not learned empathy, as his public teasing of Jane after their engagement demonstrates since it clearly makes her uncomfortable. When Jane quietly upbraids him, he teases her further, once again proving himself lacking empathy. However, "Emma's feelings were chiefly with Jane," demonstrating that Emma has learned empathy (393).

Like Buddhism arguing that compassion for others leads to happiness, Austen links them in her happy ending. When her own engagement to Mr. Knightley removes all egocentric anxiety over competition, Emma's compassion for Harriet solidifies as among her first thoughts are how "to do her best by Harriet," "to spare her from any unnecessary pain," and "how to make her any possible atonement" (357). Emma's only regret now is her "pain of having made Harriet unhappy" (380) with Austen once again using emotive language to describe Emma's response. Having learned her lesson of empathy and compassion, Emma gets her happy ending, with Robert Martin again proposing to Harriet and Harriet accepting. Relieved of pain and guilt, Emma asks, "What had she to wish for? ... Nothing, but that the lessons of her past folly might teach her humility and circumspection in future" (389).

Not everyone shares Emma's growth in empathy and compassion, and Austen alludes to less happiness for those characters. Mr. Woodhouse remains a static character who accepts his daughter's marriage only because someone has been breaking into poultry-houses in the neighborhood, and he is desirous of Mr. Knightley's protection as his son-in-law and new resident at Hartfield. We are to understand a continued life of nervousness for Mr. Woodhouse. Mrs. Elton, a lesser version of Emma in terms of her cluelessness and script writing who never learns, is "very much discomposed indeed" by news of the engagement (384) and ends the novel excluded and complaining. Frank, as noted, continues egocentric, teasing Jane and more interested in congratulating himself on his own engagement than in hearing about Emma's. Our last view of Jane is with her forced smile and lowered self-conscious voice, which subtly does not bode well for her own happiness married to Frank, something Mr. Knightley predicts unless Jane's goodness rubs off on Frank. Frank's lucky circumstances give him a shot at happiness but not a guarantee like Emma's. Austen's narrator closes the novel by promising that "the wishes, the hopes, the confidence, the predictions of the small band of true friends who witnessed the ceremony, were fully answered in the perfect happiness of the union" (396).

It is perhaps easy to be happy when one's every wish comes true, and everything comes tidily together. While we can admire Emma's increase in compassion and follow her lead, Austen's heroines who take on the job of true enlightenment under duress show us how to be happy even in unhappy circumstances.

# Six

# Catherine as Child of Nature in the Consumer Culture of *Northanger Abbey*

"We need to recognize and identify the spiritual and material foods we have ingested that are causing us to suffer."
—Thich Nhat Hanh, *The Heart of the Buddha's Teaching*

"Dress was her passion."
—Jane Austen, *Northanger Abbey*

"Dear Miss Morland, consider the dreadful nature of the suspicions you have entertained. What have you been judging from?"
—Jane Austen, *Northanger Abbey*

The second Noble Truth is that we can understand the source of our suffering. This is the subject of *Northanger Abbey* with its focus on consumption. Austen sets the novel in Bath, a city devoted to the consuming of water for health and of material goods for pleasure. She fills the novel with characters engaged in consuming, whether that be fashion, picturesque landscapes, or novels. Like Buddhist psychology, Austen recognizes that what we consume forms our habits; our habits generally lead to misperceptions and, not surprisingly, to suffering.

As with *Sense and Sensibility*, Austen displaces our main character, sending young Catherine Morland to Bath with her childless neighbors the Allens. There, she discovers the friendship of Isabella Thorpe, a consummate flirt who introduces her to Gothic novels and who later becomes temporarily engaged to Catherine's brother who has formed a friendship with Isabella's brother, John Thorpe. She also meets Henry Tilney, who will become her love interest, and visits the Tilney family at their home, Northanger Abbey. General Tilney, thinking her wealthy, first encourages a match with his son, and, when he learns she is not, dismisses her from the abbey unceremoniously. Catherine interprets the world through a Gothic lens after reading *The Mysteries of Udolpho*, and her reading habits allow our narrator to expound upon the benefits of novel reading even as Catherine misreads thanks to the Gothic. All the while, Austen fills her novel with shopping, discussions of shopping, and less obvious versions of consumption, such as novel reading.

Literary critic Susan Zlotnick notes that the "pleasures and pains of living in a market economy consume the characters" of the novel (277). Mrs. Allen lives for dress, Isabella offers herself on the marriage market, John Thorpe prides himself on his horses and carriage—the price be damned!—and General Tilney clearly lives to (over) consume with Zlotnick labeling him a "shopaholic patriarch" (285). Bath itself had become a tourist trap of sorts, with many smart shops to while away the days when not tending to health or dancing. Mrs. Allen expresses her pleasure over this, telling Henry Tilney, "Bath is a charming place, sir; there are so many good shops here" (51). Though Austen is said to have disliked Bath, she was not anti-shopping and enjoyed a fine piece of muslin herself.[1] In and of itself, consumption is not the problem.

In fact, from a Buddhist perspective, consumption is unavoidable given Buddhism's broad definition of consuming. The Buddha taught that nothing can survive without food. This "food" is referred to as "the Four Kinds of Nutriments" by Thich Nhat Hanh in his secular updating of the Buddha's fifth precept to living an ethical life. The nutriments are the literal foods that we eat, impressions made by the outside world on our senses, "volition, and consciousness" (*Mindfulness Survival Kit* 103).

We consume with all of our senses. This means that we consume food and drink, conversations, social media, articles, books, etc.—and, importantly, all of the emotions contained therein. If a colleague is brimming over with anger and venting, we consume that anger, for example. This means we should try to be in environments that offer wholesome "food" and, if not, must find ways to protect ourselves.

*Volition* refers to our aspiration and deepest desires—the intent behind our actions. For instance, one could donate to a worthy cause because of a genuine desire to help or in a public fashion in order to impress. The money will go to the cause either way, but the intent will feed the person's habit energy of wishing to be generous or of longing for recognition or power; the effect is the same for the charity but not for the donor. We are fed by our volition; desire is not bad, but what we desire makes us healthy or not; desiring worldly power does not make us happy but desiring to be compassionate does. An unwholesome or unexamined volition can drive us blindly toward goals that will lead to suffering for ourselves and others.

And we feed off of our own thoughts and feelings—our consciousness. Western science confirms that much of how we know the world comes from internal processing, not directly from our senses. The majority of input to the part of the brain responsible for processing visual information "comes from internal memory stores and perceptual-processing modules (Raichle 2006). Your brain simulates the world—each of us lives in a virtual reality that's close enough to the real thing that we don't bump into the furniture" (Hanson 43). In addition, we are all filled with anger, desire, love, compassion, kindness, etc. We consume whichever of these emotions we nurture with our attention. If we are often nurturing anger, we become angry people, putting ourselves at risk and even harming others in our company who will be subject to that energy of anger. We feed off of our emotions, memories, and ideas, so we must consume mindfully. Doing so is an example of Right Action in the Eightfold Path that leads us away from suffering.

When we use the word *psychology* in the West, we can mean many approaches from Freudian to evolution to cognitive-behavioral. Similarly, Buddhism, with its differing schools of thought, varies somewhat in its understanding of the mind. However, there is a shared foundation with an emphasis on consumption, perception, and suffering. The model used here is from Thich Nhat Hanh's "Fifty Verses on the Nature of Consciousness." Thich Nhat Hanh composed the "Fifty Verses" based upon central teachings of the Buddha that were finally put into writing 500 years after his death and upon texts from the Mahayana tradition with the aim of capturing "in a nutshell" the central tenets of Buddhist psychology.

While Buddhists argue against relying upon concepts, they simultaneously recognize that we need concepts in order to understand anything, particularly anything as complex as the human mind.

Therefore, Buddhist psychology explains the workings of our mind as divided into different consciousnesses, in the case of "The Fifty Verses," eight of them.

Before discussing the different consciousnesses, however, we need to understand the five aggregates. Throughout, keep at the forefront the essential notion of what Thich Nhat Hanh calls *interbeing*. Even as there are categories and classifications and seemingly different steps to perceiving and understanding the world, none of this is linear; all are co-dependent. The four nutriments, five aggregates, and eight consciousnesses flow together like a body of water.

The five aggregates are an excellent example of this. Aggregate means parts making up a whole, so the five aggregates make up each human being, once again emphasizing that there is no central inherent self that we can point to and say that is me. They consist of form (body), feelings, perceptions, formations, and consciousness. The first two are self-explanatory, and perceptions will become clear during the discussion of consciousness. The word formation is similar to aggregate: parts making up a whole. A tree is roots, trunk, branches, bark, leaves, soil, water, etc.; all of these elements must come together to form what we call a tree. In the same way, there are mental formations; ideas, feelings, and thoughts arise due to a combination of factors, connected to consciousness.

The first five consciousnesses are the obvious ones: our senses. We take in the world via our eye, nose, tongue, ear, and body consciousnesses. In other words, we see, smell, taste, hear, and feel. Yet very rarely do we do this straightforwardly thanks to the other three consciousnesses: mind, manas, and store.

*Store consciousness* is at the base of all, as its name implies, so is the best place to start explaining how thoughts, emotions, and actions are produced by the mind. Within store consciousness rest the seeds that form the 51 mental formations, such as pride, sloth, craving, wrath, guile, and greed as well as joy, compassion, humility, kindness, and love. The seeds come from our ancestors, our culture, and our personal experience.

Seeds are planted in the consciousness even before birth passed down from ancestors in ways similar to DNA. We inherit mannerisms, talents, physical traits and even values from generations of ancestors, and the experiences of parents transmit to the baby in the womb. Seeds can be like DNA where there may be a history of mental illness or alcoholism in a family, but the switch, so to speak, may not be triggered so that the gene does not get expressed. The child of an alcoholic is not inevitably fated to be one also. In the same way, a seed may be present from an ancestor in store consciousness, but the conditions necessary for its manifestation do not occur. Another example might be the colloquialism that talent skips generations. The seed was always there, but the conditions were not ripe until a subsequent generation. The study of epigenetics is a good example. Science has demonstrated that trauma can be passed from one generation to the next. DNA expression changes thanks to traumatic experiences such as being held a prisoner of war or in rats via shock therapy that then are transmitted to the next generation though that generation did not experience the trauma personally.

Seeds are present from our culture—collective consciousness— as well. Our notions of beauty and taste are a product of our culture, something that the disciplines of advertising and marketing understand. For example, in marketing, there is a term called top of mind awareness, referring to a brand being the first to come to mind within its particular category or industry. In the South, people will say Coke when what they mean are sodas. Culturally, Coke has top of mind awareness for Southerners; it's the first thought Southerners have when they think of sodas or soft drinks (or maybe pop for someone who lives outside the South). The stock market is another example where daily decisions are made about what companies are valuable. Money itself and how we value it is a fiction given that money now translates into numbers that appear on bills or in bank accounts. In this way, though we believe we are making choices based on individual preferences, we are operating from ideas—seeds—planted by the culture in which we live. Such mindless living can create much suffering. The collective consciousness holds great power in a consumer culture like most of us live in today.

Along with seeds from ancestors and culture, our personal experience adds to our store consciousness with everything we encounter leaving some sort of trace even if we are not aware. A man may have had a bad experience with a dog when a young boy on a walk in his neighborhood. He was so young that he has no memory of the event, but as a man he dislikes dogs due to that experience.

These seeds of which we are unaware become habit energies that determine our thoughts, feelings, and actions if we do not use mindfulness. When we react habitually, we create and strengthen neural pathways so that rather than reacting to the moment we are in, the well-used neural pathway determines our response. A comparable image is a green space at a park where people have walked the same path over and over creating what we call in the South a cow path. We habitually step along that same path from habit energy.

In this way, store consciousness serves as a kind of garden with seeds sprouting depending on the attention we give them. If we nurture compassion, then compassion grows. If we nurture anger, then anger grows and affects our body accordingly perhaps with increased blood pressure, a scowl, and reddened complexion. As Rick Hanson explains, "What flows through your attention sculpts your brain" (189).

In some ways, store consciousness is comparable to Freudian ideas of the unconscious in that we are not cognitively aware of it. It differs from the Freudian unconscious that holds repressed ideas too uncomfortable for us to process. Instead, store consciousness is "indeterminate," because the seeds are both wholesome and unwholesome. *Wholesome* means of benefit to all as opposed to unwholesome, which is harmful to ourselves and others. Store consciousness never rests and is always working, even during sleep, and always changing. This mutability allows store consciousness to be "unobstructed" so that there is the possibility of clarity and transformation that reduces suffering. We cannot transcend human nature and remove the seed of anxiety, for example, but while anxiety will always be present, mindfulness can return anxiety to its seed state rather than a fully grown plant that harms ourselves and others.

Visualize manas consciousness as resting on store consciousness. It is the source of delusion because it is here that we find clinging to the idea of a solid, inherent, and stable self. Thich Nhat Hanh labels manas consciousness as "the lover" in that manas looks for those aspects of store consciousness that define an acceptable self and pursues and clings to them. The concept of manas consciousness shares aspects of evolutionary psychology in that manas consciousness's function is self-preservation. It operates blindly and instinctively. In this way, manas consciousness is always false and delusional because it rests on ignorance: the idea of a stable self. Manas craves the stable self that does not exist, a craving that never, thus, can be filled. Like store consciousness, manas never stops operating; it is always thinking, discriminating, reasoning, and grasping. Manas is indeterminate—neither inherently wholesome nor unwholesome—like store consciousness but obscured by ignorance;

because it's indeterminate, though, it can change and stop clinging and discriminating.

The next layer, so to speak, is mind consciousness. While store consciousness is a kind of basement, according to Thich Nhat Hanh, mind consciousness serves as a living room. This is the consciousness of which we are aware and is responsible for all action of body, speech, and mind. Like manas, mind consciousness is responsible for naming, evaluating, judging, thinking, discriminating, etc. It can perceive directly (either correctly or not) and infer (either correctly or not). Mind consciousness has the potential to perceive clearly in interacting with the sense consciousnesses. However, mind consciousness often gets things wrong thanks to the operation of manas with which it interacts.

For instance, a woman's mind consciousness could encounter a yellow rose via eye consciousness and label it correctly as a yellow rose. However, manas may interact with mind consciousness to create a sense of anger or sadness as she remembers back to prom when she wanted a corsage that matched a pink dress and ended up with clashing yellow roses. Suddenly, the yellow rose means feeling disappointed, slighted by a thoughtless date, and, perhaps, even unloved by the boyfriend who did not care enough to pay attention. In this example, we can see how the different levels of consciousness interact with the sense consciousness bringing attention to the flower, mind consciousness labeling the flower as a yellow rose, and manas touching the seeds of disappointment, sadness, or anger in store consciousness because of a memory that made the woman feel threatened. That is suffering, and it is not caused by the rose but by a narrative created by mind consciousness thanks to manas clinging to a wronged sense of self and reliving a painful memory unnecessarily. Here, we see the levels of nutriment with a sense impression as well as the mind feeding off of consciousness, reliving a negative experience.

At the level of sense consciousness, we can find "suchness," experiencing things purely in and of themselves. I see a cat through eye consciousness. I hear a meow through ear consciousness. I feel the cat rub against my leg with body consciousness. Once mind consciousness gets involved, we can stay at that level and directly perceive, or our preferences start to kick in with the potential for suffering. If one likes cats, then pleasure follows, which is not a problem at all as long as one does not cling to that pleasure so that pleasure turns to regret when we must move away from the cat. If one does not like cats, then aversion may rise up so that uncomfortable feelings in the body may arise in response. Therefore, it matters what we consume and how we consume it.

That is where mindfulness enters. Merely being aware of how the mind works allows us to see the source of suffering. We can drop the story about the yellow roses because we recognize it is a story. We can let go of strong preferences that make a quick encounter with a cat either pleasurable or painful. Right Action allows us to consume what is wholesome, Right View recognizes the role of mind consciousness in tending to the garden of store consciousness, and Right Mindfulness puts our attention on wholesome seeds, encouraging their growth.

But, often, we consume the wrong things and without awareness—just like the characters in *Northanger Abbey*.

Austen opens her novel by warning us that "[n]o one who had ever seen Catherine Morland in her infancy, would have supposed her born to be an heroine" (37), but, of course, she is the heroine of *Northanger Abbey* just as each of us is the protagonist of our own stories. Catherine's story is as much her story as a story about stories and a demonstration of how we humans write our own daily narratives that have the power to make us and others suffer—or not. What we consume and how we consume it determines the nature of those stories.

Consumption, in its broadest sense, is emphasized from the start. Readers get more background on Catherine's childhood than on any other Austen heroine. From the beginning, we learn that she "was fond of all boy's plays" (37), that "she had no taste for a garden; and if she gathered flowers at all, it was chiefly for the pleasure of mischief" (38), and that she "loved nothing so well in the world as rolling down the green slope at the back of the house" (39). She is a child of nature who also loves to draw though she does so without instruction picking up any scrap of paper available for the fun of it.

Austen gives specifics on her more formal education (such as it is) as well. Her mother taught her the "Beggar's Petition," often used for elocution lessons and which she fails to memorize; "The Hare and the Friends," a contemporary and cautionary fable; and French. Like most girls, she receives music lessons, which she dislikes, and "Mrs. Morland, who did not insist on her daughters being accomplished in spite of incapacity or distaste, allowed her to leave off." Her father teaches her "writing and accounts" (38), and Catherine "shirked her lessons" whenever possible. The narrator expresses her surprise that "with all these symptoms of profligacy at ten years old, she had neither a bad heart nor a bad temper." Catherine has benefited from lacking the conventional education of a proper young lady, instead enjoying robust physical health and showing herself "very kind to the little ones" (39).

Continuing that theme, Catherine prefers "cricket, baseball, riding on horseback, and running about the country at the age of fourteen, to books—or at least books of information—for provided that nothing like useful knowledge could be gained from them, provided they were all story and no reflection, she had never any objection to books at all" (39–40). What follows are a series of quotes from eighteenth-century writers Alexander Pope, Thomas Gray, and James Thomson, and from Shakespeare as memorized passages heroines would find "serviceable" and "soothing in the vicissitudes of their eventful lives" (40). The implication, of course, is that Catherine has no deep knowledge here and is regurgitating information without investment.

Read with the necessary dose of irony, this is no criticism as the lack of a lady's education is no real loss. Critics have long debated whether Austen is a conservative or feminist. Conservatives argue that her plots all contain conventional marriages at the end whereas others say the feminism, like much about Austen is subtle, comparing her to the much more vocal feminist Mary Wollstonecraft. Wollstonecraft, who died shortly after giving birth to the famous author of *Frankenstein*, Mary Shelley, wrote *A Vindication of the Rights of Woman* where she famously argued that women were not naturally inferior to men but educated to be so. Thanks to the biography written by her husband after her death that chronicled her less than ladylike personal life, Wollstonecraft was widely castigated, so it would make sense that Austen might choose a more subtle approach in her critique of girls' and women's educations. While clearly not arguing that Catherine's education is ideal, Austen appears to be endorsing Wollstonecraft's argument that girls should be allowed to run and play. And while Catherine's education certainly does make her naive, it also teaches her wholesome volition; she is kind, openhearted and honest.

Austen uses setting and plot to further emphasize the theme of consumption, sending Catherine to Bath with her neighbors the Allens. The city of Bath sits upon hot springs used since the Roman empire for health. By the time Austen is writing, Bath was a resort town that commercialized health. Mr. Allen, the chief property owner around Fullerton and suffering from the rich man's disease of gout, visits Bath to drink and bathe in the sulfur water. Recognizing the money to be made, Bath appealed to more than patients and was a hot spot, not merely a hot springs.

By the time of the Allens' visit (and Austen's residency there), Bath, during the proper season, was the sight of fireworks, balls, circulating libraries, bookshops, theaters, and masquerades. The spas themselves appealed to the taste of those who could afford more luxurious care. Private baths opened a little after the mid-eighteenth century, relegating the public baths to "hospital invalids" and "persons of the lower class of life" by the beginning of the nineteenth (Cottom 161). In keeping with the emphasis on consumerism rather than wholesome consumption for medical purposes, Mr. Allen's health is little discussed, and primarily readers hear about his card playing. There is only a quick comment from Mrs. Allen "that it is much better to be here than at home at this dull time of the year. I tell him he is quite in luck to be sent here for his health" (76).

It is Mrs. Allen who is in luck given her "passion" is dress. The narrator's contempt for Mrs. Allen begins from her first introduction, describing her as "one of that numerous class of females, whose society can raise no other emotion than surprise at there being any men in the world who could like them well enough to marry them." Mrs. Allen lacks "beauty, genius, [and] accomplishment" (44). Austen's "numerous" points to Mrs. Allen as being a representative of a common vacuousness among women, one that clearly derives from a collective consciousness that emphasizes teaching women to consume material goods rather than enlarging their minds.

Though Austen describes Mrs. Allen as having "a most harmless delight in being fine," the results of this exclusive focus on appearance are not entirely harmless. Her superficiality prevents any real connection or empathy with others. We see this when she reunites with an old acquaintance after lamenting once again that she did not know anyone in Bath (and we see it later upon Catherine's return home from the abbey).[2] When she and Mrs. Thorpe catch up on the previous 15 years, certainly neither engages in Right Speech but talk "both together, far more ready to give than to receive information, and each hearing very little of what the other said" (54). Mrs. Allen's delight rests in part on having "found these friends by no means as expensively dressed as herself" (58). While this might, indeed, seem harmless, from a Buddhist perspective, it demonstrates ignorance— seeing the self as separate and superior, which can only create suffering. This is manas at work.

At a practical level, there is also harm, for the Thorpe family becomes the primary companions of Mrs. Allen and Catherine; as Catherine's guardian in Bath, Mrs. Allen owes her due diligence to assure her new friendship is with someone who will not mar her character or lead her into harm. She repeats exactly this same mistake when learning about the Tilney family. The only real intelligence she offers Catherine after a long conversation about the Tilney family is that "Miss Tilney was in a very pretty spotted muslin, and I fancy, by what I can learn, that she always dresses very handsomely." Though being told "a great deal about the family," she remembers little other than learning of Miss Tilney's mother that she spent £500 on wedding clothes (88).

With a light touch, Austen also allows us to see how Mrs. Allen's poor guardianship holds the possibility of imperilment for Catherine. When arriving in Bath, Mrs. Allen refuses to enter society until days of shopping have caught her up in fashion. When she and Catherine finally attend an assembly, they arrive late due to Mrs. Allen's fussing over her appearance and, therefore, into a crowd through which Mrs. Allen moves with "more care for the safety of her new gown than for the comfort of her protege" leaving Catherine to cling to her arm in order to stay by her side (45). Later, when Catherine appeals to Mrs. Allen during her frantic apology to Henry Tilney at the theater, Mrs. Allen's only response is, "My dear, you tumble my gown" (109) rather than offering Catherine support or advice. Because Henry is an honorable gentleman who finds Catherine charming, there is no harm. However, the reputation of a young woman was paramount; Catherine should be comporting herself with more dignity, something a proper guardian would ensure.

The danger to reputation surfaces more clearly with John Thorpe. Knowing Austen's subtlety, we want to note that upon meeting Catherine, Thorpe brags of his horse, telling her to "look at his loins" (68), implying Thorpe could be a potential sexual threat. In keeping with the horse motif, Thorpe convinces Catherine to go via an open carriage ride on an adventure. Catherine, having made other plans, shares her reservations about going, but Mrs. Allen tells her to do as she pleases. When Thorpe, Isabella, and James urge her,

Mrs. Allen tells Catherine to go. Catherine is committing multiple faux pas in accepting, both in breaking an engagement (though Thorpe lied to her saying the Tilneys were not coming for a prearranged walk) and in riding off with Thorpe though her brother and Isabella were in the carriage behind them. Doing so signals a potentially romantic relationship. As a parody of Gothic tropes pointing to Thorpe as not a gentleman, he refuses to stop and allow Catherine to leave the carriage though she implores him. "Mr. Thorpe only laughed, smacked his whip, encouraged his horse, made odd noises, and drove on" (104).

While we don't really fear for Catherine's safety, the hints are there, and they all point to the poor guardianship of Mrs. Allen. When Catherine turns down the invitation for a second carriage ride, Mr. Allen congratulates her on her good sense, saying "going to inns and public places together! It is not right," and asks Mrs. Allen if she agrees. She replies, "Yes, very much indeed. Open carriages are nasty things. A clean gown is not five minutes wear in them. You are splashed getting in and getting out; and the wind takes your hair and your bonnet in every direction" (118). Catherine is aghast that Mrs. Allen advised her to go on the first ride and tells her, "I had always hoped you would tell me if you thought I was doing wrong," but once again, Mrs. Allen can only view life through the seed of vanity and appearance and defends herself saying, "You know I wanted you, when we first came, not to buy that sprigged muslin, but you would. Young people do not like to be always thwarted" (119). Mrs. Allen's emphasis on material consumption makes her oblivious to all else and opens the possibility of great suffering, though thanks to the comic nature of the novel, this is only hinted at.

When explaining the idea of collective consciousness, Thich Nhat Hanh uses fashion as an example. He writes that while we may feel we are expressing our individuality in choosing a certain style of clothing, really it is an expression of the collective consciousness. After all, we cannot buy what is not produced, so fashion is determined by designers, stylists, advertisers, consumers, etc. Mrs. Allen attempts to express individuality via her fashion choices but, in doing so, she demonstrates her vacuity and lack of mindfulness. Austen offers commentary here on a society that pushes women to consume material goods. Doing so undercuts human connection both to others and to the self.

While fashion may be a form of art, with Isabella Thorpe, we get artifice, for she is a consumer who offers herself as an object to purchase on the marriage market. Mrs. Allen is clueless, but Isabella purposely operates from a mercenary volition without caring how she harms others.

Catherine, in contrast, operates consistently from a place of honesty with the narrator telling us she "could not tell a falsehood even to please Isabella" (87), so she fails to recognize her friend's lack of authenticity. We readers, however, see it immediately thanks to our narrator. Early in their friendship, the two meet in the Pump Room with the narrator telling us that Isabella arrived five minutes earlier than Catherine. Isabella scolds Catherine, complaining she has been waiting "at least this age!" and telling Catherine she has been there at least half an hour, which we readers know to be untrue. During the same visit, Isabella explains she is determined to show men that women are capable of deep and true friendship, citing her defense to a man of a Miss Andrews as proof. She then proceeds to criticize Miss Andrews as "amazingly insipid" (63). These less harmful instances hint at much worse examples of artifice to come.

Isabella flirts and calls attention to herself from the start given that her volition—one she gained from the collective consciousness—is to find a husband who can support her in style. When Catherine's brother arrives, though, she concentrates her powers upon him, believing James to have much better financial prospects than he does. Whereas Mrs. Allen parrots Mr. Allen because she is genuinely vacuous, Isabella purposefully echoes all that James says out of manipulation, telling Catherine, "There was not a single point in which we differed" (90).

Her valuation of James as suitor changes dramatically upon learning about his real financial value. She then turns her flirtatious attention to Captain Frederick Tilney, including in front of James after their engagement. Ironically, she suffers the same fate as James, for Captain Tilney never would consider marriage with a woman without fortune so that, ultimately, Isabella is left friendless and single.

Experience teaches kindhearted Catherine not to trust her. Upon receiving the letter from Isabella where she glosses over her treatment of Catherine's brother, Catherine sees its "shallow artifice … inconsistencies, contradictions, and falsehood" and feels "ashamed of having ever loved her" (212). Suffering is the inevitable result given that Isabella has ingested messages from her culture that her worth is only as a commodity to be sold to the highest bidder.

Isabella is also a consumer of novels with Zlotnick describing her as using the language of sentimental heroines in popular novels of the time. She also introduces Catherine to the Gothic novel, starting with the popular *The Mysteries of Udolpho* by Anne Radcliffe. Thanks to Miss Andrews, Isabella has a long reading list of more Gothic novels to consume. The Gothic characteristically includes a Gothic tyrant—a powerful male—who pursues a female victim who generally becomes a prisoner within a Gothic enclosure, such as a dungeon, or even is killed all with elements of the supernatural and a knight in shining armor (sometimes literally) who attempts to rescue the damsel. While Isabella no more believes in the sentimental rhetoric she uses than she does in the reality of the Gothic, her attraction to it points to elements of victimization and powerlessness that are part of her life as a commodity no one wishes to purchase. There is no way for Isabella to win in this game; she needs to nurture herself with a different volition.

On the other end of the spectrum from Isabella stands General Tilney who has abundant purchasing power. Yet, as a good market economy consumer should, he wants to "sell" his children on the marriage market to increase his own wealth and status. Though a fictional character from centuries earlier, General Tilney fits the Dalai Lama's observation of materialism producing anxiety, lack of contentment, vexation, and depression thanks to the constant desire for more.

Certainly, unhappiness fills the atmosphere of the Tilney home thanks to General Tilney. The General treats his children like, well, a General sending his soldiers out to conquer in order to expand his wealth. We learn at the end of the novel that he had refused Eleanor's love interest thanks to his lack of status but readily and cheerfully agrees to the marriage upon the suitor inheriting a title and fortune "and never had the General loved his daughter so well in all her hours of companionship, utility, and patient endurance, as when he first hailed her, 'Your Ladyship!'" (239). General Tilney sees Eleanor as a commodity in the same way that Isabella sees herself, only valuing her monetarily.

Austen uses the pineapple to prove that the General is watering the seed of greed and is in no need of more wealth. General Tilney wastes no time in flaunting his riches to Catherine, taking her on a tour of the abbey on her first full day and starting with his grounds, calling attention to his gardens. He assures Catherine "without any ambition of that sort himself—without any solicitude about it—, he did believe them to be unrivaled in the kingdom" (178). To emphasize the idea of kingdom and over consumption, Austen gives the General a pinery, a hothouse dedicated to growing pineapples so that, like the water in Bath, a simple form of nutriment becomes unwholesome, not as a food, but as a symbol of wealth created by the collective consciousness.

Pineapples, obviously, are not indigenous to England, requiring a more tropical climate, and were introduced to Europe by Christopher Columbus. They became particularly popular in Britain, which is apt given that Britain was on the cusp of becoming a great empire. Because they were difficult to transport across the ocean and expensive to cultivate, they were a symbol of hospitality and served by those who could afford them to guests to demonstrate not only a welcome but social status.

In the case of the General, they also symbolize a grotesque use of funds. Pineapples are slow growing, taking two to three years to mature, and required hiring attendants specifically to tend only the pineapples. The pinery was a hothouse specifically fitted up for pineapple growing and represented a huge monetary output for initial construction as well as upkeep. Christopher J. Natali estimates that a single pineapple would have cost £80 to grow, translating into modern dollars as $12,535.09. The General laments that "the utmost care" still "yielded only one hundred" pineapples in the last year.

Beyond this specific example of gross use of funds, the setting of the abbey itself teaches us about the moral implications of the General's spending. The abbey of old would have served as a place of charity, altruism, and contemplation, but all of that is wiped out by the General's conspicuous consumption. Before the Reformation under Henry VIII, monasteries served central and supportive roles in the lives of the average English citizen. Roger Moore, in an article tracing Austen's view of the Reformation, explains that, before the Reformation, a person of the General's social status and wealth likely would have offered charitable gifts to the abbey as "an institution devoted to the well-being of the entire parish in perpetuity. Now, however, Tilney's money only serves his own appetite: the great kitchen, which formerly fed not only the monks or nuns but their many guests, feeds only the Tilney family and an occasional visitor"

(68). Judging by Catherine's experience, the General bullies those guests via mealtime as he drinks cocoa—with chocolate also being expensive.[3]

The estate being a former abbey underscores the lack of mindful consumption occurring and the General's greedy volition, but the setting also plays with the Gothic because most Gothic literature was set in an earlier era in Catholic countries. Like the General, the Gothic genre is noted for its excess, which perhaps excuses Catherine for reading the General as a Gothic tyrant rather than a run-of-the-mill bully.[4] Henry fuels her imagination, teasing her about her Gothic expectations of visiting an abbey and priming her to misread. Between Henry and her too literal reading of *The Mysteries of Udolpho*, Catherine concludes that the General must be guilty of nefarious actions toward his late wife thanks in part to the General hiding away her portrait in her room rather than displaying it in the public rooms. Henry discovers her suspicions upon finding Catherine in his late mother's room searching for clues.

Upon realizing that due to her immersion in the Gothic Catherine fears that his mother has been murdered or imprisoned by his father, he asks her, "What have you been judging from?" (195). The answer, as already noted, is the Gothic. Because of her consumption of Gothic tales, she has created her own Gothic story about his parents, which Henry corrects with a rational argument embedded in history and fact, a correction that awakens her to her foolishness.

Yet we know from a previous conversation that history is a discipline that Catherine finds vexing and wearying where "the men are all so good for nothing, and hardly any women at all" (122). What Catherine recognizes and Austen played with in her *Juvenilia* are all of the voices that are unceremoniously silenced when telling the story of a country. For this reason, as many critics have noted, Henry's correction of Catherine in Mrs. Tilney's bedroom falls flat for the reader. Henry admonishes Catherine, "Remember that we are English, that we are Christians" (195).[5] A true history of England and Christianity only condemns the General and his consumption all the more as the General has wiped out the history of a holy site for his own vanity and wiped out the remembrance of his wife for his own comfort. And all of that is only possible thanks to Henry VIII wiping out the Catholic church for his own vanity, power, and comfort. History is filled with unwholesome volition and erased stories.

Henry Tilney does not see this. He is sincere in arguing that reason, education, and laws prohibit the narrative Catherine has created. This is because Henry and Eleanor escape their father's greedy volition but nonetheless inhabit a perspective without mindfulness also. More introspective than Mrs. Allen and with pure volition, they prove better friends, but Austen uses the Tilney siblings to demonstrate less obvious consumption.

We can see this on the long-awaited country walk when Henry and Eleanor expound upon the picturesque, looking at the landscape around them "with the eyes of persons accustomed to drawing" rather than taking in the view as the view, that is mindfully. Catherine laments her ignorance after listening to them and learns that "a good view were no longer to be taken from the top of an high hill, and that a clear blue sky was no longer a proof of a fine day" (124). As Waldo Glock argues, "the picturesque ... distorts reality, preventing a direct and pure appreciation of Nature" in the same way that the Gothic distorts reality, so that the Tilneys' chosen aesthetic creates its own story in the same way that Catherine's does. Many critics argue, in fact, that Catherine's immersion into the Gothic allows her to be mistaken yet more clear sighted than Henry about his father, for the General, indeed, is a tyrant, if not fully a Gothic version.[6]

Unlike Henry, Austen realizes that everyone is creating narratives based on what they have consumed. She marks the danger of that not so much with Catherine and the Gothic but with John Thorpe. Thorpe's narrative of malignant gossip drives much of the plot and creates most of the ill will within the novel. Clearly, given that he is James's school friend, it is he who misreads and misreports James's financial prospects, leading to Isabella's promise to marry and later to James's broken heart. He lies to Catherine about seeing the Tilneys walking in the opposite direction when he wants her to go on the first carriage ride, which risks her reputation and possible romance with Henry. And, in order to promote his own self-importance because he thinks of himself as Catherine's suitor and wishes to appear important to an important man, he exaggerates her wealth to the General. After creating a story that made Catherine rich far beyond expectations, when he later meets the General and knows his family will no longer be joined to hers, he equally exaggerates her poverty. He warns the General that Catherine's is a "necessitous family, numerous too almost beyond example, by no means respected in their own neighbourhood ... a forward, bragging, scheming race" (236). The last description ironically applies truly to himself and his sister.

As with Mrs. Allen's poor guardianship, Austen rescues Henry and Catherine from heartbreaking consequences with the two getting married and Catherine suffering no harm from being evicted from the abbey so unceremoniously after Thorpe's second lie about her economic status. As noted, there is no change of heart—or watering of wholesome seeds. The General is appeased by Eleanor's advantageous marriage and upon learning that Catherine will have £3,000. More importantly, after carefully looking into the matter, he discovers that the disposal of Mr. Allen's estate could be settled anywhere—including on Catherine—making it "open to every greedy speculation" (240), the same kind of speculating that a Gothic tyrant might engage in.

So, again, Catherine is not wrong in distrusting him. However, Catherine's suspicions that there is something off about the General form before she suspects him of imprisoning or murdering his wife; the roots of her discomfort are not from the Gothic but from her own observations and intuition. When the family is preparing to set off from Bath to the abbey, his overly solicitous behavior "made it impossible for her to forget for a moment that she was a visitor" (158). She witnesses the General's impatience and fussing at being late and finds her "spirits revived as they drove from the door; for with Miss Tilney she felt no restraint" (159); she feels better as soon as she is away from the General. Her instincts are good here as they are with John Thorpe, whom she dislikes upon their first meeting though she ignores her intuition as he is a friend of her brother and brother to her friend. Yes, Catherine is naive, but thanks to her volition—her consistent desire to be honest and kind—she is from a Buddhist perspective more enlightened than those around her.

From a Buddhist perspective, there is no perspective that will lead Catherine or any of us right. Buddhism is a practice, not a doctrine. Catherine is able to escape the Thorpes' clutches and see most clearly because of her lack of an education that has grown unwholesome seeds of materialism, coquettishness, greed, and pride. As a child of nature when the novel opens, she learned to live fully in the moment—mindfully.

Yet Austen also uses her novel to make the argument for novels, showing, again, that Austen is not arguing against consumption but for the right kind. *Northanger Abbey* is not anti–Gothic. It is an argument for the right practice of reading—of consuming. The novels that Austen notes in her panegyric to the genre were written by women for women. The narrator describes them as "work in which the greatest powers of the mind are displayed, in which the most thorough knowledge of human nature, the happiest delineation of its varieties, the liveliest effusions of wit and humour, are conveyed to the world in the best chosen language" (60). In this same passage, she excoriates the eighteenth-century periodical *The Spectator*. *The Spectator* and the essay from *The Mirror* that Mrs. Morland wishes Catherine to read to cure her sulking upon her return home were reputable publications containing moral lessons. Austen rejects these conduct manuals teaching rigid doctrine. Instead, she promotes *Camilla*, *Cecilia*, and *Belinda* as books capable of awakening the imagination and creating empathy in the reader.

Buddhism recommends the use of imagination in meditation. Matthieu Ricard describes the use of imagination—we might say narrative—to generate lovingkindness by thinking about a dearly loved one suffering in some way in order to produce emotion and experience compassion (qtd. in Goleman 282). Compassion is the end goal of the five precepts for ethical behavior. Of course, this is what literature does. Narrative has the power to awaken imagination, produce empathy, and generate compassion. That is why we should read novels. Austen knew this before science proved it.

For all her silliness and mistakes, Catherine, therefore, truly is a heroine, as she is at least capable of mindfulness, able to use her imagination, operates from good volition, risks embarrassment to do what is right, and is unfailingly kind and compassionate. With such a heroine, *Northanger Abbey* is indeed worth consuming.

# SEVEN

# Powerful, Not Poor
## *Fanny Price as* Bodhisattva[1]

"...through hatred, lust, and ignorance,
I've been the cause of many evils."
—Shantideva, *The Way of the* Bodhisattva

"Fanny looked on and listened, not unamused to
observe the selfishness which, more or less disguised,
seemed to govern them all, and wondering how it
would end."
—Jane Austen, *Mansfield Park*

*Mansfield Park* is a novel about selfishness. With the exception
of Fanny Price, the characters care more about the comfort of their
own worldview than about anyone else.[2] Caught by self-centered
perspectives, everyone but Fanny lacks the freedom to live a happy
life. Instead of pursuing genuine happiness, they work to fend off
personal suffering, bringing about more suffering to themselves and
others. Only Fanny, who suffers materially from the start and out-
wardly lacks freedom compared to the rest, lives mindfully and uses
her powers to alleviate the suffering of others.

In typical Austen fashion, *Mansfield Park* introduces readers to
a central family, the Bertrams, and to interlopers who best demonstrate the problems of that family. Sir Thomas Bertram and Lady
Bertram of Mansfield Park appear to possess everything necessary
for happiness through status, property, and four children. Thanks
to their good fortune, they are able to extend charity to Lady Bertram's sister, who has married unwisely and struggles financially with
too many children to raise properly. Hence, Fanny comes to live with
the Bertrams when she is 10 years old. Years pass with the Bertram

children growing older, if not wiser, and with Fanny purposely thrust into the background by most of the family to indicate her lower social position. Chaos ensues upon the removal of the patriarch, Sir Thomas; the introduction of the Crawford siblings; and Fanny's banishment from Mansfield.

No wonder Fanny Price is often referred to by Austen readers as "poor Fanny." In fact, her reputation has suffered greatly among scholars who have called her variously "poor Fanny," "prig," "monster," and more.[3] While the name-calling may differ in criticisms of Fanny, complaints against her character generally refer to her dullness and her passivity. Literary critic Lionel Trilling attributes to all detractors of Austen "the fear of imposed constraint," that is fearing the possibility that society can or even should place limits upon the individual. *Mansfield Park*, according to Trilling, is the novel most guilty in Austen's canon of creating a sense of constraint and dullness, offending our Western "modern pieties" that value action and individualism (127). Perhaps this explains why *Mansfield Park* has not been adapted as often as other Austen novels and why Fanny, as its heroine, is the least beloved.

Seeing Fanny from a different perspective than one fearing constraint, specifically an Eastern one, readers can appreciate Fanny better. Viewing Fanny from a Buddhist perspective, we can see that she has the traits of a *bodhisattva*, a figure devoted to enlightenment for the purpose of helping others.[4] A *bodhisattva* is someone who consciously aspires to awaken *bodhicitta*, the "mind of love," defined by Buddhist monk Thich Nhat Hanh as the "deep wish to cultivate understanding in ourselves in order to bring happiness to many beings" (Thich Nhat Hanh, *Heart* 62). Doing so "means surrendering completely, with an attitude of letting whatever happens happen; if it's better for me to have pleasure, let me have pleasure; if it's better to have pain, let me have pain" (Pema Chödrön, *No Time to Lose* 248). While there are *bodhisattvas* that can be invoked to support enlightenment, anyone can aspire to be one, even poor Fanny.[5]

The Buddhist text elucidating what it means to be a *bodhisattva* was written by an eighth-century Indian prince turned monk named Shantideva, a name that translates to "God of Peace." *The Way of the* Bodhisattva is based upon a speech delivered by Shantideva at Nalanda University, the largest and most powerful Indian monastery at the time. The story goes that Shantideva was lazy—quite a terrible monk. In order to either shame or motivate him to do better, the monks invited him to give a talk to the entire university, an honor usually only conferred on the best students who sat on a throne while speaking. Ostensibly, the monks made the throne even higher than typical and provided no stairs, but Shantideva had no trouble mounting the throne and then delivered the entire text of *The Way of the Bodhisattva*. His speech is not remarkable for groundbreaking new ideas as much as for being poetic, personal, and emotionally moving. As he concluded his talk with a discussion on the idea of emptiness, he began to float, eventually being so high above the monks that they could not see him and could only hear his voice; he then disappeared. He spent the rest of his life as a wandering yogi.

Like Austen, Shantideva created a text about transcending selfishness. Austen wrote during a time that emphasized newly modern ideas about the importance of the individual, hence her concern about selfishness. Likewise, Buddhism argues that an over-emphasis on the individual creates selfishness. Shantideva exhorts his audience to

> strive at first to meditate
> Upon the sameness of yourself and others.
> In joy and sorrow all are equal:
> Thus be a guardian of all, as of yourself [122].

Here, Shantideva advises empathy as a meditative practice, recognizing no distinction among all individuals. Note, however, his use of the word "first."

Since the emphasis is on "the way" and practice, empathy is an early step on the path. As previously noted, ultimately, Buddhism argues that the individual does not exist as a separate entity: it is a convenient fiction we tell ourselves to sustain our daily lives. Aronson, in reconciling modern Western ideas of self with Buddhism, explains, "Our separate and independent existences are merely figures of speech: easy to recognize, identify, and name, but no more than temporary formations, composed of the same stuff" (71). Again, the self is a story we write.

This notion of a self as separate and real is profound, which the Dalai Lama recognizes: "Grasping at this sense of self is quite instinctual" (*Practicing Wisdom* 55). Yet instinct can be transcended through recognizing that the self is a story. As Zen teacher David Loy writes in *The World Is Made of Stories*, "Like the proverbial fish that cannot see the water they swim in, we do not notice the medium we dwell in. Unaware that our stories are stories, we experience them as the world" (19). To cling to an inflexible narrative of the self—a form of attachment—creates more suffering; however, we are very prone to doing so.

Our blindness to narrative and our construction of harmful stories often come from being trapped by concepts. Pema Chödrön, in her commentary on Shantideva's text, compares being trapped by concepts to a pot being full with no room to add new ideas or opinions, a pot filled with poison where negativity prevents openness, or a pot with a hole in the bottom where distraction with our own preconceptions prevents engagement with the present moment. A closed mind "that fixates, conceptualizes, and compartmentalizes; a mind incapable of seeing things without bias," leading to "false views" will create false narratives that lead to suffering rather than approach each moment with fresh perspective (*No Time to Lose* 866).

Shantideva explicitly identifies the sense of a separate self as the creator of suffering. He offers the following dialogue to his self (what we might in modern language call the ego) as part of the section on meditative concentration:

> Let every thought of working for yourself
> Be utterly rejected, cast aside!
> ...
> Stop your whining, be of service!
> ...
> I will crush your selfish schemes! [8.170].

Shantideva knows the self will "hand me over, it is certain, / To the guards and janitors of hell" (133) through this selfish focus on only himself.

But selfishness can be transcended, and, because "suffering is the fruit of thought and action, it can be avoided" (Shantideva 8). Avoiding it means seeing the world correctly (Right View), not trapped by concepts and not creating stories that produce harm to ourselves and others. A *bodhisattva* moves beyond concepts by cultivating the *paramitas*, which literally translated means "going to the other shore." The six *paramitas* are generosity, discipline, patience, enthusiasm, meditation, and wisdom (Pema Chödrön, *No Time to Lose* 343). The *bodhisattva* practices the *paramitas* in order to heal others, that is to help those around her achieve freedom from damaging narratives, thereby eliminating suffering not only from her own life but from those around her.

*Bodhisattvas* do not create suffering or avoid it but allow the suffering produced by hardship to produce an inner softness and kindness (Pema Chödrön, *No Time to Lose* 127). Rather than running from life's suffering, a *bodhisattva* sits with it, looks deeply at it, and feels it fully. A *bodhisattva* is not a masochist who courts pain, but by not spending all of her energy avoiding pain, the *bodhisattva* can be fully present to the moment, to herself, and to those around her.[6] Thus, suffering can produce the empathy, the powerful emotion capable of bringing great healing that Shantideva urges we cultivate. Pema Chödrön explains that in cultivating *bodhicitta*, one trains to use personal fear or pain to become open to others' fear or pain (*No Time to Lose* 200).

The Bertrams instead enjoy the luxuries of life thanks to others' fear and pain via the West Indies plantation that Sir Thomas owns. Slavery is explicitly mentioned only once, but subtle references to slavery are peppered throughout the novel, and it is implied that Sir Thomas must leave Mansfield for Antigua to deal with either slave insurrections or economic changes wrought by the end of the slave trade. Many scholars speculate that Austen used the name Mansfield Park intentionally to connect to Lord Mansfield, the Lord Chief Justice and an ardent abolitionist who ruled in 1772 that an escaped slave did not have to return to slavery but could remain free in England. Others have argued that the name Mrs. Norris may have referred to a notorious John Norris, an ex-captain in the slave trade featured in Thomas Clarkson's *History of the Abolition of the Slave Trade*, a book many believe Austen read. While such connections are speculative, Fanny does explicitly ask Sir Thomas about the slave trade upon his return from Antigua. Given that his visit there is necessary due to financial circumstances and given the timing of the law's passage in 1807, it is safe to say that the Bertram family's fortune depended at least in part on slave labor. Clearly, Sir Thomas is not engaged in Right Livelihood but rather is demonstrating the same selfishness and inability to recognize interconnectedness as his empire-building nation.[7]

Given the underpinning foundation of their fortunes, it is no surprise that the Bertram household exemplifies all of the self-created miseries Shantideva argues against. To give one example, Sir Thomas, trapped thoroughly by attachment to an English-gentleman self, asks

Maria if she really wishes to marry Mr. Rushworth after he discovers for himself that Rushworth is an "inferior young man, as ignorant in business as in books, with opinions in general unfixed, and without seeming much aware of it himself" (156). Maria hesitates but responds with an immediate assertion of her willingness to continue the engagement, though the reader, unlike her father, understands that her motivation arises from the pain of rejection and her desire to leave her father's restrictive house. The narrator says of Maria, "In all the important preparations of the mind she was complete; being prepared for matrimony by an hatred of home, restraint, and tranquility; by the misery of disappointed affection, and contempt of the man she was to marry" (158).

Sir Thomas, trapped by his perspective that privileges his estate and reputation, "was satisfied; too glad to be satisfied perhaps to urge the matter quite so far as his judgment might have dictated to others ... happy to secure a marriage which would bring him an addition of respectability and influence" (157). Because of his own worldview and his selfishness, Sir Thomas only increases the suffering to come. Maria will eventually marry Rushworth only to commit adultery in a public manner that brings consequences to the entire family—as the narrator foreshadows for the reader, who, alas, knows Maria better than her father. Sir Thomas admits as much to himself after the deed, with the narrator sharing his realization that he "had been governed by motives of selfishness and worldly wisdom" (362).

The Bertrams and Crawfords, like most of us according to the Buddhist world view, continually wish to avoid suffering and pain— unlike the *bodhisattva* who is open to any experience. Avoidance, though, only magnifies suffering. To use the same example of Maria marrying Rushworth, she has trapped herself by agreeing to the engagement, which is exemplified in the scene at Rushworth's estate, Sotherton, by the locked gate on the grounds. In that scene, Maria refuses to be shut in and temporarily escapes with her future lover, Henry Crawford. However, when Henry later leaves Mansfield Park and no longer serves as the rescuer from the engagement she now regrets, Maria decides, "Henry Crawford had destroyed her happiness, but he should not know that he had done it; he should not destroy her credit, her appearance, her prosperity too" (158).

Maria escapes through the gate but is still trapped by the mindset that marriage is her rescue and refuses to see how she must create her own happiness. Rather than face potential humiliation and

prove to Henry that he has broken her heart, Maria makes her situation worse by marrying a man she dislikes. Ultimately, she allows
Henry Crawford to, in fact, "destroy her credit, her appearance, her
prosperity too." Maria must face some pain either before she marries Rushworth or after to truly escape her previous bad choice, but
she creates greater suffering for herself and all those around her by
avoiding initial pain before the marriage. According to the Dalai
Lama, Maria would be suffering from the "pervasive suffering of con-
ditioning": unexamined thoughts and emotions that guide words and
deeds (*How to Practice* 9). She lacks awareness due to the blindness
of her perspective and to her refusal to face how she has created her
own suffering.[8]

Unlike the privileged Bertram children, Fanny shares Shantideva's outsider status, and her ability to endure and end suffering owes
much to the lessons that her difficult circumstances have taught
her. Austen establishes the sources of Fanny's suffering before readers even meet her. Upon inviting her to live at Mansfield Park, Sir
Thomas explicitly draws boundaries between Fanny and her cousins: "I should wish to see them very good friends, and would, on
no account, authorize in my girls the smallest degree of arrogance
towards their relation; but still they cannot be equals. Their rank, fortune, rights, and expectations, will always be different" (8). He thus
undercuts the very premise of Buddhist enlightenment—interconnectedness—and gives license to Mrs. Norris to treat Fanny very differently from her other nieces. From the moment that Fanny arrives,
Mrs. Norris does just that, lecturing her on ingratitude when she
sees her natural sadness at being separated from her immediate family and assigning her to an attic room. We also learn that 10-year-old
Fanny is "somewhat delicate and puny," and Fanny's less than optimal health is a recurring issue throughout the novel (9). All of this
makes her poor Fanny indeed, when compared with the Bertram sisters raised in wealth and privilege.

However, Fanny's poor life circumstances create the conditions
that awaken her *bodhisattva* nature in a way not available to her coz-
ened cousins. The right relationship to suffering drives out pride,
offering humility and making us less self-centered; it creates empathy, enabling us to relate to our fellow sufferers and feel connected
with the human condition; it positions us to gain a greater understanding of cause and effect; and it creates the will to do good, incul-
cating virtues rather than causing pain (Pema Chödrön, *No Time*

*to Lose* 627–29). In his instructions on how to awaken *bodhicitta*, Shantideva writes:

> There's nothing that does not grow light
> Through habit and familiarity.
> Putting up with little cares
> I'll train myself to bear with great adversity! [6.14]

Fanny's lifelong challenges that come from her outsider status and frail health teach her how to put "up with little cares" so that she is better able "to bear with great adversity." The deprivations created by Mrs. Norris, such as the lack of a fire in the East room assigned to her for leisure hours or the long walks that she must take to fetch things for her aunt, tax Fanny's strength and make it possible for her to sit comfortably with her suffering—something that her cousins simply lack the experience to do. Pema Chödrön notes that there "is no practice more important than relating honestly and sanely with the irritations that plague us in everyday life" (*No Time to Lose* 725). While such irritations make life less pleasurable, they produce the conditions that make happiness possible.

The relative isolation that Fanny experiences due to her social status also teaches her to be comfortable with being alone and undistracted from the present moment. When on the road to visit Sotherton, Mr. Rushworth's estate, she "was not often invited to join in the conversation of the others, nor did she desire it. Her own thoughts and reflections were habitually her best companions" (64). Fanny wastes no energy on forcing her way into a conversation or on bitterness about not being included; rather, she uses the opportunity for self-reflection that leads to self-understanding not available to any other characters in the novel.[9]

We see the contrast repeatedly and early. For example, when Fanny sits abandoned in an enclosed area of the grounds at Sotherton, Julia, who has also been left behind by the young people, finds her and takes out her bad temper on Fanny saying, "Such a penance as I have been enduring, while you were sitting here so composed and so happy! It might have been as well, perhaps, if you had been in my place, but you always contrive to keep out of these scrapes." Fanny, of course, rarely gets her own way and must almost always be at the beck and call of her aunts, so the charge is completely unfair. But it is precisely not being able to get her way that prepares Fanny for this conversation. With a lifetime of living at others' whims, Fanny knows better than to overreact to Julia's rude comment. She refuses to increase suffering through a story that increases her victimhood.

In addition, Fanny at this moment is far from happy, which Julia entirely fails to notice. Fanny bears the attack with patience: "This was a most unjust reflection, but Fanny could allow for it, and let it pass; Julia was vexed, and her temper was hasty, but she felt that it would not last" (80). Unlike her cousin, Fanny reads Julia correctly and also makes allowances for her as she has observed already that Julia is unsuccessfully competing with her sister for status and male attention. She recognizes Julia's mood as impermanent, not as something to fixate on.

Austen directly links Maria's and Julia's bad choices to the endless flattery and favoritism given to them by their Aunt Norris, noting that Julia's less harmful choices come from being "less the darling of that very aunt" causing her "to think herself a little inferior to Maria" so that "her education had not given her so very hurtful a degree of self-consequence." Maria, the cousin who suffers least growing up, consequently causes the most suffering for everyone. Austen even lays some of the blame on Maria for Julia's elopement, telling the reader, "She had not eloped with any worse feelings than those of selfish alarm. It had appeared to her the only thing to be done. Maria's guilt had induced Julia's folly" (366).

Shantideva addresses the problems with praise:

> Veneration, praise, and fame
> Serve not to increase merit or my span of life
> Bestowing neither health nor strength
> And nothing for the body's ease [6.90].

Praise brings no benefit. Yet praise has been the mainstay of the Bertram girls' education, and it has left them vulnerable to envy and to the flattery of Henry Crawford. In this way, Mrs. Norris has done more harm to her favorite nieces than to Fanny in spite of her unkind treatment, for "troublemakers" require "the exercise of patience," allowing for the tormented to be clean and pure while the tormenter creates a personal hell for herself (Pema Chödrön, *No Time to Lose* 751). This is certainly true of Fanny and Mrs. Norris by the novel's end, with Fanny's patience producing happiness and Mrs. Norris in a hell of her own making, choosing exile with Maria after her infidelity. Perhaps this explains Fanny's seeming "almost as fearful of notice and praise as other women were of neglect" (155).

In addition to differences in how they are treated within the family, the Bertram sisters and Mary Crawford experience strong health compared with Fanny's frailty, which ultimately benefits Fanny. Buddhism does not vilify the body. Importantly, the Buddha rejected the extreme asceticism he had undergone as part of his quest for enlightenment, advocating instead for a more balanced approach—the Middle Way. The problem is not the body per se but our attachment to the body. As the introduction to *Way* states, "The body has its place and value, but the mind must be freed from an obsessive and enslaving preoccupation with it" (12). Such preoccupation can lead to not distinguishing between happiness and pleasure. Shantideva writes:

> All the joy the world contains
> Has come through wishing happiness for others.
> All the misery the world contains
> Has come through wanting pleasure for oneself [8.12].

Happiness can be achieved without sensual pleasure, and sensual pleasure can come at the cost of happiness, for the temporary pleasant body sensation may come at an emotional cost or at the expense of integrity. The problem is attachment, or in Tibetan *shenpa*. Dzigar Kongtrul describes attachment as "the 'charge' behind emotions: the charge behind 'I like and don't like,' the charge behind self-importance itself" (qtd. in *No Time to Lose* 257–8). The focus on one's own comfort and pleasure undercuts the ability to care for others and empathize with them. It leads to egocentrism as we seek to avoid those things we don't like and to cling to those that we do.

*Mansfield Park*'s best example of pleasure-seeking egocentrism is Mary Crawford, particularly in the scene where she keeps Fanny's horse well into Fanny's scheduled riding time. "Active and fearless ... strongly made," Mary finds "pure genuine pleasure" in the exercise and assures Edmund that the long ride has not tired her in the least (53). "I am very strong. Nothing ever fatigues me, but doing what I do not like" and then wishes Fanny a "pleasant ride." Edmund, when asking Fanny when he might next offer the horse to Mary, notes, "*She* rides only for pleasure, *you* for health" (emphasis in original 53). Mary later claims that "resting fatigues me" (76).

Mary's constant desire for pleasure and activity leads directly to her selfishness, both keeping the horse from Fanny, whose health consequently suffers, and in leaving Fanny behind at Sotherton when she ventures off with Edmund. Though sounding ironic, Miss

Crawford admits as much in her apology to Fanny when returning her horse: "I have nothing to say for myself—I knew it was very late, and that I was behaving extremely ill; and, therefore, if you please, you must forgive me. Selfishness must always be forgiven you know, because there is no hope of a cure" (54). But, of course, the practice of a *bodhisattva* is exactly the cure for selfishness. Seduced by her pleasurable company, Edmund also becomes shortsighted and selfish, for in his efforts to please Mary, he forgets Fanny. Again, there is nothing wrong with activity—with riding or walking—other than it leading to egocentric pleasure in one's own bodily activity and thereby to lack of empathy for others.

This becomes yet more exaggerated with the least likable character of the novel: Mrs. Norris. While Mary's active, witty nature that veers into occasional indiscretion may be excused and even admired by some, Mrs. Norris is so universally disliked that J.K. Rowling named Argus's Filch's spying cat after her. As with Mary Crawford, Austen immediately describes Mrs. Norris as having "a spirit of activity" which stems from ego (4). She exemplifies "the three main bases of self-importance: attachment to possessions, body, and merit" with her obsessive parsimoniousness, her pride in her physical endurance, and her need to call attention to all of her acts of merit (Pema Chödrön, *No Time to Lose*, 257). Examples abound, but one that will do is her response to Sir Thomas's return from the West Indies:

> She was vexed by the *manner* of his return. It had left her nothing to do. Instead of being sent for out of the room, and seeing him first, and having to spread the happy news through the house, Sir Thomas, with a very reasonable dependance (*sic*) perhaps on the nerves of his wife and children, had sought no confidant but the butler, and had been following him almost instantaneously into the drawing-room. Mrs. Norris felt herself defrauded of an office on which she had always depended, whether his arrival or his death were to be the thing unfolded; and was now trying to be in a bustle without having anything to bustle about, and labouring to be important where nothing was wanted but tranquility and silence [emphasis in original 141].

Austen's narrator makes clear that Sir Thomas's safe arrival home or death makes no difference to Mrs. Norris. What matters is her own active importance in the event. She is active and lacks all empathy. She is purely selfish, only interested in the appearance of doing good. When Sir Thomas gently confronts Mrs. Norris with the impropriety of the playacting in his absence, she defends herself by praising her "*general* attention to the interest and comfort of his family, much exertion and many sacrifices to glance at in the form of hurried walks and sudden removals from her own fireside" and, most importantly, her "active" matchmaking that brought about the engagement of Maria to Mr. Rushworth, an undertaking that results in disaster (emphasis in original 148).

Certainly, Austen is not rejecting activity completely, nor is she endorsing indolence, for Lady Bertram is no model. She is a static character until the very end of the novel, so an early description of her holds true throughout almost the entirety of the story. Austen describes her thus:

> To the education of her daughters, Lady Bertram paid not the smallest attention. She had not time for such cares. She was a woman who spent her days in sitting nicely dressed on a sofa, doing some long piece of needlework, of little use and no beauty, thinking more of her pug than her children, but very indulgent to the latter, when it did not put herself to inconvenience, guided in everything important by Sir Thomas, and in smaller concerns by her sister. Had she possessed greater leisure for the service of her girls, she would probably have supposed it unnecessary, for they were under the care of a governess, with proper masters, and could want nothing more [16].

As a static character, almost a stereotype, Lady Bertram feels almost like a concept herself. She represents all that was wrong with the superficial education women received during Austen's time. Through her proscribed ladylike laziness, Lady Bertram fails to educate her children in morality or critical thinking, leading to the crisis ahead.

Between Mrs. Norris and Lady Bertram, Austen, Buddha-like, presents an endorsement of a middle way of "thoughtful rest" while rejecting "the dangers of thoughtless restlessness" (Tanner 173). Fanny's isolation and lack of endurance create opportunities for her to live comfortably with her own thoughts and company, so she has learned the art of the pause. Rather than responding immediately to what is happening around her, she has developed powers of observation and the ability to refrain from merely responding or reacting impulsively. When she begins to feel envy after Edmund agrees to act in *Lovers' Vows*, "reflection brought better feelings" (125). When she becomes anxious about the rehearsal where Mary Crawford and Edmund will perform their parts together, she honors "her wish to retreat, and she worked and meditated in the East room" (132). When speaking to Edmund about how Mary can't understand why she won't accept Henry's proposal, she responds only "after a pause of recollection and exertion" (277). While readers and critics have complained of Fanny's passivity and seen her quiet acceptance in such examples as defeatism, her ability to withdraw and respond with calm detachment indicates an aspirant moving toward enlightenment.

The contrast between Fanny's "thoughtful rest" and Mary's "thoughtless restlessness" appears when the two sit together in Mrs. Grant's shrubbery. Austen guides the reader in how to interpret the interaction by explaining that it was "an intimacy resulting principally from Miss Crawford's desire of something new" (162). Even an attempt at friendship comes from Mary's restlessness. As the women sit together, Fanny, struck by the beauty of her natural surroundings, verbalizes her admiration and philosophizes. "Miss Crawford, untouched and inattentive, had nothing to say" (163). Fanny, after a pause, once again admires the scene, explaining, "when I am out of doors, especially when I am sitting out of doors, I am very apt to get into this sort of wondering strain." Mary responds, "I see no wonder in this shrubbery equal to seeing myself in it" (164). She then quickly follows up with snide, materialistic comments about the Rushworths. While Fanny demonstrates a sense of connection, Mary concentrates on herself as an individual, and her comments about the Rushworths show her solipsism and lack of empathy. The conversation proves Fanny's ability to be in the moment and value it, whereas Mary relapses "into thoughtfulness" unable to appreciate her surroundings, preferring her own thoughts, her own narrative of a possible future with Edmund—if he changes as she directs.

To reinforce the value of being still in a thoughtful manner, Austen gives her readers Tom Bertram. Tom spends most of the novel as the disappointing, profligate older son. His expenses cost Edmund the Mansfield Park living—that is, the position of parish clergy with a guaranteed income and housing, that must now be sold to Dr. Grant to cover Tom's debts. When Sir Thomas confronts him with this, "Tom listened with some shame and some sorrow; but escaping as quickly as possible, could soon with cheerful selfishness reflect" on a list of excuses (19). We see Tom escaping his father, his responsibility, and his appropriate feelings of shame and sorrow in order to immediately revert to his selfish nature. The verb *reflect* is truly ironic. Through costing the living for Edmund, Tom is indirectly responsible for causing most of the Bertrams' woes by introducing the Crawfords into the narrative. In addition, he directly introduces theatricals to

Mansfield Park during Sir Thomas's absence, which leads to further chaos and opportunities for Henry to seduce Maria.

But Tom's illness changes him; he regains his health "without regaining the thoughtlessness and selfishness of his previous habits. He was the better for ever for his illness. He had suffered, and he had learnt to think, two advantages he had never known before" (363). Like Shantideva, Austen here links suffering to the ability to pause and think and labels suffering itself as an advantage. Shantideva concurs:

> The cause of happiness is rare,
> And many are the seeds of suffering!
> But if I have no pain, I'll never long for freedom [6.12].

Pain, suffering, and illness have value as motivation to achieve spiritual freedom.

Fanny's freedom comes from her liminal status; she is not firmly fixed in any class or place, being both family but not immediate family, both resident and visitor. This prevents her from being caught by concepts, unlike the other characters who are pigeonholed into their various roles. Mary Crawford expresses confusion over Fanny's status, asking "is she out, or is she not? I am puzzled.—She dined at the parsonage, with the rest of you, which seemed like being *out*; and yet she says so little, that I can hardly suppose she *is*" (emphasis in original 39). Mary tries to fix Fanny's status by determining whether or not she is on the marriage market. A discussion follows between Mary and Tom about the usually clear distinctions between in or out and how awful it is when such decorum is violated. Fanny, however, is neither in nor out. The distinction that Sir Thomas draws so early and that is so carefully reinforced by Mrs. Norris remains firm until Sir Thomas returns from the West Indies, and even then, Fanny is not recognized as a rightful, full member of the family until after Maria's adultery, so she is never forced to deal with the trials of being in or out.

Fanny escapes the kind of damage inflicted upon the Bertram sisters by their education as proper ladies, one that traps them by a society that carves out narrow limits for their lives. Fanny lives a life without expectations, surprised, for example, when she realizes she is to lead the ball as Sir Thomas's niece. Rather than seeing the ball as part of the machinations of matchmaking that it is, Fanny is free to see it as a dance. And while she feels self-conscious as a young woman not used to public appearances, she does not see herself as being on display as a possible mate. This liminality is a hallmark of the *bodhisattva*. The Dalai Lama describes the *bodhisattva* as being in an in-between state as she does not enter nirvana or "solitary peace" but chooses cyclical existence out of a sense of altruism (*Practicing Wisdom* 83). She is enlightened without opting for the award of enlightenment, which is an escape from this world's suffering.

Unlike Fanny, for the other residents of Mansfield Park, ideas about a stable self come burdened with expectations and definitions of what is expected of a lady or a gentleman. This is in contrast with the Buddhist path to happiness, which involves dropping "our ideals of who we think we ought to be, or who we think we want to be, or who we think other people think we want to be or ought to be" (Pema Chödrön, *When Things Fall Apart* 120). All of the Bertram children attempt escape: Maria and Julia via men; Tom via his profligate lifestyle; and even Edmund, temporarily, via acting in the play (even though he does so for "noble" reasons). Because they cannot escape the roles thrust upon them by their social positions, the ladies and gentlemen take on different roles via *Lovers' Vows*.

However, adopting a role is a pleasurable escape, not a true path to happiness, and the playacting exemplifies when each character becomes the most selfish, which we can see from the moment the idea is proposed. In introducing the idea, Mr. Yates is filled with self-pity that playacting had been canceled due to a death in the family when he was visiting other friends. Mr. Yates expresses his desire that the death could have been ignored a few days so that the play could have proceeded, it "being only a grandmother, and all that happening two hundred miles off" (97). From this ignominious start, the play produces only problems. Those who act in it (or wished to in Julia's case) are unkind, unobservant, angry, and/or jealous. Fanny, who avoids prescribed, predetermined roles in life, refuses to act and, thereby, escapes the dangers of the play's narrative.

Any play would do to emphasize role playing, but Austen's choice of *Lovers' Vows* foreshadows the adultery and scandal to come between Maria and Henry while giving them the excuse to interact in a personal, inappropriate manner for a gentleman and an engaged lady. The disruption of Sir Thomas's rooms to become a theater serves as warning of the disruption to come to Mansfield.

We can see this most clearly in comparing Julia and Fanny as "two solitary sufferers," each feeling jealousy but experiencing it in such a different manner. Julia loses her preferred role to her sister and must watch her act intimate scenes with Henry Crawford, the man they both desire. Julia responds by refusing to participate, which might be a good solution, but she finds no peace, for "her heart was sore and angry, and she was capable only of angry consolations" (127). She makes "no endeavour at rational tranquility for herself" (125). While Julia removes herself physically from the play, she stays mired in the scene of suffering, nurturing anger rather than seeking peace. Only Fanny sees this. Those around Julia are, to return to the metaphor from Pema Chödrön's commentary on *The Way of the* Bodhisattva, full pots: "The inattention of the two brothers and the aunt to Julia's discomposure, and their blindness to its true cause, must be imputed to the fulness of their own minds. They were totally pre-occupied" (128). Alas, with the exception of Fanny, everyone surrounding Julia is self-centered and selfish.

Fanny, though, is a witness to all and perceives everyone correctly because she is not caught by jealousy or any given role. She observes correctly that "far from being all satisfied and all enjoying, she found everybody requiring something they had not, and giving occasion of discontent to the others" (129). Her conclusions come not just from observation, however, as everyone turns to her with their problems.

Fanny enacts in the *Lovers' Vows* rehearsals the Eightfold Path. Deep listening is the foundation for Right Speech, and "Fanny, being always a very courteous listener, and often the only listener at hand, came in for the complaints and distresses of most of them" (129). Thanks to her liminal status, she engages in Right View and Right Thinking—correct perception not marred by concepts—throughout the novel. As explored previously, Fanny continues to use Right Mindfulness, looking within to understand the cause of her suffering. When Edmund accepts a role in the play after protesting about how wrong it is to act, she finds that "her indifference to the danger was beginning to fail her," that she "was at first in some danger of" envy, and that she is "agitated" and "anxious" (124, 125, 131). Unlike Julia, Fanny sits with her suffering, examines it, and is then free from it, finding peace, which she achieves via Right Diligence— that is applying herself earnestly to the endeavor with good intent. Lastly, she shows Right Concentration, not escaping as everyone else is but staying present, which allows her to see the suffering of all, and engages in Right Livelihood, offering her time and service with compassion, for example memorizing Mr. Rushworth's lines in an effort to help him "in her pity and kind-heartedness" (130). In this way, while the others seek pleasure, Fanny continues to offer happiness, defined by Thich Nhat Hanh as benefiting and nourishing everyone (*Heart* 78).

Those characters who do enjoy the play perform as directors and actors in their everyday lives. Mrs. Norris happily participates behind the scenes, oblivious to any impropriety and certainly unworried about Sir Thomas's wishes. Long before the play, Austen describes Mrs. Norris in rather theatrical terms referring to "her love of directing" (7). Henry Crawford is by far the best actor, which gives insight into someone who lives a part rather than reflecting on his own character. Fanny is "the only one of the party who found anything to dislike" in Henry (92). But the narrator assures us that she is quite correct, telling the reader that Henry lacks "the habit of examining his own motives, and reflecting to what the indulgence of his idle vanity was tending; but, thoughtless and selfish from prosperity and bad example," Henry knowingly plays games with Maria and Julia, just as he will attempt to do later with Fanny (91). He does so via the overt acting of scenes in the play, but also through staging scenes in daily life, for example, reading the Shakespeare play aloud, performing conversations for Fanny's benefit, insisting on helping during the card game at the Grants, and having Mary offer Fanny a chain for her pendant to trick her into accepting a gift and thereby be in his debt. These characters who are acting scripts are caught by narrative, unlike Fanny, the constant observer who sees "all that was passing before her" (145).

Because Fanny operates in the moment responding to her circumstances with flexibility and engages in self-reflection, the charge that she is a self-righteous prig is wrong. And rather than being a sadomasochistic victim, as some charge, Fanny exhibits humility and quiet self-confidence by the end of the novel. Faced with the bullying and intimidation by Sir Thomas calling her ungrateful and selfish in her refusal of Henry Crawford, Fanny stands her ground, knowing that she and Henry could not make each other happy. Certainly, the argument exists that it is her love for Edmund preventing her acquiescence to the engagement rather than internal conviction, but Fanny is also clear in knowing that Edmund wants Mary, not her. Her refusal comes at great cost to herself and to her family, whom Henry could help with his funds. It comes from a sense of what is right, not hope for a future with Edmund.

It is also true that Fanny begins to see Henry in a more positive light when in Portsmouth, which serves only as a refutation of those critics who argue that Fanny is boorish in being always and only right. Rather, Fanny struggles throughout the novel but properly as any aspirant would in facing difficult emotions. And she does continue to resist the seductive Crawfords, refusing their offer to return her to Mansfield and choosing to remain with her family, even at the cost of her health. Instead, she turns her *bodhisattva* nature to good use, resolving the disruptive dispute between her two sisters through her gift and lifting up Susan through the subscription to the lending library and through quiet conversation.

None of this makes Fanny unique. Buddhists believe that everyone has Buddha nature within them, and anyone who chooses to awaken *bodhicitta* and achieve enlightenment out of altruism can become a *bodhisattva*. Fanny is fortunate in the life circumstances that offer her freedom not available to the other characters. Julia, Maria, and Mary are educated in how to be proper young ladies—an education that ultimately traps them socially and in how they view the world; they psychologically limit themselves. Mrs. Norris addresses Sir Thomas's concerns about bringing Fanny to Mansfield Park by saying, "Give a girl an education, and introduce her properly into the world, and ten to one but she has the means of settling well" (5). While Mrs. Norris, of course, means settling into a good marriage, Austen implies that these women are settling for an inferior education.

Education for proper ladies, as Mary Wollstonecraft argued in *Vindication of the Rights of Woman* only 22 years earlier, did more harm than good, training them only to catch husbands. Sir Thomas echoes these thoughts in lamenting the education of his daughters, deciding "they had never been properly taught to govern their inclinations and tempers," for he "had meant them to be good," but "that with all the cost and care of an anxious and expensive education," his daughters had learned lady's manners only (364).

Similarly, though Edmund is guilty of looking for ways to excuse Mary's behavior when smitten with her, he is not wrong in blaming her thoughtlessness on a poor education and role models. While some critics see Fanny as Edmund's mere cipher, with his taking charge of her education, she benefits greatly from her deep reading and his guidance. Shantideva argues for the importance of teachers, and while Edmund's infatuation with Mary blinds him for a while, he is still an excellent model of many attributes of enlightenment. For example, he is the only member of the Bertram family to see Fanny's distress upon moving to Mansfield Park, offering deep listening and compassion.[10] Most importantly, Fanny as student clearly surpasses Edmund as teacher with her clarity of vision and self-discipline.

In an August 2014 *Los Angeles Review of Books* piece, Anna Keesey describes her movement from dislike of Fanny as "Anglican doormat" to an appreciation of her as "a hero on a winged horse," offering with her "stillness" an antidote for our times where "rough beasts are aslouch on the road to many Bethlehems" (qtd. in Troost and Greenfield 29). Perhaps our modern pieties have changed so that Fanny and *Mansfield Park* no longer offend. With Robert Wright's *Why Buddhism Is True* on *The New York Times* bestseller list and *Time* devoting a special issue to mindfulness in 2017, we may be at a cultural moment where our own perspectives have shifted in such a way that we can see Fanny Price anew and appreciate her *bodhisattva* nature. We might even have something to learn from her about cultivating a bit of *bodhicitta* ourselves.

# EIGHT

## *Persuasion*

### Why I Didn't Want to Be Anne Elliot and Why I Now Aspire to Be Her

"Encountering sufferings will definitely contribute to the elevation of your spiritual practice, provided you are able to transform the calamity and misfortune into the path."
—The Dalai Lama, *Essential Wisdom*

"Abandon all hope ye who enter here."
—Dante, *The Divine Comedy*

As I said in my preface, this project started with Anne Elliot. *Persuasion* is the book I could read during the worst of my troubles, and Anne was the answer to the BuzzFeed quiz asking which Jane Austen heroine are you—four times. I took it four times. Why didn't I want to be Anne? Let's be honest. Who would want to be Anne? A former student of mine, knowing about my project and wishing to read some Austen beyond *Pride and Prejudice*, began *Persuasion* and had to stop about 50 pages in because she could not bear the meanness of the novel. Anne is unappreciated, overlooked, and undervalued. No one listens to her; no one truly knows her. Her family neglects her spitefully (Elizabeth) or, at best, benignly (Mary). She serves as the recipient of others' confidences but has no one to whom she may speak. Her former lover returns only to torment her with cold civility and flirtations with other women to her very face. She seemingly is passive and accepting of this awful treatment. I repeat: Who would want to be Anne? But, of course, I was. Like Anne, I wished to be useful, but my efforts were not always appreciated, particularly by my mom, simply because, thanks to her dementia, she could not. Perhaps most importantly, I was like Anne because I could not change my circumstances. The only real choice each of us had was in our response.[1]

The Buddha taught that life will metaphorically shoot arrows at us. We are going to feel pain, and that is out of our control. However, it is human nature to shoot a second arrow at ourselves via our reaction to the pain of the first. Instead of simply being aware of the first arrow, acknowledging the pain, and, thereby, removing the arrow, we create more pain for ourselves. We ask, why am I always getting shot by arrows? Who shot this arrow at me? Why didn't that other person get shot by the arrow? Why do I feel so bad about this arrow? And on. This is the choice point.[2] Pain is inevitable in life, but do we create suffering by wallowing in the pain, or do we find a way to remove it? Anne Elliot accepts her suffering—the external circumstances over which she has no control—but she does not work to make her suffering worse. In spite of her difficult circumstances, Anne finds equanimity and, ultimately, happiness. So who wants to be Anne Elliot? I do. I think we all should.

Let's start with why I didn't want to be Anne. *Persuasion* begins by demonstrating Anne's powerlessness. She is the middle daughter of a vain nobleman obsessed with status. She is likely facing spinsterhood at the age of 27, having refused two proposals, one from a man she genuinely loved and still does. Her mother died when Anne was only 14, so she shares her home with her unloving father, Sir Walter, and her older sister, Elizabeth, whose personality mirrors her father's. Neither understands nor appreciates Anne. Her younger sister, Mary, having married the other man whose proposal Anne refused, lives close by but communicates primarily to complain and demand. Anne's only friend is a woman her parents' age, Lady Russell, the same person who persuaded her to reject the proposal of her soulmate, Frederick Wentworth, eight years previous. Wentworth, as a member of the navy, has literally sailed out of her life.

Wentworth's dismissal serves as perfect evidence of how little Anne's own feelings were considered throughout her life. Sir Walter greeted the news of Anne and Frederick's engagement with coldness. Lady Russell actively persuaded the then 19-year-old Anne to break her engagement. Lady Russell's "pardonable pride" guided her to believe that young Anne would be throwing herself away on a man "who had nothing to recommend him, and no hopes of attaining affluence, but in the chances of a most uncertain profession" (55). Yet Wentworth's confidence in his abilities was part of his appeal for Anne. For Lady Russell, "his sanguine temper, and fearlessness of mind, operated very differently on her. She saw in it but an aggravation of evil. It only added a dangerous character to himself. He was brilliant, he was headstrong.—Lady Russell had little taste for wit; and of anything approaching to imprudence a horror. She deprecated the connexion [*sic*] in every light" (56). Lady Russell rejected Wentworth based on her own personal views and preferences, not through an understanding of Anne's character. Her objections are based upon pride, money, status, her own ideas of ideal manhood and happiness, and fear, not a consideration of what would make Anne truly happy. Lady Russell embodies Thich Nhat Hanh's contention that "if you do not give right attention to the one you love, it is a kind of killing" (*Heart* 65). Though Lady Russell loves Anne, she failed at Right Action and became the source of Anne's suffering. All of this serves as the backstory represented in the first few chapters before Anne's circumstances take another turn for the worse, leaving her not only powerless but hopeless.

But hopelessness is not bad. Western culture values hope and encourages us to have it, seeing it as the opposite of despair, as a motivation to strive and reach goals. Hence Dante's famous line from *The Divine Comedy* about abandoning hope as he enters Hell. Hope can be Hell from a Buddhist perspective. Pema Chödrön teaches that "hope and fear is a feeling with two sides. As long as there's one, there's always the other.... Hope and fear come from feeling that we lack something; they come from a sense of poverty" (88). To hope means to wish for something we don't have; it means not valuing the present moment and not finding happiness in our lives exactly as they are. Anne does not hope, nor does she despair. Losing Wentworth causes great initial emotional pain resulting in Anne's "early loss of bloom and spirits" (57).

Yet, having lost everything, Anne can be content. Contentment comes when we realize we have nothing to lose, according to Pema Chödrön. Contentment results from sitting with our loneliness, boredom, anxiety—any unpleasant emotion—without working to distract ourselves through materialism or through, as she puts it, "our Very Important Storylines" those internal stories we tell ourselves that inflict the second arrow, creating drama and distracting us from the reality of our feelings (114). So Anne lacks hope. Importantly, she lacks fear.

Anne's outsider status within her family stems exactly from this ability. Her other family members choose material comfort and distraction over Right View, resulting in the creation of a great deal more suffering for everyone. When the novel begins, thanks to her father's profligacy, the family's fortunes falter, leading to the need to change lifestyles. Options include severe budgetary cutbacks while staying at Kellynch Hall or moving and renting the estate. In making this major life decision, neither Elizabeth nor Sir Walter consider Anne's perspective or ideas—or, frankly, consider her at all. In fact, Elizabeth's recommendation to save money is to not bring Anne a gift from London as is the usual practice. When things come to the point where action is absolutely necessary, Sir Walter and Elizabeth consult their longtime family friend Lady Russell, who does think to ask Anne's opinion, though she was never "considered by the others as having any interest in the question" (43). Lady Russell "in a degree" was "influenced by her, in making out a scheme of retrenchment" (43). Anne's lack of importance is highlighted by the retrenchment scheme to relocate to Bath, the least attractive to Anne of the available options. Even Lady Russell actively opposes Anne's preference for a small house nearby and favors Bath because she herself is fond of it "and disposed to think it must suit them all" (45). And not only must Anne live in the one place she does not like, Elizabeth further insults her by choosing Mrs. Clay, the daughter of the family's lawyer, as her companion over her sister. Lady Russell rightly sees this as an "affront" to Anne, though "Anne herself was become hardened to such affronts" (62). While Anne does not heighten her own pain by wallowing in the insult of Elizabeth preferring Mrs. Clay, she does recognize that Mrs. Clay is a widow who wishes to attract Sir Walter's attention (a gold digger, to be anachronistic) and thereby serves as a potential threat to the family.

To Anne's hopeless situation, therefore, is added uncertainty as the family faces an uncertain future.[3] Pema Chödrön writes that life is our greatest teacher and that life's greatest lesson is to live comfortably with uncertainty. "Sticking with that uncertainty, getting the knack of relaxing in the midst of chaos, learning not to panic—this is the spiritual path" (*When Things Fall Apart* 35). On its surface, *Persuasion* is not a spiritual book. Yet, if we take Chödrön's definition of the spiritual path, we certainly can characterize Anne's journey as a spiritual one. She successfully lives with uncertainty. We all must, but we pretend otherwise. Anne does not pretend. She sees with great clarity life's uncertainty and admirably relaxes into it. Anne accomplishes all of this calmly. She is not always happy; that is impossible. But she is capable of and willing to flow with the universe and to trust her own feelings.

The grinding day-to-day suffering experienced by Anne thus far described takes place within the first three chapters of the book, hence my former student putting the novel down after 50 pages because it was too depressing. Granted, Anne's circumstances are not impossible. She is not deathly ill. She is not being physically abused. She is not destitute. Yet her circumstances are precisely of the nature to cause great personal pain, in part because on the surface, they do not appear all that bad: daughter of a nobleman who must move from her estate to a lovely house in the pleasure city of Bath. In this way, Anne's suffering mirrors the kind of suffering experienced by most of us—not earth shattering, not obviously apparent, but nonetheless ripe with anxiety and pain. Psychologists tell us that day-to-day long-term stress can damage the brain.[4] A life of enduring daily pain (emotional or physical), poverty, or disease changes our brains negatively more so than the major events of suffering we struggle to avoid such as the loss of a loved one.

I believe my attraction to *Persuasion* during the period I couldn't read came from an unconscious recognition of and appreciation for seeing how Austen's novels are so much about this kind of quiet suffering with *Persuasion* serving as a model to cope—in a Buddhist-like manner. Anne doesn't lie to herself, trying to sugarcoat her circumstances or alleviate pain by pretending she will marry well out of it (as her sister Elizabeth does). She's aware that she is, by her culture's terms, a spinster living with an unkind family, facing genteel poverty, and silently carrying the burden of unrequited love in isolation. She's aware and brave.

Buddhists believe that this capacity lives within all of us, that each person has the Buddha within. That is the main lesson of the Buddha's teachings, that all humans are capable of transforming and transcending suffering just as he had done. Anne displays these virtues of a Buddha from the very beginning. Thich Nhat Hanh offers two questions that we must ask ourselves in order to move beyond suffering: What conditions already exist in life that bring happiness? What nourishes joy in me and others? Anne successfully asks and answers these questions. Anne's sole recourse for happiness is herself. In yet another instance of Anne being overlooked, we hear her thoughts about playing piano while visiting her sister Mary's in-laws: "She knew that when she played she was giving pleasure only to herself; but this was no new sensation" (73). It's important to note that Anne thinks this with no self-pity and finds happiness in noting the "fond partiality" for performances of the daughters of the house she's visiting.[5] Throughout the novel, Anne refers to her actions as a duty and finds joy in performing these actions such as being willing to listen or to visit a sick friend. She finds joy in Right Action.

In another example of Anne's early Buddhahood, when Lady Russell consults Anne about the family's finances, Anne demonstrates Right Livelihood in place of her irresponsible father. As a nobleman holding an estate, Sir Walter has a societal obligation to all of his dependents, including not only his family but also tenants, cottagers, and the tradesman with whom he deals. Instead, he has incurred debt and refuses to reduce the pomp and circumstance of the lifestyle befitting a nobleman. Upon learning of the debt, Anne "considered it as an act of indispensable duty to clear away the claims of creditors, with all the expedition which the most comprehensive retrenchment could secure, and saw no dignity in anything short of it" (43). Anne recognizes that her father's selfish choices have created hardship for those to whom he owes money, hence calling upon him to meet his duty—to exhibit Right Livelihood—a proposal Lady Russell does not even bother to make because she knows that Sir Walter would never consider it.

While Elizabeth and Sir Walter distract themselves from spiritual poverty through snobby materialism, Mary turns to "Very Important Storylines" with herself starring as the central sufferer at all times. The Buddha argued that craving is one of our main sources of suffering. Mary embodies this notion, always wanting just one more thing to make her happy, making herself and those around her miserable in the process. While Anne truly is neglected, Mary always thinks herself so.

This unhappy grasping is best exemplified during the scene that occurs at a resting place midway through a long walk. Mary finds a comfortable seat and is perfectly happy until the rest of the walking party except for Anne disperses. "Mary was happy no longer; she quarreled with her own seat,—was sure Louisa had got a much better somewhere,—and nothing could prevent her from going to look for a better also." Having moved to find Louisa, "Mary sat down for a moment, but it would not do; she was sure Louisa had found a better seat somewhere else, and she would go on" (109). Though it is a simple thing, the inability to find comfort in her resting place says volumes about Mary's inability to rest within the comfortable circumstances of her own life. She consistently lives life feeling a sense of lack.

Mary writes before the family leaves Kellynch insisting on Anne's visit because she believes herself once again unwell and "cannot possibly do without Anne" (61). Elizabeth replies "nobody will want" Anne in Bath, so Anne willingly agrees to go to Mary "glad to be thought of some use, glad to have anything marked out as a duty" (61). As noted, the word *duty* appears throughout the novel, with Anne embracing each opportunity to practice Right Action and connecting it to the emotion of being glad. In fact, the return of Anne's "early bloom and spirits" that make her cousin Mr. Elliot notice her before even knowing her identity, comes from performance of duty rather than reconciliation with Wentworth.

The duty of caring for Mary primarily consists of listening to everyone's complaints, thereby practicing Right Speech. Mary complains, well, about everything but particularly about her husband Charles' parenting; about Charles' mother, Mrs. Musgrove, as a grandparent, Mrs. Musgrove's governance of her servants, and Mrs. Musgrove's neglect in giving Mary precedence in company; as well as about her own health. Charles and Mrs. Musgrove, meanwhile, complain about Mary's mothering. Mrs. Musgrove lays out charges of misbehavior against Mary's servant. And Louisa and Henrietta Musgrove (Charles' sisters) ask Anne to correct Mary's public claim to precedence at social events. "How was Anne to set all these matters to right? She could do little more than listen patiently, soften every grievance, and excuse each to the other, give them all hints of forebearance necessary between such near neighbours [*sic*], and make those hints broadest which were meant for her sister's benefit" (72).

This "little more" that Anne can do perfectly fits Thich Nhat Hanh's description of Right Speech, which first involves deep listening. Because merely being heard will greatly alleviate suffering, just by listening patiently, Anne ameliorates the suffering of the Musgrove family. Right Speech also means delivering a message appropriately for the listener. He gives the example of a *bodhisattva* named Wondrous Sound from the *Lotus Sutra* who was able to speak to each person in his or her own language. Anne speaks in Mary's language by giving broad hints, knowing that direct confrontation will accomplish nothing with her sister.

Austen's use of free indirect discourse for her narrative style underscores Anne's difference from Mary in not creating "Very Important Storylines" via dwelling on insults and thereby inflicting the second arrow.[6] Upon her eventual arrival in Bath to rejoin her family, Anne overhears Elizabeth urging Mrs. Clay to stay as her companion by assuring her that Anne "is nothing to me, compared with you" (158). Austen records no response to Elizabeth's cruelty, no reference to Anne's thoughts or feelings upon hearing her sister's dismissal of any familial affection. Instead, Elizabeth's comment is immediately followed by Sir Walter's attempts to get Mrs. Clay to stay also and Anne's astute observation of Mrs. Clay's response to praise of her "fine mind." Anne's suspicions regarding Mrs. Clay's matrimonial schemes are heightened when Sir Walter recommends Gowland lotion to Anne based upon its success in lessening Mrs. Clay's freckles. Elizabeth had previously dismissed Anne's warnings about Mrs. Clay as husband hunter by citing her freckles as the guarantee preventing a match between Mrs. Clay and Sir Walter, who cannot abide them.

Anne shoots no second arrow by ruminating over Elizabeth's insult, reliving that moment of unkindness repeatedly. Nor does she get carried away with fear over the possibility of Sir Walter marrying Mrs. Clay. Instead she notes that the "evil of the marriage would be much diminished, if Elizabeth were also to marry. As for herself, she might always command a home with Lady Russell" (159). Anne's refusal to concentrate on the unkindness of her family frees her from great suffering. She has saved herself from "ruminating on the toxic food of our consciousness" through the practice of Right Concentration (Thich Nhat Hanh, *Silence* 52).

Wentworth's reintroduction into Anne's life appears at first only to bring pain, but, as a Buddha figure, Anne faces this painful challenge with calm. Pema Chödrön argues that "those events and people in our lives who trigger our unresolved issues could be regarded as good news" (*When Things Fall Apart* 38). Anne is capable of this kind of open attitude in her refusal to hold grudges or become angry in spite of Wentworth's unkindness. On that first night of his visit to the Musgroves while Anne stays at her sister's to care for her injured nephew, she can't help but compare his choice to ignore her with her own response if circumstances had allowed a renewal of their relationship. When Wentworth declines coming to the cottage the next day, "Anne understood it. He wished to avoid seeing her. He had enquired after her, she found, slightly, as might suit a former slight acquaintance"—this from a former fiancée (84). Austen allows her reader here to imagine clearly the incredible depths of quiet pain Anne endures in this moment as she learns of the charming ease with which the love of her life ignores her. The next day, Mary tells her of Wentworth's comment, "You were so altered he should not have known you again." This leaves Anne with a feeling of "silent, deep mortification" (85). Things only become worse for Anne as the two are constantly thrown together but never move beyond civility, a condition of being "worse than strangers, for they could never become acquainted. It was a perpetual estrangement" (88). Anne hears "the same voice" and discerns "the same mind" but cannot move beyond politeness.

Anne also suffers from being in company completely ignorant to her pain other than the man causing it (though Wentworth's anger blinds him to this), since no one there knows about their brief engagement. Austen highlights Anne's alienation during a gathering at the Musgroves by describing the tears in her eyes and her wish to be unobserved while playing piano so that the others can dance in contrast with the "merry, joyous party" with no one "in higher spirits than Captain Wentworth" (95). Wentworth's boisterousness contrasts strongly with his "studied politeness" with Anne such that "Anne did not wish for more of such looks and speeches. His cold politeness, his ceremonious grace, were worse than any thing" (96). The sadness of Wentworth's absence can be nothing compared to the heartbreak of his nearly daily presence.

When Wentworth eventually shows some signs of warming up to her, she does not obsess over these moments or read too much into them. She feels happy over signs of his respect and perhaps friendship when, for example, he intervenes as her nephew clings to her or when he ensures her a ride with his sister when she is tired from a long walk. Only when there are clear signs of his renewed interest does Anne use her successful Theory of Mind skills to see this, and, even then, she continues calm.

Nowhere can we see Anne's ability to be present and not create narrative that increases suffering as with the many opportunities to watch Wentworth with the flirtatious Henrietta and Louisa. She not only witnesses the interactions of the three but also must entertain her sister and brother-in-law asking her to support their opinions about which sister Wentworth likes better. Anne incorporates Right View throughout, which allows for her successful use of Theory of Mind. Rather than allowing jealousy to color her perceptions, Anne successfully reads Frederick's attentions to Louisa and Henrietta: "while she considered Louisa to be rather the favourite, she could not but think, as far as she might dare to judge from memory and experience, that Captain Wentworth was not in love with either." At the same time, Austen makes clear that this is not wishful thinking, for Anne is willing to acknowledge that the flirtation "might, probably must, end in love with some" (105). Like everyone else, she misreads Wentworth's grief over Louisa's injury due to a fall as coming from affection rather than a sense of guilt since he failed to catch her. However, even here, she does not come to conclusions. She does not ruminate over the inevitability of Wentworth and Louisa's engagement but recognizes it is possible.

Thich Nhat Hanh recommends in following Right Thinking always to ask, "Are you sure?" Anne sees that the answer is no, that she's not sure, so she does not create a scenario for heartbreak that may not happen. Anne's successful engagement with Right Thinking explains why she is the one character to keep a cool head upon Louisa's fall. The irony of the sheltered woman visiting Lyme for the first time directing the ship's captain on how to handle an emergency should not be lost on us. Throughout all of her interactions with Wentworth and the Musgrove sisters, Anne demonstrates Right Action and Right Diligence, never making an effort to undercut Henrietta or Louisa or using her energy in a jealous manner.

To contrast Anne's negotiation of romantic sorrow, we have Benwick, the other sufferer of a broken heart who, unlike Anne, wallows in his grief, purposely shooting the second arrow that first has pierced him in the form of the death of his fiancée. Wentworth "considered his disposition as of the sort which must suffer heavily, uniting very strong feelings with quiet, serious, and retiring manners, and a decided taste for reading, and sedentary pursuits" (118). The description of Benwick could just as easily be of Anne, and she sees the parallel between them immediately, reflecting "he has not, perhaps, a more sorrowing heart than I have" (118).

Like with Mary, in her interactions with Benwick, Anne masters Right Speech. As the others are entertained by Wentworth's and Harville's stories of adventures, "it fell to Anne's lot to be placed rather apart with Captain Benwick; and a very good impulse of her nature obliged her to begin an acquaintance with him" (121). Austen explicitly notes Anne's good intentions: "and besides the persuasion of having given him at least an evening's indulgence in the discussion of subjects, which his usual companions had probably no concern in, she had the hope of being of real use to him in some suggestions as to the duty and benefit of struggling against affliction" (121).

Anne and Benwick's conversation gives Austen an opportunity to discuss consumption as she does in *Northanger Abbey*. We learn that Benwick reads only Romantic poetry, with the titles of poems by Sir Walter Scott and Lord Byron being explicitly given as favorites. Benwick "shewed [*sic*] himself ... intimately acquainted with all the tenderest songs of the one poet, and all the impassioned descriptions of hopeless agony of the other; he repeated, with such tremulous feeling, the various lines which imaged a broken heart, or a mind destroyed by wretchedness" (121). Benwick consumes material meant to exaggerate his heartbreak rather than to mend his heart. Upon hearing about Benwick's reading preferences, Anne recommends more prose such as moral essays, letters, and memoirs "as calculated to rouse and fortify the mind by the highest precepts, and the strongest examples of moral and religious endurances" (123). Here, Anne urges Benwick to use Right Diligence, to make an effort to move beyond his suffering rather than inflicting the second arrow through his reading.

Anne briefly falls into a similar experience with poetry upon a walk where she first recites to herself nature poetry while enjoying the beauty of the autumn day. Upon hearing Wentworth and Louisa flirting, however, "Anne could not immediately fall into quotation again. The sweet scenes of autumn were for a while put by—unless some tender sonnet, fraught with the apt analogy of the declining year, with declining happiness, and the images of youth and hope, and spring, all gone together, blessed her memory." In the very next sentence, though, "she roused herself" (107). So, even as Anne indulges in self-pity in most understandable fashion, the lapse is very short. Unlike Benwick, she does not increase her suffering.

Benwick wallows in his suffering because he receives a kind of pleasure in having his situation observed and remarked upon; he basks in others' pity. During their conversation, Benwick appears "not pained but pleased with this allusion to his situation" and takes Anne's advice "with a shake of the head, and sighs which declared his little faith in the efficacy of any books on grief like his" (122). Anne laughs at herself later for "coming to Lyme, to preach patience and resignation to a young man whom she had never seen before; nor could she help fearing, on more serious reflection, that, like many other great moralists and preachers, she had been eloquent on a point in which her own conduct would ill bear examination" (122). Yet Anne need not fear, for she is indeed an exemplar of Buddha nature.

In one way, Anne appears to fail at achieving Buddhahood, and that is through attachment. After all, she fails to move on romantically after her broken engagement. We humans, as social animals, are prone to romantic attachment; this is timeless and universal. Beyond romantic attachment, though, we are simply prone to attachment: to ego, to material goods, etc. Such attachment creates craving and suffering, however, as we make the object of our concentration our lack and what we cannot have. All of us at some point in our lives have become attached to someone or something we could not have. Capitalism is predicated upon human desire and attachment. If not true love, everyone has wanted a certain car, house, accessory, or fashion trend. Anne is not unusual in her attachment in literature or in life.

Books on dealing with grief, breakups, smart women, and bad choices spill from our modern bookshelves, and perhaps a modern-day version of Anne would have gotten over Wentworth. Anne hints as much when comparing her situation to Benwick's. "I cannot believe his prospects so blighted for ever. He is younger than I am; younger in feeling, if not in fact; younger as a man. He will rally again" (118–9). Similarly, when defending women's constancy to Harville, Anne supports that argument by telling him, "We cannot help ourselves. We live at home, quiet, confined, and our feelings prey upon us. You are forced on exertion. You have always a profession, pursuits, business of some sort or other, to take you back into the world immediately, and continual occupation and change soon weaken impressions" (236). Austen as narrator further implies the truth of this by saying time had not been enough to rid Anne of her attachment; she lacked help in the form of "novelty or enlargement of society," and "no second attachment, the only thoroughly natural, happy, and sufficient cure, at her time of life" tempted her (57). A woman today could have turned her attention to her education or career or expanded her social circle through dating. Perhaps.

Yet Austen undercuts her own argument pretty thoroughly

through Wentworth, a man as active as a man could be as his constant telling of his adventures shows. Those adventures and time do nothing to end his attachment to Anne to whom he confesses his love eight and a half years later. If Anne were to sit on a modern-day therapist's couch, no doubt the therapist would see her eight-and-a-half-year attachment to one man as unhealthy and attempt to cure her. Likely, the therapist would see her as suffering from low self-esteem. Given her family's treatment of her, low self-esteem makes sense as a diagnosis.

But I don't think Anne suffers from low self-esteem, and I don't think there's anything wrong with her attachment. If there were, Austen wouldn't reward her for her feelings. Austen allows us into Anne's head. She never describes herself negatively. She doesn't even blame herself. She doesn't subscribe to the worldview of her father and Elizabeth as we can see, and she asserts herself accordingly, visiting Mrs. Smith, as described below, rather than visiting the great relations over whom her family fawns. She, therefore, also does not subscribe to their view of her. In recognizing how wrong they are about the world, she sees that their dismissal of her also is wrong. Anne is offered the opportunity of a second attachment, but Austen says no man ever lived up to the standard set by Wentworth; Anne esteems herself too much to settle and refuses Charles Musgrove's proposal (which she was clearly right in doing).

Even as she stays attached to the man from her past, she doesn't live in the past. Anne is not trapped by her attachment. It doesn't hinder her from living her life. Her life circumstances themselves are limiting, but this has much more to do with living as a single woman in a stratified patriarchal culture than her continued love of Wentworth. Anne's decisions are not clouded by her love of Wentworth at all. Since, as Thich Nhat Hanh states, "equanimity is an aspect of true love," the equanimity Anne feels throughout proves that her love for Frederick is true and pure (*Heart* 218).

Rather than Anne serving as a lesson on attachment, we get Wentworth who inflicts his own second arrow via attachment to anger. His resentment toward Anne painfully prolongs the years-long separation of the two. He admits to Anne that he "had imagined himself indifferent, when he had only been angry" and recognizes that his "attempts to attach himself to Louisa Musgrove" were disguised "attempts of angry pride" (244). Wentworth admits that this angry attempt could have permanently separated himself from his true love, telling Anne, "I had not considered that my excessive intimacy must have its danger of ill consequence in many ways; and that I had no right to be trying whether I could attach myself to either of the girls, at the risk of raising even an unpleasant report, were there no other ill effects. I had been grossly wrong, and must abide the consequences" (245). When Louisa falls and everyone assumes a near engagement between her and Wentworth, he realizes that he must offer himself to her upon her recovery should she wish it as a matter of honor, making a union with Anne impossible. Even when freed from such an entanglement, Wentworth allows jealousy of Mr. Elliot to prevent his declaration of love to Anne. When comprehending that Anne would have accepted him years earlier if he only had asked, Wentworth acknowledges, "I shut my eyes, and would not understand you, or do you justice.... Six years of separation and suffering might have been spared.... I must learn to brook being happier than I deserve" (249). Fortunately for Wentworth, Austen rewards Anne with their marriage, so Anne earns him his happiness, deserved or not.

The logical match for Anne, of course, the one that should have broken Wentworth's hold on her heart, is Mr. William Elliot, the heir to Kellynch Hall. Though guilty of ill treating Sir Walter before the novel begins, Mr. Elliot appears as the golden child in Bath, winning over everyone with his insight and good breeding. He is the doll of Lady Russell who observes his attention to Anne and eagerly awaits an engagement that would return Anne to her rightful home and to her mother's place as lady of the house.

Beneath the polished golden veneer, however, Mr. Elliot embodies the same corrupt values as Sir Walter and Elizabeth—only worse. And, ultimately, it is her continued attachment to Wentworth that saves her from a disastrous match with Mr. Elliot that would have truly ruined her happiness in the same way her mother's was ruined in marrying Anne's father. It's important to note that her love of Wentworth is only partially responsible for saving her from Mr. Elliot's charms as Anne reflects to herself, "She could never accept him. And it was not only that her feelings were still adverse to any man save one; her judgment on a serious consideration of the possibilities of such a case, was against Mr. Elliot" (172). Anne, due to her adept Theory of Mind, sees Mr. Elliot's lack of authenticity even before she has evidence of it. Because her quest is spiritual, not material, she is not blinded by the prestige and return to her beloved home to be gained by marrying Mr. Elliot but sees him clearly.

Anne's consistently astute Theory of Mind comes from her ability to be friends with her thoughts and feelings.[7] One of Anne's consistent practices in dealing with her feelings is to give herself space and time for awareness. She does not immediately react but steps back and labels, just as a good Buddhist would. This happens at a number of pivotal moments in the book, for example when Wentworth lifts her bothersome, clinging nephew off of her while she attempts to nurse the injured nephew. Anne feels overcome and leaves the room to process. Similarly, after reading Wentworth's letter declaring his love, Anne struggles to process everything, with Austen's narrative voice telling us, "Half an hour's solitude and reflection might have tranquilized her" (240). Pema Chödrön emphasizes the importance of refraining, "not habitually acting out impulsively" (75). "If we immediately entertain ourselves by talking, by acting, by thinking—if there's never any pause—we will never be able to relax" (*When Things Fall Apart* 76). In this way, Anne has the advantage over us since there is no temptation to immediately text her BFF about Wentworth's latest doings or post updates to her status on Facebook depending on whether Wentworth is flirting with Henrietta or Louisa. Anne allows for quiet contemplation of her genuine emotions, or Right Mindfulness.

Yet Thich Nhat Hanh also argues that we need to share our insights in community, something Anne fails to do until she meets the other obvious sufferer within the novel, Mrs. Smith. The introduction of Mrs. Smith is a turning point for Anne in the novel when she overtly rejects the chosen companion of her father and sister, the upper-class Lady Dalrymple, for, as Sir Walter calls her "a Mrs. Smith. A widow Mrs. Smith ... this old lady" (169), referring to a woman in her early thirties. While Anne still does not confide her feelings about Wentworth, with Mrs. Smith, she is able to put her own situation into context, to learn the truth conclusively about Mr. Elliot, and to gain insight into suffering itself.[8] As the Dalai Lama teaches, learning of others' suffering will give us much-needed perspective, which Anne gains from Mrs. Smith.

Austen devotes several pages to Anne's musings over Mrs. Smith's suffering, with Anne wondering over how "neither sickness nor sorrow seemed to have closed her heart or ruined her spirit" (166). Thich Nhat Hanh, as previously mentioned, argues that an open heart—not doctrine—is necessary to enlightenment. Anne concludes that Mrs. Smith's positive disposition comes not from fortitude but from the "power of turning readily from evil to good" and an elasticity of mind that prevents her from brooding (167). Mrs. Smith, to use Buddhist terms, does not inflict a second arrow. Like Anne, she finds joy in doing small things such as talking to her nurse and crafting small items for sale to support herself.

In her conversation with Wentworth about Lyme, Anne articulates her own ability to find joy in suffering. When Wentworth expresses surprise over her desire to see Lyme again after "the horror and distress" of her first visit, Anne replies, "The last few hours were certainly very painful, ... but when pain is over, the remembrance of it often becomes a pleasure. One does not love a place the less for having suffered in it, unless it has been all suffering, nothing but suffering—which was by no means the case with Lyme" (193). Anne understands that suffering is part of experience but need not define an entire experience. She recognizes the first Noble Truth.

In the same way, Anne refuses to regret her choice or her consequent suffering as a result of refusing Wentworth, telling him upon their reconcilement, "I must believe that I was right, much as I suffered from it.... I should have suffered more in continuing the engagement than I did even in giving it up, because I should have suffered in my conscience" (248). Anne understands that suffering is not only inevitable, it also brings us joy. She intuitively understands as well what the Dalai Lama teaches, that motivation is everything, and since her actions sprung from good intentions, she need not feel regret (*Art of Happiness* 533).

The novel closes, of course, with the traditional happy marriage ending. Those who caused Anne the most unhappiness end the story themselves unhappy with Mr. Elliot running off with Mrs. Clay; Elizabeth, who had hopes of Mr. Elliot, a spinster still at age 29; and Sir Walter intelligent enough to be somewhat mortified. Mrs. Smith's fortunes mend thanks to Wentworth's diligence on her behalf in recovering some part of her late husband's estate. Austen writes ironically that Mrs. Smith "might have been absolutely rich and perfectly healthy, and yet be happy. Her spring of felicity was in the glow of her spirits" (253).

Anne's happiness rests "in the warmth of her heart" now happier still with the returned affection of Wentworth. However, importantly, this is not a fairy-tale ending, as the uncertainty that Anne has so successfully navigated from the start of the book follows her in her marriage to the ship's captain.[9] Anne's "dread of a future war" was "all that could dim her sunshine" (253). Anne has married a sailor, not a landed gentleman as happens in all of Austen's previous books. The joy implies the possibility of suffering, yet we need not worry, for Anne Elliot Wentworth is the Buddha. She knows how to find her own happiness.

I no longer aspire to be Anne Elliot. Since we all have the Buddha within, already I am Anne Elliot. I'm very happy about that.

# Conclusion

"If the world is made of stories, stories are not just stories. They teach us what is real, what is possible."
　　　　—David Loy, *The World Is Made of Stories*

"Of course it is happening inside your head, Harry, but
why on earth should that mean that it is not real?"
　　　　—J.K. Rowling, *Harry Potter
　　　　and the Deathly Hallows*

The Buddha taught that suffering is universal. So are stories.
Whether oral or written, every culture has had stories. All major religions, including Buddhism, teach through stories. Evolutionary psychology has asked why stories are universal. Are they a psychological
adaptation? Or do they exist to support an adaptation? What is the
purpose of stories? We can speculate about the purpose. We know
that they can be good for us.

The mere universality of a trait does not qualify it to be called an
adaptation. For something to qualify as an adaptation, it must provide an evolutionary advantage. As mentioned previously, humans
developed a preference for sweet-tasting food because sweet food
is less likely to be poisonous; that makes the preference an evolutionary adaptation because it benefited the species by increasing the
likelihood of survival. Anxiety is a psychological adaptation for similar reasons; being in tune with our environment and wary of threats
benefits the species. Stories must offer a similar benefit to be an
adaptation. It could be instead that stories grew from or to support a
psychological adaptation.

Possibly, stories arose out of the adaptation of anxiety. The
research of Alexa Tullett and colleagues demonstrates that humans
are so keen on creating order and having the world make sense that

we will make up stories, even implausible ones, to offer explanations in order to impose a sense of order. This imposed order pushes back against the anxiety created by randomness. As a species, we don't tolerate randomness well, so we have created science, religion, and folklore to explain everything from floods to sacrifice. For example, we find the story of the flood in the Bible with the narrative of Noah's ark as well as in the oldest surviving piece of literature, *Gilgamesh*. Each version solves the problem of randomness by giving a clear cause for the flood, either God's or the gods' displeasure with humans. The same is true of the bubonic plague that hit Europe during the medieval era. Looking to Christianity for an explanation, literature of the period often invoked the story of Job from the Bible to figure out why they were being punished. After all, if one can locate the source of the suffering to be an action of some kind, one can avoid that action in the future—no more flood or plague. The story can provide a sense of control even if patently false.

Stories and art in general may be a byproduct of our overly developed brains. Brian Boyd calls humans "superpredators" who ended up with spare time once we were able to dominate our environment and not spend all of our time searching for food. Other mammals adapted to use spare time to create spare energy, that is through extra sleep. However, our large brains eat up much of our own energy even when resting, so more sleep as an adaptation makes less sense for humans. Instead art—stories in particular—can work with other adaptations to support us evolutionarily and to exercise our brains to help us navigate socially, which is important because we are social animals.

In fact, Maja Djikic defines fiction by its emphasis on the social world. Unlike nonfiction, fiction can be about anything, ranging from wars to genetics; we get information from nonfiction but not the benefits offered by fiction. Research shows that reading a short story as compared to an essay increases social reasoning. Given the argument that we developed our powerful brains to navigate the social world, stories may have come along to teach us how to navigate better and with lower stakes. If we get it wrong when deciding the butler did it in an Agatha Christie novel, there's no harm done, but we don't want to misjudge character so badly in our daily lives.

Another possible evolutionary purpose of stories is to develop the adaptation of empathy. Reading fiction allows us into the thoughts and feelings of others, allowing for perspective taking that is less easy in everyday life. Unlike daily living, fiction offers direct access to motivation, secrets, and even an understanding of the character's emotions that she may not understand herself. We know Elizabeth Bennet likes Darcy before she does. Recent brain research found that the Harry Potter books build brain health and empathy. Children who read and identified with Harry Potter were more accepting of marginalized groups (Stefanski). And, of course, J.K. Rowling publicly acknowledges her debt to Austen, while those of us who love both Rowling and Austen can't miss the similarities.

It makes sense that fiction can enhance our empathy since our brains process fiction in much the same way as they process reality. Studies involving MRIs show a change in brain activity when carefully reading great works of literature. Michigan State professor Natalie Phillips in conjunction with Stanford's Center for Cognitive and Biological Imaging conducted an experiment in which graduate students working to attain their Ph.D. in literature were asked to read Austen's *Mansfield Park* projected inside an MRI. The students were directed to read first casually and then with close attention as if they were reading for deep analysis. The neuroscientists predicted very little difference, but data demonstrated that the brain lit up when the students were reading carefully as compared to casually. Even parts of the brain responsible for movement and touch were affected, demonstrating scientifically that readers physically responded to the use of their imaginations when reading Austen (Jones).

Other studies confirm these findings. Another placed participants in an MRI while reading a short story and discovered that as people read about a character grasping something the area of their brain that would process physically grasping something themselves lit up. If a character moved to a new scene, the part of the brain that deals with analyzing visual scenes became active. As we read fiction, our brains simulate the events about which we are reading. Similar responses were found when reading poetry. The poetry of John Keats, an early nineteenth-century Romantic writing around the same time as Austen, affects parts of the brain that process not only reading but those usually activated by music, introspection, and memory (Djikic and Oatley 499–500).

Connecting quite literally in a physical manner to literature enhances the brain's ability to empathize with those encountered in everyday life. This has societal consequences as further research using MRI technology demonstrates that the septal area of the brain, which is associated with prosocial behavior and the helping of others, lights up as well when empathy is engaged (Morelli).

The Greeks seem to have understood this intuitively, inscribing above library doors "medicine for the soul." In 1916, Samuel Crothers coined the term *bibliotherapy*, referring to the idea of reading as a cure (Pehrsson and McMillen). Hospital librarians in the United Kingdom began using books as healing tools in the 1920s (Brewster). One of the early researchers of bibliotherapy described six objectives for the practice. Reading fiction

- allows the reader to see that she is not alone in having a particular problem;
- demonstrates there is more than one solution to the problem;
- provides access to the motives of the characters within their defined context;
- humanizes and makes more concrete moral values;
- offers facts that might help in solving the problem experienced by the reader; and
- inspires the reader to realistically face the problem faced by the character [Brewster, "Medicine" 115].

Such healing reading generally requires guidance. Various programs have existed within the UK for the last few decades, including a 2016 initiative called Reading Well, created by the Reading Agency. This particular program created reading lists for adolescents in response to concern about mounting mental health problems for that age group. Librarians and health professionals provided reading suggestions ranging from self-help to literature. The program encompasses the three varieties of bibliotherapy: self-help, developmental (for children), and creative (fiction).

Bibliotherapy has demonstrated proven results in helping with anxiety and depression. Studies document positive results such as improved self-awareness, empathy, knowledge of other cultures, appreciation of one's own ethnicity and cultural identity, clarification of developing values, better coping and problem-solving skills, and opportunities for fruitful discussions in organized programs that include group participation (Pehrsson 403). And reading has the obvious benefits of increasing vocabulary and literacy. With this goal, one program in Liverpool concentrates on the classics with a leader reading aloud in order to build confidence with readers who would never feel they could tackle Dickens or Austen on their own (Brewster, "Prescription" 404). When combined with traditional therapy, bibliotherapy extends the time that clients engage in self-reflection beyond the therapy session with the counselor (Levitt 329).

The effects can be even more long lasting. Studies found that reading fiction initially prompted readers to have a greater sense of possible ways to respond to problems and to increase possible choice options consistent with their values. With time, readers reflected upon their experience or even re-read leading to purposeful personal development as they used these stories as guidance moving forward. The process was active with readers constructing meaning and organizing narrative selectively based upon their personal experience (Levitt et al. 347).

The healing from bibliotherapy involves four components: identification, catharsis, insight, and projection or universalization. The reader needs to be able to identify with the main character or events, either through similarity of gender, socio-economic background, ethnicity, culture, or ways of thinking and feeling. There must be a connection. This is why the chosen reading material matters; the potential for identification is important.

With this identification, catharsis is possible. As the character faces challenges and succeeds in overcoming them, the reader's own emotions are heightened and released; it's a purging of emotion, something Aristotle argued centuries ago as an essential ingredient of tragedy. Reading about the experiences of a character with whom we identify allows us to feel those strong emotions at a distance and, therefore, feel safe while exploring the difficult thoughts and feelings we are processing ourselves. Identification and catharsis allow for insight, an emotional awareness that the readers can address and solve the problem in their own lives.

The last component is variably called *projection* or *universalization*. The readers can now picture a better future and feel a sense of optimism while also feeling connected to the larger world with the recognition that they are not alone in their suffering (Stewart and Ames). This connection is thanks to the hippocampus operating so that we identify with fictional characters and believe ourselves transported spatially into a narrative world (Cheetham et al.).

Such transportation can occur across cultures and time. We experience the benefits of reading fiction and make those connections in spite of what seem like obvious differences between our own lives and those of fictional characters. For example, Peruvian writer Mario Vargas Llosa, who won the Nobel Prize for Literature in 2010, cites the nineteenth-century French novel *Madame Bovary* as healing his suicide ideation. At a time when he considered suicide himself, he read about the main character's painful death from poisoning herself, which put his own suffering into perspective and beat back the urge to kill himself (Detrixhe 64). Less dramatically, in a survey of English majors who graduated from my university, several noted that they were surprised by the benefits of reading older British literature; they had not expected to see themselves and feel connected to characters and situations from centuries before. Doing so made them feel less lonely.

This is the purpose of bibliotherapy: allowing perspective taking and connection so that we can understand the human condition, develop empathy, feel less lonely, and have confidence to solve our own problems. "Such developments occur in unique individual ways, and change is not a result of explicit intentions to make the reader think or act in certain ways. The effects of literature and other art forms rather take place because of their nondirective influence, opening to change by presenting a multitude of possible selves" (Punzi and Hagen 50).

Or as Sir Philip Sidney put it in the English Renaissance, literature can do what other disciplines of learning cannot. Stories both teach and delight. We often are learning without realizing it thanks to our pleasure in reading, and authors are writing stories that may be teaching though that was not their conscious purpose.

A fair amount of recent press coverage has examined reading and mental health, with Austen's name appearing pretty often. A June 2015 *The New Yorker* piece called "Can Reading Make You Happier?" by Ceridwen Dovey answers that question with an introduction to bibliotherapy. The article centers around the practice of Ella Berthoud and Susan Elderkin, friends who met as Cambridge University undergraduates and began the practice of prescribing books to each other to heal emotional wounds.

Berthoud, an artist and art teacher, and Elderkin, a writer and writing teacher, began their bibliotherapy practice in England's School of Life and have now published a book titled *The Novel Cure, from Abandonment to Zestlessness: 751 Books to Cure What Ails You.* Those who seek bibliotherapy fill out a questionnaire asking about reading habits and what is troubling in their lives at that moment. In return, they get reading lists. Berthoud and Elderkin's book has the following Austen recommendations. To cure arrogance, read *Pride and Prejudice*; for being a daddy's girl, read *Emma*; and for looking for Mr. or Mrs. Right, read both. Two other Austen novels make top-10 lists: *Persuasion* to get your female partner interested in fiction and *Sense and Sensibility* to drown the sound of snoring.

While Austen didn't write six novels as bibliotherapy textbooks, we know via *Northanger Abbey* that she understood the value of reading and that the reading material mattered. She explores that same argument less forcefully in all of her novels.

In *Pride and Prejudice*, there is much discussion of books, with Bingley apologizing for the lack of books in his own library and Mr. Darcy proclaiming, "I cannot comprehend the neglect of a family library" after noting that the one at Pemberley has been the work of many generations (26). When debate arises over the accomplishments of women, Darcy adds, "and to this she must yet add something more substantial, in the improvement of her mind by extensive reading" (27). Readers are to remember this later when Miss Bingley "quite exhausted by the attempt to be amused with her own book, which she had only chosen because it was the second volume of his" yawns and puts it aside (37). Mr. Collins also reads, refusing to touch the novel that is clearly from a circulating library and choosing Fordyce's *Sermons*, reading it in a monotonous voice that leads to Lydia interrupting him three pages in. There are many references to Mary reading and basing her moralisms upon that reading, but we don't get titles, and Austen describes Mary's responses in a tone of sarcasm to indicate no deep knowledge.

*Sense and Sensibility* mentions specific authors as well with Edward teasing Marianne that if she came into money, she would buy all the books of James Thomson, William Cowper, and Sir Walter Scott—all writers whose works appeal to emotions and all poets (though Scott is well known for his novels). Marianne fears that Edward will make a poor husband given his unspirited performance reading Cowper aloud. Willoughby, of course, agrees with all of her opinions on great literature with Cowper's and Scott's names appearing yet again, and he reads with the sensibility that Edward lacks. Marianne uses her reading to deepen her misery rather than alleviate it after Willoughby leaves, reading only the same books that the two looked at together.

Mr. Knightley laments Emma's lack of reading to Mrs. Weston.

Emma draws up excellent reading lists and never follows through. The book that she compiles is of riddles and leads to much mischief. And Emma uses the notion of reading literature in order to snobbishly denigrate Harriet's love interest when Harriet tells her that Mr. Martin reads agricultural reports. However, as readers ourselves, we see that Mr. Martin's taste is superior to Harriet's, as he has read Oliver Goldsmith's *The Vicar of Wakefield*, a canonical novel still taught today, but not the Gothic romances Harriet mentions.

Edmund helps in Fanny's education and development from the start in *Mansfield Park* by recommending books. Fanny mirrors this with her own sister upon returning home, using her funds to join the circulating library and sharing her love of reading with Susan. We get a glimpse into her reading habits when Edmund visits the East room (Fanny's little white attic) and teases her about taking a visit to China with Lord Macartney or perhaps reading George Crabbe, famous for his pastoral poetry, or Samuel Johnson, a writer so central to the eighteenth century that it has sometimes been referred to as the age of Johnson. Johnson compiled the first reliable English dictionary and published a series of periodicals, including a famous piece titled "On Fiction" where he argued for the necessary moral purpose of literature. Henry Crawford's reading of a speech from Shakespeare meets its purpose of capturing Fanny's attention, though she is greatly reluctant to offer it, and Edmund notes that Shakespeare is familiar enough to all that he is widely quoted. Of course a book—the play *Lovers' Vows*—proves a great catalyst of action and a measure of morality.

*Persuasion*'s opening sentence is about reading—or lack thereof: "Sir Walter Elliot, of Kellynch Hall, in Somersetshire, was a man who, for his own amusement, never took up any book but the Baronetage," which is referred to as "the book of books" in describing Elizabeth to demonstrate how she shares her father's shallow values (35). Captain Benwick, like Marianne, uses poetry to extend his grief, leading to Anne's suggestion that he broaden his reading to include "works of our best moralists, such collections of the finest letters, such memoirs of characters of worth and suffering," as might "rouse and fortify the mind by the highest precepts" (122). However, in her argument with Captain Harville about who is more constant in love, men or women, Anne applies "no reference to examples in books. Men have had every advantage of us in telling their own story" (237).

Having covered reading in *Northanger Abbey* extensively in that chapter, I won't repeat myself except to note that Austen uses that novel to make a clear argument in favor of reading and reading well. But the short summaries above show that she is making that same argument throughout all her novels. Austen would never have used the term *bibliotherapy*, but she knew that novels had the power to form and demonstrate character, meant in the broadest sense of the pun.

Not surprisingly, Austen's works have been a staple of bibliotherapy going back to World War I. The American Library Association's "War Service Library" program collected over 100 million books and magazines between 1917 and 1920 to distribute to soldiers. Copies of Shakespeare and Austen still exist from that effort. In World War II, Penguin Books in 1942 selected 120 titles to distribute to soldiers, which included *Northanger Abbey* and *Persuasion* (Barchas).

Perhaps the most famous example is a fictional one. Writer Rudyard Kipling captured Austen as bibliotherapy in his story "The Janeites." The short story, published in magazines in May 1924, takes place shortly after the war has ended with veterans sharing cleaning duties at a Masonic Lodge. Recounting his wartime experience, the character Humberstall shares being part of the Janeites, a group of soldiers who bonded over reading Austen. When asked about Austen, he responds, "Jane? Why, she was a little old maid 'oo'd written 'alf a dozen books about a hundred years ago. 'Twasn't as if there was anythin' to 'em, either. I know. I had to read 'em. They weren't adventurous, nor smutty, nor what you'd call even interestin." He expands by explaining, "I mean that 'er characters was no use! They was only just like people you run across any day." Yet the very commonness of these characters make them ones with which he and his fellow soldiers could identify, which Humberstall obviously did as he goes on to talk about Henry Tilney, for example, as if he were someone he had met personally. Reading Austen bonds these men at a time when loneliness, fear, and the unknown were paramount. And, unlike his earlier dismissal, Humberstall tells his fellow veterans that "I read all her six books now for pleasure 'tween times in the shop; an' it brings it all back—down to the smell of the glue-paint on the screens. You take it from me, Brethren, there's no one to touch Jane when you're in a tight place. Gawd bless 'er, whoever she was" (n.p.).

Kipling's use of Austen for the story came not merely from knowing about her books being distributed to soldiers, though, for

Austen's novels had proven personally therapeutic for him. Visiting Bath in 1915, Kipling reread all of Austen's novels expressing his increased admiration for her. In 1917, his son John was reported killed in the war. The diary of Kipling's wife reflects that he was reading Austen aloud to her and their daughter in the months after John's death "to their great delight"—an echo of Sidney's "teach and delight" and the power of literature to offer solace (Lewis and Kieffer).

The seminal work that all literary critics must cite when working on eighteenth-century novels is Ian Watt's *The Rise of the Novel*. There, Watt's defining characteristic of what he argues is a new genre is realism, and he concludes his book by pointing to Austen as best at capturing real life. Her contribution is, to use the phrase of Kipling's Humberstall, to create characters who were only "just like people you run across any day," that is, characters with whom we can identify.

What novels do as an art form is what humans do every day: We create stories and live that as our reality. Unfortunately, our brains do not have a hidden Austen who will create the promised happy ending. The fictional reality our mind produces generally creates our suffering.

Buddhism finds truth in shining the bright light on harmful stories, and that allows us to live in reality and, thereby, find nirvana. Buddhist scholar Robert Thurman has called the Buddha "the ultimate realist." This is not a rejection of stories. The Buddha taught via stories. Rather, to live in reality is to recognize that we are creating stories and not to get trapped in them. In the same way that it matters what fiction we read and how, it matters to recognize the fiction of our own lives and to choose reality, or suchness, as Mahayana Buddhism calls it. With the recognition that we operate in a world of signs, we can escape signs. We can, as *The Diamond Sutra* teaches, use the word rose and realize that we are only using a word, a sign, but know that the reality of the rose is empty.

Fictional stories allow for empathy and connection to alleviate suffering, but Buddhism allows for awakening to the stories we live every day that can make us suffer or not. The Eightfold Path creates the possibility of awakening to our own stories—the cause of suffering—so that we can narrate our world differently or better yet, escape narration, at least for a while.

Much of this comes from the most popularly studied aspect of the Eightfold Path: mindfulness gained via the practice of meditation. Studies of dedicated meditators show brain changes in much the same way that careful reading of fiction does. Changes occur in the parietal lobe, which is activated during times of loneliness. Meditators show a decrease in activation and feel more connected. While depression shrinks the hippocampus, it shows signs of growth for meditators (Fayed). Like stories, meditation also enhances empathy, changing the neural circuitry that is activated during empathy. Meditation has been shown to reduce the stress response to adversity or a sense of threat, allowing room for empathy and compassion (Mascaro et al.). This leads to more pro-social behavior.

If evolution teaches us how to read the world for the species to survive, and bibliotherapy teaches us to read to be happy as individuals, Buddhism teaches us to read so that all may be happy. Thurman says it's our duty to be happy. To take the vow to be a *bodhisattva* is to take the vow to be happy, for we cannot help others with their suffering if we continue to suffer ourselves.

Ultimately, then, both Austen and the Buddha teach the same things: not to get caught by stories and that our duty is to be happy. If we are happy, we are good to each other, and since we are all connected, my happiness is your happiness and yours is mine.

# Epilogue

It took me five years to write this book. Life was busy and challenging. I taught a lot of extra classes to make up for the loss of income due to divorce. I cared for a close family member who struggled with chronic illness. Both of my parents had dementia. Both died. With other Floridians, I dealt with tropical storms and hurricanes. My ceiling collapsed—right on top of me. (And I don't care what my insurance company claims; of course it was because of the hurricane.) Like all of us, I'm living through a global pandemic.

I write that not to complain but to share that I'm more at peace and happier than I've been in my life—yes, during the global pandemic.

The Buddha and Austen were right about suffering and the cure for suffering.

Where I see this clearly in my own life is in my mother's dementia and death. Mom was still high functioning when she had a TIA on July 27, 2019. Ironically, I had just finished reading the preface to this book at a gathering of writing friends in my home when I got the call that Mom was in the emergency room. My daughter, then 15, and I rushed over while my amazing friends cleaned up the party and got my daughter's friend home.

That time in the emergency room is a fond memory. Mom was the most cheerful, optimistic, and loving person, qualities enhanced by her dementia because dementia had released her from anxiety. We talked animatedly and joked. We were happy to be together. Her test results were fine, so we took her back to the assisted living facility in the early morning hours of July 28. I tucked her into bed, and we said goodnight.

The major stroke came a few hours later, and we would never have another conversation. She was still alert when I saw her that morning, but she could no longer speak. I spent five days with her at the hospital, and she died under hospice care back in her room at Arden Courts on August 15. I sat by her side singing to her.

That, too, is a bittersweet memory as I felt honored to guide her through a peaceful death.

Mom was my best friend, and I suffered. But I'd learned to suffer, and, thanks to understanding impermanence, I knew my suffering wouldn't last forever. I will always miss Mom, but I know deeply that she is still with me, that she endures.

Even more importantly, Austen and Buddhism taught me during Mom's life to let go of the fear that overtook me with her diagnosis of dementia. That fear built a wall between us. Releasing the fear allowed me a closeness with her stronger than any I had experienced—which is saying a lot given the lifelong closeness of our relationship. Dementia allows a person to be truly present, and I allowed myself to be truly present with Mom. The last part of her life was our happiest together for which I have great gratitude.

Anecdotally, then, I assure you that mindfully releasing the narrative works. Austen gives us happy endings. Buddhism teaches us that we can create happiness for ourselves and others.

# Chapter Notes

## Introduction

1. Even psychologically, the eighteenth century argued for moderation. In *Essay*, Locke claimed that reason and imagination were on a continuum with the possibility of madness if one lost grounding in reason.

2. For more on the rise of the novel, see Ian Watt's *The Rise of the English Novel: Studies in Defoe, Richardson, and Fielding* (University of California Press, 2001); Michael McKeon's *The Origins of the English Novel, 1600–1740* (Johns Hopkins University Press, 2002); Lennard Davis's *Factual Fictions: The Origins of the English Novel* (University of Pennsylvania Press, 1996).

3. Excellent discussions of Austen's use of Theory of Mind can be found in Lisa Zunshine's *Why We Read Fiction: Theory of Mind and the Novel* (Ohio State University Press, 2006) and "Mind Plus: Sociocognitive Pleasures of Jane Austen's Novels," *Studies in the Literary Imagination*, vol. 42, no. 2, 2009, pp. 103–23.

## Chapter One

1. Maner and Kenrick have similar findings, claiming that social anxiety disorder "is one of the most prevalent mental disorders, ranking third among all psychiatric conditions (lifetime prevalence 13.3%; Kessler et al., 1994). Anxiety disorders cost the American health care system approximately $68.1 billion annually (Greenberg et al., 1999). Among the anxiety disorders, SAD accounts for a substantial percentage of those costs" (126). Jon K. Maner and Douglas T. Kenrick, "When Adaptations Go Awry: Functional and Dysfunctional Aspects of Social Anxiety," *Social Issues and Policy Review*, vol. 4, no. 1, 2010, pp. 111–42, at 126.

2. Felicia Pratto, "Sexual Politics: The Gender Gap in the Bedroom, the Cupboard, and the Cabinet," *Sex, Power, Conflict: Evolutionary and Feminist Perspectives*, eds. David M. Buss and Neil M. Malamuth (Oxford University Press, 1996), pp. 179–230.

## Chapter Two

1. "When the Chinese describe the Yang aspects of the cosmos it was male and fiery, rockets and explosions; the Yin was female and earthy, Jane Austen and cream teas." Daniel Keown, *The Spark in the Machine: How the Science of Acupuncture Explains the Mysteries of Western Medicine* (Singing Dragon, 2014), p. 89.

2. The language and order here is from Thich Nhat Hanh's *The Heart of the Buddha's Teaching: Transforming Suffering into Peace, Joy, and Liberation* (Broadway Books, 1999).

## Chapter Three

1. Erin Stackle notes that Elizabeth's ego blocks her ability to perceive well. "Elizabeth's blindness is inveterate. She tends to think well of those who please her or flatter her vanity, and badly of those who pain her or challenge her confidence. But she remains convinced that she is an excellent judge of character, and continues confidently asserting her judgments to vanishingly rare opposition" (205). Erin Stackle, "Jane Austen's Aristotelian Proposal: Sometimes Falling in Love Is Better Than a Beating," *Philosophy and Literature*, vol. 41, no. 1A, 2017, pp. 195–212.

2. Richard Dawson notes that humility is required to see that someone else's assumptions may be right so that conversation can be effective (199). Richard Dawson, "'The Power of Conversation': Jane Austen's *Persuasion* and Hans-Georg Gadamer's Philosophical Hermeneutics," *Fictional Characters, Real Problems: The Search for Ethical Content in Literature*, ed. Garry L. Hagberg (Oxford: Oxford University Press, 2016), pp. 194–208.

3. Michael Giffin argues that the leitmotif of volume one of the novel is Elizabeth telling Jane "one knows exactly what to think" and that for volume two, it is the reversal of this very idea—one does not know what to think (102). Michael Giffin, *Jane Austen and Religion: Salvation and Society in Georgian England* (Palgrave Macmillan, 2002).

4. David Simpson argues that learning successful conversation is a theme in all of Austen's novels and this knowledge must be tempered by the use of writing. "The power of the voice, in Austen's world, must be disciplined by and tested against the power of writing, embodied in books and letters and assembled personal testimonies" (n.p.). David Simpson, "The Cult of 'Conversation,'" *Raritan: A Quarterly Review*, vol. 16, no. 4, 1997, pp. 75–85.

5. I wrote previously about the intrasexual competition in *Pride and Prejudice*. Kathryn Duncan and Michael Stasio, "An Evolutionary Approach to Jane Austen: Prehistoric Preferences in *Pride and Prejudice*," *Studies in the Novel*, vol. 39, no. 2, 2007, pp. 133–46.

6. Rachel Brownstein aptly notes this is an attempt to protect her own ego. Rachel Brownstein, "Jane Austen: Irony and Authority," *Women's Studies*, vol. 15, 1988, pp. 57–70.

## Chapter Five

1. A recent study also proves Austen's claim about Emma's lack of likability incorrect. Readers clearly identify Emma as a conventional protagonist with whom they can identify. See Joseph Carroll, John A. Johnson, Jonathan Gottschall, and Daniel Kruger, "Graphing Jane Austen: Agonistic Structure in British Novels of the Nineteenth Century," *Scientific Study of Literature*, vol. 2, no. 1, 2012, pp. 1–24.

2. Timothy Peltason includes an analysis of Mr. Woodhouse in his article about Austen's novels; he argues that Mr. Woodhouse is representative among characters throughout Austen's work who are "deficient in imaginative consciousness" (621) to demonstrate how Austen argues for the "value of a full and busy mind" (629). See "Mind and Mindlessness in Jane Austen," *The Hudson Review*, vol. 67, no. 4, 2015, pp. 609–33.

## Chapter Six

1. Clair Hughes reminds readers that the novel's setting, Bath, "had lately undergone a frenzied building and rebuilding program and was now an elegant city full of shops for the consuming middle classes, and of places to display their purchases" (187). Clair Hughes, "Talk about Muslin: Jane Austen's *Northanger Abbey*," *Textile: Cloth and Culture*, vol. 4, no. 2, 2006, pp. 184–97.

2. "Mrs. Allen's and Isabella's obsession with clothes and headgear is not only boringly self-centered for others to listen to (although entertaining to read about), but indicates a

lack of discernment—'a displacement of concern'" (Tanner 60). Tony Tanner, *Jane Austen* (Harvard University Press, 1986). "When Mrs. Allen hears of the General's brutality to Catherine, she deplores it in the same breath as she tells Catherine that she has had "that frightful great rent in my best Mechlin [a kind of lace] so charmingly mended (Austen 1995 1798)" (Hughes 196).

3. Maggie Lane also argues that the General's epicureanism is symbolic of his moral shortcomings in "The French Bread at Northanger." *Persuasions*, no. 20, 1998, pp. 135–45.

4. For more on Gothic excess, see Susan Allen Ford's "A Sweet Creature's Horrid Novels: Gothic Reading in *Northanger Abbey*," *Persuasions: The Jane Austen Journal On-Line*, vol. 33, no. 1, 2012.

5. See Roger E. Moore, "The Hidden History of *Northanger Abbey*: Jane Austen and the Dissolution of the Monasteries," *Religion & Literature*, vol. 43, no. 1, 2011, pp. 55–80, and Mary Spongeberg, "History, Fiction, and Anachronism: *Northanger Abbey*, the Tudor 'Past' and the 'Gothic' Present," *Textual Practice*, vol. 26, no. 4, 2012, pp. 631–48.

6. For example, see Miriam Rheingold Fuller, "'Let me go, Mr. Thorpe; Isabella, do not hold me!': *Northanger Abbey* and the Domestic Gothic," *Persuasions*, no. 32, 2010, pp. 90–104.

## Chapter Seven

1. A version of this chapter was printed under the title "Powerful Not Poor: Reading Fanny Price from a Buddhist Perspective," *Studies in Religion and the Enlightenment*, vol. 2, no. 1, 2020.

2. Amy J. Pawl argues that the "cardinal Austen sin [is] selfishness" (315) in "Fanny Price and the Sentimental Genealogy of *Mansfield Park*," *Eighteenth-Century Fiction*, vol. 16, no. 2, 2004, pp. 287–315. Tony Tanner says of *Mansfield Park* that "it is a book about the difficulty of preserving true moral consciousness amid the selfish manoeuvring and jostling of society" (171).

3. Linda Troost and Sayre Greenfield's "A History of the Fanny Wars," *Persuasions*, no. 36, 2014, pp. 5–33 best captures the many negative opinions of poor Fanny through careful documentation of reactions to Fanny throughout the centuries.

4. In *Jane Austen and the Theatre* (Cambridge University Press, 2002), Penny Gay calls her a "true Christian heroine" (118).

5. An aspiring *bodhisattva* can invoke the "four great *bodhisattvas*—Avalokiteshvara (Regarder of the Cries of the World), Manjushri (Great Understanding), Samantabhadra (Universal Goodness), and Kshitigarbha (Earth Store)." Thich Nhat Hanh, "*Dharma* Talk: Cultivating Our *Bodhisattva* Qualities," *The Mindfulness Bell*, no. 22, 1998, https://www.mindfulnessbell.org/archive/2016/01/dharma-talk-cultivating-our-bodhisattva-qualities-2?rq=dharma%20talk%20bodhisattva.

6. Anne K. Mellor and Alex L. Wilson accuse Fanny of "intense masochism" (228). I disagree. As an aspiring *bodhisattva*, Fanny does not court or enjoy pain; rather, she understands how to manage it and does not flee from the inevitable suffering in life. "Austen's Fanny Price, Grateful Negroes, and Stockholm Syndrome," *Persuasions*, vol. 34, 2012, pp. 222–35.

7. For more on the slave trade in *Mansfield Park*, see Sarah Parry, "Mansfield Park vs. Sotherton Court: Social Status and the Slave Trade," *Persuasions*, vol. 35, no. 1, 2014; John Wiltshire, "Decolonising *Mansfield Park*," *Essays in Criticism: A Quarterly Journal of Literary Criticism*, vol. 53, no. 4, 2003, pp. 303–22; Ruth Perry, "Austen and Empire: A Thinking Woman's Guide to British Imperialism," *Persuasions*, vol. 16, 1994, pp. 95–106; Laurie Kaplan, "The Rushworths of Wimpole Street," *Persuasions*, vol. 33, 2011, pp. 202–14; and Stephanie Howard-Smith, "'Hearty Fow Children': The Penrhyns, Pugs, and *Mansfield Park*," *Persuasions*, vol. 35, 2013, pp. 191–99.

8. In *No Time to Lose*, Pema Chödrön states, "Expecting lasting happiness from a shift

in outer circumstances will always disappoint us" (735). Pema Chödrön, *When Things Fall Apart: Heart Advice for Difficult Times* (Shambhala, 2011, ebook).

9. Dawn Potter believes "among all the major characters in *Mansfield Park*, she is the only one who studies her own personality" (612). Dawn Potter, "In Defense of Dullness or Why Fanny Price Is My Favorite Austen Heroine," *Sewanee Review*, vol. 116, no. 4, 2008, 611–18. Pema Chödrön notes that such powers of self reflection are essential for enlightenment: "In all kinds of situations, we can find out what is true simply by studying ourselves in every nook and cranny" (*When Things Fall Apart* 149).

10. Jane McDonnell notes that Edmund is the only character in *Mansfield Park* to foster her intellectual growth and to esteem her sensitivity and "spirituality." "'A Little Spirit of Independence': Sexual Politics and the Bildungsroman in *Mansfield Park*," *Novel*, vol. 17, no. 3, 1984, pp. 197–214. For another defense of Edmund's education of Fanny, see Marija Reiff, "The 'Fanny Price Wars': Jane Austen's Enlightenment Feminist and Mary Wollstonecraft," *Women's Studies*, vol. 45, 2016, pp. 275–90.

## *Chapter Eight*

1. Mona Scheuermann notes that *Persuasion* is the grimmest of Austen's novels: "There is a strong sense of mortality in *Persuasion* which has not been obvious in earlier Austen novels. Things change; people change. People age, they decay, they get sick, they even die" (143).

2. See Tara Brach, *True Refuge: Finding Peace and Freedom in Your Own Awakened Heart* (Bantam, 2012).

3. Jeff Nunokawa points out this kind of uncertainty is a pattern in Austen: "As much as the novels affirm the continuing tenure of the social world at large, they decline to offer it to any of the particular characters who collectively constitute it" (3). "Speechless in Austen," *Differences: A Journal of Feminist Cultural Studies*, vol. 16, no. 2, 2005, pp. 1–36.

4. S. Chetty et al., "Stress and Glucocorticoids Promote Oligodendrogenesis in the Adult Hippocampus," *Molecular Psychiatry*, vol. 19, 2014, pp. 175–83.

5. Mona Scheuermann interprets the scene similarly in *Reading Jane Austen*.

6. Free indirect discourse refers to a style of third-person narration that allows readers to get inside characters' heads that simultaneously captures the characters' point of view or style of thinking. Austen was a pioneer of the method. For more on Austen's style, see John Sutherland's *How to Read a Novel: A User's Guide* (St. Martin's Griffin, 2007).

7. Lisa Zunshine refers to the scene in Molland's when Anne sees Wentworth in Bath as the best example Austen creates of a character's astute use of Theory of Mind. *See Why We Read Fiction: Theory of Mind and the Novel* (The Ohio State University Press, 2006).

8. K.K. Collins argues that Mrs. Smith is a problematic character with no real purpose, but I see her as thematically important in understanding suffering. See "Mrs. Smith and the Morality of *Persuasion*," *Nineteenth-Century Fiction*, vol. 30, no. 3, 1975, pp. 383–87.

9. Valerie Shaw believes that Anne and Wentworth gain "a maturity earned by the suffering they have both endured" (301) but not necessarily a tidy happy ending, arguing that "Anne Elliot does not marry into safety and sameness, but into risk." The ending's "impulse is not towards stasis and calm, but towards movement and change" (301). "Jane Austen's Subdued Heroines," *Nineteenth-Century Fiction*, vol. 30, no. 3, 1975, pp. 281–303.

# Bibliography

American Psychological Association. "Anxiety." http://www.apa.org/topics/anxiety/.

Anxiety and Depression Association of America. "Facts and Statistics." https://adaa. org/about-adaa/press-room/facts-statistics.

Aronson, Harvey B. *Buddhist Practice on Western Ground: Reconciling Eastern Ideals and Western Psychology*. Shambhala, 2004.

Auerbach, Emily. *Searching for Jane Austen*. University of Wisconsin Press, 2004.

Austen, Jane. *Emma*. Ed. Alistair M. Duckworth. Bedford/St. Martin's, 2002.

———. *Mansfield Park*. Ed. James Kinsley. Oxford University Press, 2003.

———. *Northanger Abbey*. 2nd edition. Ed. Claire Grogan. Broadview, 2002.

———. *Persuasion*. Ed. D.W. Harding. Penguin, 1985.

———. *Pride and Prejudice*. Ed. Donald Gray. W.W. Norton, 2001.

———. *Sense and Sensibility*. Ed. Kathleen James-Cavan. Broadview, 2001.

Austen, Jane, and Seth Grahame-Smith. *Pride and Prejudice and Zombies*. Quirk Books, 2009.

Austin, Michael. *Useful Fictions: Evolution, Anxiety, and the Origins of Literature*. University of Nebraska Press, 2010.

Bajerski, Michał. "'I Understand You, So I'll Not Hurt You with My Irony': Correlations between Irony and Emotional Intelligence." *Psychology of Language and Communication*, vol. 20, no. 3, 2016, pp. 235–54.

Barash, David P. *Buddhist Biology: Ancient Eastern Wisdom Meets Modern Western Science*. Oxford University Press, 2014.

Barchas, Janine. "G.I. Jane: Austen Goes to War." *JHU Press Blog*, April 23, 2014. https://jhupress.wordpress.com/2014/04/23/g-i-jane-austen-goes-to-war/.

Beck, Charlotte Joko. *Everyday Zen: Love and Work*. Ed. Steve Smith. Harper San Fransisco, 1989.

Berthoud, Ella, and Susan Elderkin. *The Novel Cure, from Abandonment to Zestlessness: 751 Books to Cure What Ails You*. Penguin, 2014.

Boyd, Brian. "Jane Meet Charles: Literature, Evolution, and Human Nature." *Philosophy and Literature*, vol. 22, no. 1, 1998, pp. 1–30.

Brach, Tara. *True Refuge: Finding Peace and Freedom in Your Own Awakened Heart*. Bantam, 2012.

Brewster, Liz. "Books on Prescription: Bibliotherapy in the United Kingdom." *Journal of Hospital Librarianship*, vol. 9, 2009, pp. 399–407.

———. "Medicine for the Soul: Bibliotherapy." *Aplis*, vol. 21, no. 3, 2008, pp. 115–19.

Brontë, Charlotte. Excerpt of letter to George Lewes, January 12, 1848. https://pemberley.com/janeinfo/janeart.html.

Brooks, Alison Wood. "Get Excited: Reappraising Pre-Performance Anxiety as Excitement." *Journal of Experimental Psychology*, vol. 143, no. 3, 2014, pp. 1144–58.

Brownstein, Rachel. "Jane Austen: Irony and Authority." *Women's Studies*, vol. 15, 1988, pp. 57–70.

Carroll, Joseph, John A. Johnson, Jonathan Gottschall, and Daniel Kruger. "Graphing Jane Austen: Agonistic Structure in British Novels of the Nineteenth Century." *Scientific Study of Literature*, vol. 2, no. 1, 2012, pp. 1–24.

Cheetham, Marcus, Jürgen Hänggi, and Lutz Jancke. "Identifying with Fictive Characters: Structural Brain Correlates of the Personality Trait Fantasy." *Scan*, vol. 9, 2014, pp. 1836–44.

Chetty, S., Aaron R. Friedman, Kereshmeh Taravosh-Lahn, Elizabeth D. Kirby, Christian Mirescu, Fuzheng Guo, Danna Krupik, Andrea Nicholas, Anna Geraghty, Amrita Krishnamurthy, Meng-Ko Tsai, David Covarrubias, Alana Wong, Darlene Francis, Robert M. Sapolsky, Theo D. Palmer, David Pleasure, and Daniela Kaufer. "Stress and Glucocorticoids Promote Oligodendrogenesis in the Adult Hippocampus." *Molecular Psychiatry*, vol. 19, 2014, pp. 175–83.

Chödrön, Pema. *No Time to Lose: A Timely Guide to the Way of the* Bodhisattva. Shambhala, 2017. ebook.

_____. *When Things Fall Apart: Heart Advice for Difficult Times.* Shambhala, 2011. ebook.

Collins, K.K. "Mrs. Smith and the Morality of *Persuasion*." *Nineteenth-Century Fiction*, vol. 30, no. 3, 1975, pp. 383–87.

Cottom, Daniel. "In the Bowels of the Novel: The Exchange of Fluids in the Beau Monde." *NOVEL: A Forum on Fiction*, vol. 32, no. 2, 1999, pp. 157–86.

The Dalai Lama. *The Essential Dalai Lama: His Important Teachings.* Ed. Rajiv Mehrotra. Penguin, 2005.

_____. *His Essential Wisdom.* Ed. Carol Kelly-Gangi. Fall River Press, 2007.

_____. *How to Practice: The Way to a Meaningful Life.* Ed. and trans. Jeffrey Hopkins. Atria Books, 2002.

_____. *Practicing Wisdom: The Perfection of Shantideva's Bodhisattva Way.* Ed. Jinpa Thuten. Wisdom Publications, 2004.

The Dalai Lama, and Howard Cutler. *The Art of Happiness.* 10th Anniversary edition. Penguin, 2009. ebook.

Dante Alighieri. *The Divine Comedy.* Ed. Robin Kirkpatrick. Penguin, 2013. ebook.

Dawson, Richard. "'The Power of Conversation': Jane Austen's *Persuasion* and Hans-Georg Gadamer's Philosophical Hermeneutics." *Fictional Characters, Real Problems: The Search for Ethical Content in Literature.* Ed. Garry L. Hagberg. Oxford University Press, 2016, 194–208.

Detrixhe, Jonathan J. "Souls in Jeopardy: Questions and Innovations for Bibliotherapy with Fiction." *Journal of Humanistic Counseling, Education and Development*, vol. 49, 2010, pp. 58–72.

De Waal, Frans. "The Evolution of Empathy." *Greater Good Magazine: Science-Based Insights for a Meaningful Life.* September 2005. https://greatergood.berkeley.edu/article/item/the_evolution_of_empathy.

Djikic, Maja, and Keith Oatley. "The Art in Fiction: From Indirect Communication to Changes of the Self." *Psychology of Aesthetics, Creativity, and the Arts*, vol. 8, no. 4, 2014, pp. 498–505.

Djikic, Maja, Keith Oatley, and Mihnea C. Moldoveanu. "Reading Other Minds: Effects of Literature on Empathy." *Scientific Study of Literature*, vol. 3, no. 1, 2013, pp. 28–47.

Dovey, Ceridwen. "Can Reading Make You Happier?" *New Yorker*, June 9, 2015, n.p.

Duncan, Kathryn, and Michael Stasio. "An Evolutionary Approach to Jane Austen: Prehistoric Preferences in *Pride and Prejudice*." *Studies in the Novel*, vol. 39, no. 2, 2007, pp. 133–46.

Epstein, Mark. *Thoughts without a Thinker: Psychotherapy from a Buddhist Perspective.* Basic Books, 1995.

Fayed, Nicolás, Yolanda Lopez del Hoyo, Eva Andres, Antoni Serrano-Blanco, Juan Bellón, Keyla Aguilar, Ausias Cebolla, and Javier Garcia-Campayo. "Brain Changes in Long-Term Zen Meditators Using Proton Magnetic Resonance Spectroscopy and Diffusion Tensor Imaging: A Controlled Study." *PLoS One*, vol. 8, no. 3, 2013, pp. 1–14.

Ferguson, Cristopher J. "Is Reading 'Banned' Books Associated with Behavior Problems in Young Readers? The Influence of Controversial Young Adult Books on the Psychological Well-Being of Adolescents." *Psychology of Aesthetics, Creativity, and the Arts*, vol. 8, no. 3, 2014, pp. 354–62.

Ford, Susan Allen. "A Sweet Creature's Horrid Novels: Gothic Reading in *Northanger Abbey*." *Persuasions: The Jane Austen Journal On-Line*, vol. 33, no. 1, 2012.

Fresco, David M., Nathan L. Williams, and Nicole R. Nugent. "Flexibility and Negative Affect: Examining the Associations of Explanatory Flexibility and Coping Flexibility to Each Other and to Depression and Anxiety." *Cognitive Therapy Research*, vol. 30, 2006, pp. 201–10.

Fuller, Miriam Rheingold. "'Let me go, Mr. Thorpe; Isabella, do not hold me!': *Northanger Abbey* and the Domestic Gothic." *Persuasions*, no. 32, 2010, pp. 90–104.

Gay, Penny. *Jane Austen and the Theatre.* Cambridge University Press, 2002.

Geary, David C. *The Origin of the Mind: Evolution of Brain, Cognition, and General Intelligence.* American Psychological Association, 2005.

Giffin, Michael. *Jane Austen and Religion: Salvation and Society in Georgian England.* Palgrave Macmillan, 2002.

Gino, Francesca, Alison Wood Brooks, and Maurice E. Schweitzer. "Anxiety, Advice, and the Ability to Discern: Feeling Anxious Motivates Individuals to Seek and Use Advice." *Journal of Personality and Social Psychology*, vol. 102, no. 3, 2012, pp. 497–512.

Glock, Waldo. "Catherine Morland's Gothic Delusions: A Defense of *Northanger Abbey*." *Rocky Mountain Review of Language and Literature*, vol. 32, no. 1, 1978, pp. 33–46.

Gohmann, Joanna M. "Colonizing through Clay: A Case Study of the Pineapple in British Material Culture." *Eighteenth-Century Fiction*, vol. 31, no. 1, 2018, pp. 143–61.

Goleman, Daniel. *Destructive Emotions: How Can We Overcome Them? A Scientific Dialogue with the Dalai Lama.* Bantam Books, 2003.

Gray, Sarah A.O., Christopher W. Jones, Katherine P. Theall, Erin Glackin, and Stacy S. Drury. "Thinking across Generations: Unique Contributions of Maternal Early Life and Prenatal Stress to Infant Physiology." *Journal of the American Academy of Child & Adolescent Psychiatry*, vol. 56, no. 11, 2017, pp. 922–29.

Greenwald, Anthony G. "The Totalitarian Ego: Fabrication and Revision of Personal History." *American Psychologist*, vol. 35, no. 7, 1980, pp. 603–18.

Hanson, Rick. *Buddha's Brain: The Practical Neuroscience of Happiness, Love, and Wisdom.* New Harbinger, 2009.

Howard-Smith, Stephanie. "'Hearty Fow Children': The Penrhyns, Pugs, and *Mansfield Park*." *Persuasions*, vol. 35, 2013, pp. 191–99.

Hughes, Clair. "Talk about Muslin: Jane Austen's *Northanger Abbey*." *Textile: Cloth and Culture*, vol. 4, no. 2, 2006, pp. 184–97.

Iyengar, Sheila. *The Art of Choosing.* Twelve, 2011.

James-Cavan, Kathleen. "Introduction." *Sense and Sensibility.* Ed. Kathleen James-Cavan. Broadview, 2001, pp. 7–33.

Johnson, Daniel Clinton, and Lisa Barbanell Johnson. "Reinventing the Stress Concept." *Ethical Human Psychology and Psychiatry*, vol. 12, no. 3, 2010, pp. 218–31.

Johnson, Samuel. "Vanity of Human Wishes." Ed. Jack Lynch. http://jacklynch.net/Texts/vanity.html.

Jones, Josh. "This Is Your Brain on Jane Austen: The Neuroscience of Reading Great Literature." *Open Culture*, July 14, 2015. https://www.openculture.com/2015/07/this-is-your-brain-on-jane-austen-the-neuroscience-of-reading-great-literature.html.

Kaplan, Laurie. "The Rushworths of Wimpole Street." *Persuasions*, vol. 33, 2011, pp. 202–14.

Kaptchuck, Ted J. *The Web That Has No Weaver: Understanding Chinese Medicine.* McGraw-Hill, 2000. ebook.

"Keats 200." John Keats Bicentenary. https://johnkeats200.co.uk/1817/200-years-ago-keats-writes-o-life-sensations-rather-thoughts/

Keltner, Dacher. *Born to Be Good: The Science of a Meaningful Life.* W. W. Norton, 2009.

Kenrick, Douglas R., Norman P. Li, and Jonathan Butner. "Dynamical Evolutionary Psychology: Individual Decision Rules and Emergent Social Norms." *Psychological Review*, vol. 110, no. 1, 2003, pp. 3–28.

Keown, Daniel. *The Spark in the Machine: How the Science of Acupuncture Explains the Mysteries of Western Medicine.* Singing Dragon, 2014.

Kipling, Rudyard. "The Janeites." Eds. Lisa Lewis and George Kieffer. http://www.kiplingsociety.co.uk/rg_janeites1.htm.

Knox-Shaw, Peter. *Jane Austen and the Enlightenment.* Cambridge University Press, 2004.

Lane, Maggie. "The French Bread at Northanger." *Persuasions*, no. 20, 1998, pp. 135–45.

Langer, Ellen J. *On Becoming an Artist: Reinventing Yourself through Mindful Creativity.* Ballantine, 2006.

Levitt, Heidi, M., Woraporn Rattanasampan, Suwichit Sean Chaidaroon, Caroline Stanley, and Tamara Robinson. "The Process of Personal Change through Reading Fictional Narratives: Implications for Psychotherapy Practice and Theory." *The Humanistic Psychologist*, vol. 37, 2009, pp. 326–52.

Lewis, Lisa, and George Kieffer. "Introduction," "The Janeites." The Rudyard Kipling Society. http://www.kiplingsociety.co.uk/rg_janeites1_p.htm.

Locke, John. *An Essay Concerning Human Understanding.* Generic NL Freebook, nd. netlibrary.

"Love and the Brain." *On the Brain* newsletter, Harvard Medical School. https://neuro.hms.harvard.edu/harvard-mahoney-neuroscience-institute/brain-newsletter/and-brain/love-and-brain.

Loy, David. *The World Is Made of Stories.* Wisdom Publications, 2010.

Magee, Leanne, Thomas L. Rodebaugh, and Richard G. Heimberg. "Negative Evaluation Is the Feared Consequence of Making Others Uncomfortable: A Response to Rector, Kocovski, and Ryder." *Journal of Social and Clinical Psychology*, vol. 25, no. 8, 2006, pp. 929–36.

Maner, Jon K., and Douglas T. Kenrick. "When Adaptations Go Awry: Functional and Dysfunctional Aspects of Social Anxiety." *Social Issues and Policy Review*, vol. 4, no. 1, 2010, pp. 111–42.

Markle, D. Thomas. "The Magic That Binds Us: Magical Thinking and Inclusive Fitness." *Journal of Social, Evolutionary, and Cultural Psychology*, vol. 4, no. 1, 2010, pp. 18–33.

Mascaro, Jennifer S., James K. Rilling, Lobsang Tenzin Negi, and Charles L. Raison. "Compassion Meditation Enhances Empathic Accuracy and Related Neural Activity." *Social Cognitive & Affective Neuroscience*, vol. 8, 2013, pp. 48–55.

McDonnell, Jane. "'A Little Spirit of Independence': Sexual Politics and the Bildungsroman in *Mansfield Park.*" *Novel*, vol. 17, no. 3, 1984, pp. 197–214.

Mellor, Anne K., and Alex L. Milsom. "Austen's Fanny Price, Grateful Negroes, and the Stockholm Syndrome." *Persuasions*, 34, 2012, pp. 222–35.

Moore, Roger E. "The Hidden History of *Northanger Abbey*: Jane Austen and the Dissolution of the Monasteries." *Religion & Literature*, vol. 43, no. 1, 2011, pp. 55–80.

Morelli, Sylvia A., Lian T. Rameson, and Matthew D. Lieberman. "The Neural Components of Empathy: Predicting Daily Prosocial Behavior." *Social Cognitive & Affective Neuroscience*, vol. 9, no. 1, 2014, pp. 39–47.

Moses, Carole. "Jane Austen and Elizabeth Bennet: The Limits of Irony." *Persuasions*, 25, 2003, pp. 155–64.

Natali, Christopher J. "Was *Northanger Abbey*'s General Tilney Worth His Weight in Pineapples?" *Persuasions*, vol. 40, 2019, n.p.

Nowak, Martin, with Roger Highfield. *SuperCooperators: Altruism, Evolution, and Why We Need Each Other to Succeed.* Free Press, 2012.

Nunokawa, Jeff. "Speechless in Austen." *Differences: A Journal of Feminist Cultural Studies*, vol. 16, no. 2, 2005, pp. 1–36.

Parry, Sarah. "Mansfield Park vs. Sotherton Court: Social Status and the Slave Trade." *Persuasions*, vol. 35, no. 1, 2014.

Pawl, Amy J. "Fanny Price and the Sentimental Genealogy of *Mansfield Park*." *Eighteenth-Century Fiction*, vol. 16, no. 2, 2004, pp. 287–315.

Pehrsson, Dale-Elizabeth, and Paula S. McMillen. "A National Survey of Bibliotherapy Preparation and Practices of Professional Counselors." *Journal of Creativity in Mental Health*, vol. 5, 2010, pp. 412–25.

Peltason, Timothy. "Mind and Mindlessness in Jane Austen." *The Hudson Review*, vol. 67, no. 4, 2015, pp. 609–33.

Perry, Ruth. "Austen and Empire: A Thinking Woman's Guide to British Imperialism." *Persuasions*, vol. 16, 1994, pp. 95–106.

Petrarch, Francesco. "Sonnet 17." Trans. A.S. Kline, Francesco Petrarch, and Laura deNoves. https://petrarch.petersadlon.com/canzoniere.html?poem=17.

Pope, Alexander. "Epistle I." *Essay on Man*. Representative Poetry Online. University of Toronto Libraries.

Potter, Dawn. "In Defense of Dullness or Why Fanny Price Is My Favorite Austen Heroine." *The State of Letters*, 2008, pp. 611–18.

Pratto, Felicia. "Sexual Politics: The Gender Gap in the Bedroom, the Cupboard, and the Cabinet." *Sex, Power, Conflict: Evolutionary and Feminist Perspectives*. Eds. David M. Buss and Neil M. Malamuth. Oxford University Press, 1996, pp. 179–230.

Punzi, Elisabeth, and Niclas Hagen. "The Incorporation of Literature into Clinical Practice." *The Humanistic Psychologist*, vol. 45, no. 1, 2017, pp. 49–61.

Ray, Joan Klingel. "Do Elizabeth and Darcy Really Improve 'on Acquaintance'?" *Persuasions*, 35, 2011, pp. 34–49.

Rector, Neil, Nancy L. Kogovski, aand Andrew G. Ryder. "Social Anxiety and the Fear of Causing Discomfort to Others: Conceptualization and Treatment." *Journal of Social and Clinical Psychology*, vol. 25, no. 8, 2006, pp. 906–91.

Reiff, Marija. "The 'Fanny Price Wars': Jane Austen's Enlightenment Feminist and Mary Wollstonecraft." *Women's Studies*, vol. 45, 2016, pp. 275–90.

Reniers, Renate L.E.P., Birgit A. Völlm, Rebecca Elliott, and Rhiannon Corcoran. "Empathy, ToM, and Self–Other Differentiation: An fMRI Study of Internal States." *Social Neuroscience*, vol. 9, no. 1, 2014, pp. 50–62.

Rowling, J.K. *Harry Potter and the Deathly Hallows*. Scholastic, 2013.

_____. *Harry Potter and the Sorcerer's Stone*. Scholastic, 1997.

Salzberg, Sharon. *Real Love: The Art of Mindful Connection*. Flatiron, 2017.

Scheuermann, Mona. *Reading Jane Austen*. Palgrave Macmillan, 2009.

Shantideva. *The Way of the Bodhisattva*. Trans. and ed. Padmakara Translation Group. Shambhala, 2006.

Shaw, Valerie. "Jane Austen's Subdued Heroines." *Nineteenth-Century Fiction*, vol. 30, no. 3, 1975, pp. 281–303.

Simpson, David. "The Cult of 'Conversation.'" *Raritan: A Quarterly Review*, vol. 16, no. 4, 1997, 75–85.

Smith, Adam. "Cognitive Empathy and Emotional Empathy in Human Behavior and Evolution." *The Psychological Record*, vol. 56, no. 1, 2006, pp. 3–21.

Spongeberg, Mary. "History, Fiction, and Anachronism: *Northanger Abbey*, the Tudor 'Past' and the 'Gothic' Present." *Textual Practice*, vol. 26, no. 4, 2012, pp. 631–48.

Stackle, Erin. "Jane Austen's Aristotelian Proposal: Sometimes Falling in Love Is Better Than a Beating." *Philosophy and Literature*, vol. 41, No. 1A, 2017, pp. 195–212.

Stefanski, Will. "Science Has Made a Fascinating Discovery about Fiction Readers." The Literacy Site. https://blog.theliteracysite.greatergood.com/fiction-readers/.

Stewart, Pearl E., and Gwendolyn Parker Ames. "Using Culturally Affirming, Thematically Appropriate Bibliotherapy to Cope with Trauma." *Journal of Child Adolescent Trauma*, vol. 7, 2014, pp. 227–36.

"Subhasita, Sutta: Well-Spoken." Trans. Thanissaro Bhikkhu. https://www.accesstoinsight.org/tipitaka/kn/snp/snp.3.03.than.html.

Sutherland, John. *How to Read a Novel: A User's Guide*. St. Martin's Griffin, 2007.

Tannen, Deborah. *You Just Don't Understand: Women and Men in Conversation*. William Morrow, 2001.

Tanner, Tony. *Jane Austen*. Harvard University Press, 1986.

Thich, Nhat Hanh. "*Dharma* Talk: Cultivating Our *Bodhisattva* Qualities." *The Mindfulness Bell*, vol. 22, 1998. https://www.mindfulnessbell.org/archive/2016/01/dharma-talk-cultivating-our-bodhisattva-qualities-2.

_____. "*Dharma* Talk: Does Buddhism Support Romantic Love?" The Thich Nhat Hanh Foundation. February 7, 2018. https://thichnhathanhfoundation.org/blog/2018/2/7/does-buddhism-support-romantic-love.

_____. *The Diamond That Cuts Through Illusion*. Parallax Press, 2006.

_____. *The Heart of the Buddha's Teaching: Transforming Suffering into Peace, Joy, and Liberation*. Broadway Books, 1999.

_____. *Living Buddha, Living Christ*. Riverhead Books, 2007.

_____. *Mindfulness Survival Kit*. Parallax Press, 2013.

_____. *Silence*. Harper One, 2015.

Thurman, Robert. "Great Physician and Mind Scientist for Trying Times." Buddhafest 2020.

Todd, Andrew, Alison Wood Brooks, Mattias Forstmann, Pascal Burgmer, and Adam D. Galinsky. "Anxious and Egocentric: How Specific Emotions Influence Perspective Taking." *Journal of Experimental Psychology*, vol. 144, no. 2, 2015, pp. 374–91.

Trilling, Lionel. "Mansfield Park." *Jane Austen: A Collection of Critical Essays*. Ed. Ian Watt. Prentice-Hall, 1963, pp. 124–40.

Troost, Linda, and Sayre Greenfield. "A History of the Fanny Wars." *Persuasions*, vol. 36, 2014, pp. 15–33.

Tulletti, Alexa, Aaron C. Kay, and Michael Inzlicht. "Randomness Increases Self-Reported Anxiety and Neurophysiological Correlates of Performance Monitoring." *Social Cognitive and Affective Neuroscience*, vol. 10, no. 5, 2015, 628–35.

Wallace, B. Allan. *Meditations of a Buddhist Skeptic: A Manifesto for the Mind Sciences and Contemplative Practice*. Columbia University Press, 2012.

Wallentin, Mikkel, Arndts Simonsen, and Andreas Højlund Nielsen. "Action Speaks Louder than Words: Empathy Mainly Modulates Emotions from Theory of Mind-Laden Parts of a Story." *Scientific Study of Literature*, vol. 3, no. 1, 2013, pp. 137–53.

Watson, Mary. "A Defense of Edward Ferrars: Austen's Hero as a Nexus of *Sense and Sensibility*." *Persuasions*, vol. 32, 2011, n.p.

Watt, Ian. *The Rise of the Novel: Studies in Defoe, Richardson and Fielding*. University of California Press, 2001.

Wei, Meifen, Kelly Yu-Hsin Liao, Tsun-Yao Ku, and Phillip A. Shaffer. "Attachment, Self-Compassion, Empathy, and Subjective Well-Being among College Students and Community Adults." *Journal of Personality*, vol. 79, no. 1, 2011, pp. 191–221.

Williams, Sarah. "Meaningful Gazes: Looking at Narrative in Chapter 15 of *Pride and Prejudice*." *Persuasions* 36, 2014, pp. 202–10.

Wiltshire, John. "Decolonising *Mansfield Park*." *Essays in Criticism: A Quarterly Journal of Literary Criticism*, vol. 53, no. 4, 2003, pp. 303–22.

Wright, Robert. *Why Buddhism Is True: The Science and Philosophy of Meditation and Enlightenment*. Simon & Schuster, 2017.

Zionkowski, Linda. "*Emma* and the Problem of Advice." *Persuasions*, vol. 33, 2011, pp. 223–37.

Zlotnick, Susan. "From Involuntary Object to Voluntary Spy: Female Agency, Novels, and the Marketplace in *Northanger Abbey*." *Studies in the Novel*, vol. 41, no. 3, 2009, pp. 277–92.

Zunshine, Lisa. *Why We Read Fiction: Theory of Mind and the Novel*. The Ohio State University Press, 2006.

# Index